PATTERN OF DECEPTION

PATTERN OF DECEPTION

The Media's Role in the Clinton Presidency

By Tim Graham

MEDIA RESEARCH CENTER ■ Alexandria, Virginia

Media Research Center
113 South West Street, Second Floor
Alexandria, Virginia 22314

Copyright ©1996 by the Media Research Center

ISBN 0-9627348-3-7

Cover Photo Courtesy of the Bettman Archive
Typeset in Arrus and Onyx

Printed in the United States of America
First Edition, March 1996

About the Media Research Center

Founded in 1987, the Media Research Center (MRC) is dedicated to bringing political balance to the nation's news and entertainment media. A balanced, impartial news media should provide equal time and equal weight to both sides of an issue, offer the best arguments forwarded by both sides, and give the public the fullest and fairest sense of political debates, so that it can decide which side makes the more persuasive case. The MRC works to bring balance by identifying and exposing examples of liberal media bias.

To identify bias, MRC staff members comb daily through the nation's most influential newspapers and news magazines. Summaries of all network TV stories are entered into the MRC Media Tracking System, a comprehensive computer filing system. In fact, the MRC is the only organization with a complete tape library of network news and interview programs from late 1987 to the present. The MRC uses these research tools to analyze short-term and long-term patterns of bias in the news media.

The result of the MRC's work is a mountain of evidence to support charges of bias. The key to the MRC's effectiveness is the ability to prove bias by using scientific content analysis, and perhaps more convincingly, word-for-word quotes from the media. Facts, not rhetoric, prove bias.

To distribute our findings to members of the media, the Washington political community, radio talk show hosts, newspaper columnists, and the public, the MRC publishes three newsletters analyzing the news media:

■ *MediaWatch,* a monthly that reviews news coverage of politics and current events by the national television networks, major newspapers and news weeklies.

■ *MediaNomics,* a supplement to *MediaWatch* issued by the MRC's Free Enterprise and Media Institute, which focuses on news coverage of America's business and economic systems.

■ *Notable Quotables,* published every other week, highlights bias simply by quoting media figures' most biased, outrageous, or humorous quotes, letting their own words demonstrate their bias.

In 1995, the MRC's Entertainment Division launched the Parents' Television Council in Los Angeles to promote family-friendly programming in prime time, in addition to issuing special in-depth reports analyzing the content of programming on specific issues. The PTC's *Family Guide to Prime Time Television* is a comprehensive study that allows parents to make informed decisions about what shows are appropriate for their children.

Books produced by the Media Research Center include *And That's The Way It Isn't,* a reference guide of studies proving liberal bias; *How To Identify, Expose, and Correct Media Bias,* by Brent Baker, which explains how to monitor what people across the country can do about bias or misinformation in their local media; and *Out of Focus,* by Burton Yale Pines and Timothy Lamer, a study of reporting on the free enterprise system.

The Creators Syndicate distributes to newspapers across the country a twice-weekly column from MRC chairman L. Brent Bozell III. Special articles from the MRC have appeared in *The Wall Street Journal, Chicago Tribune,* the Cleveland *Plain Dealer,* the *Los Angeles Times, National Review* magazine, and many other publications.

MRC spokesmen appear regularly on radio talk shows and have appeared on numerous television programs including ABC's *Good Morning America,* NBC's *Today,* CNN's *Crossfire* and *Reliable Sources,* CNBC's *Cal Thomas, Tim Russert, Rivera Live* and *Charles Grodin* shows, The Christian Broadcasting Network's *The 700 Club,* and the *Fox Morning News.*

Acknowledgments

The heart of this book comes not from the author, but from the relentless daily monitoring of our team of media analysts, who spend most of their days watching television to identify the media's bias, and also, on occasion, to note their fairness. Steve Kaminski, our most senior analyst, joined us early in 1992 to help us analyze most of the events of this book as they unfolded. Two former analysts, Andy Gabron and Mark Honig, relieved me of my study compilation duties for a few months during the writing of this book, and their research efforts are included, as is the work of present analyst Clay Waters. Our newest analysts -- Geoffrey Dickens, Gene Eliasen, and Jim Forbes -- complete a hard-working, reliable team.

Other former analysts who helped out with the primary research for this book include Nicholas Damask, Jim Heiser, Sally Hood, Kristin Johnson, Marian Kelley, Gesele Rey, Mark Rogers, and Bill Thompson. Interns during this period included Joe Busher, Deanna Ducher, David Felton, Melissa Gordon, Cameron Humphries, Anna Johnson, Mario Lopez, David Muska, Patrick Pitman, Jim Renne, Rebecca Swaddling, Stephanie Swafford, and Robert Dale Vane.

Brent H. Baker, the editor of *MediaWatch*, is the primary force behind our news analysis. Not only does his tireless work on editorial and administrative details make the rest of us look hopelessly lazy, his editorial judgments on this book and our newsletters have been invaluable.

L. Brent Bozell III, the Chairman of the Media Research Center, a leading light in the conservative movement, had the idea for this book, and allowed me to realize it. I thank him for the opportunity and hope it will help strengthen the organization he built from the ground up. Great thanks also go to our Board of Directors: William Rusher, Harold Simmons, Leon Weil, and Curtin Winsor. The fundraising team of Richard Kimble, Larry Gourlay, and Scott Waller makes everything we produce possible, as do the many generous donors to the MRC across the country.

Tim Lamer, who runs our Free Enterprise and Media Institute, served this book both as a media analyst and as a study director. Tom Johnson, our in-house Strunk and White, applied his copy editing skill to every page of this book. After all the editing, Kathy Ruff handled the marketing plans to insure this book would make its way to readers, with help from Carey Evans, Kerrie Mahan, and Pete Reichel.

My friend Henry Payne, a nationally syndicated editorial cartoonist for Scripps-Howard Newspapers, drew the distinctive illustration of the White House that marks the sections of this book. It's a very small demonstration of his talent, for he is not among the forgettable flock of yuk-yuk gag artists in his field today. He is the complete political cartoonist -- a solid draftsman, probing wit, and investigative journalist. I also must thank my cover artist, who asked for no credit -- you know who you are, and you're good. Susan Hankoff-Estrella of Cactus Design gave me design suggestions for the inside of this book.

Finally, I thank my parents, Jim and Ann Graham of Viroqua, Wisconsin, for all their love and support. If they hadn't allowed me to watch television and read the World Book encyclopedia at the same time, I might never have been qualified for this job. To my wife, Laura, and my son, Benjamin, my most heartfelt thanks for their understanding during a few months of ridiculous hours. They may joke that media bias is my life, but they are.

Tim Graham
March 1996

FOREWORD

By L. Brent Bozell III

Throughout the 1996 campaign, I predict Bill Clinton will rationalize, with one remarkably consistent answer, the public's love-hate relationship with him. It has nothing to do with personal qualities, from his awesome political energy to his disturbing sincerity on every position he takes, in the moment that he's taking it. Clinton believes that the end of the strategic certainties of the Cold War, paired with increasing economic anxiety, have driven the American people to apathy and cynicism. Never mind that he fought against the strategic imperatives of the Cold War in his youth, or that his party thrives on economic anxiety as its calling card for Big Government. He has suggested that when people vote again, it will not be a referendum on his presidency, but an opportunity to choose the candidate who will calm their anxieties about the future.

That is a clever way of packaging the 1996 decision outside of Clinton's personality and his record, but there is some truth in it. The end of the Cold War did suggest to the American people that a Democrat wouldn't have to look good driving a tank to be trusted with the keys to the Pentagon. As for economic anxiety, twelve years of Republican chief executives allowed many Americans to forget why Jimmy Carter's disastrous record led them to pull the lever for Reagan in 1980 despite all the caricatures of a war-mongering grandpa with his finger on the button. Clinton was certainly a cultural creature of his times. His confessional campaign -- with its savvy exploitation of bear-hugging town meetings, sunglassed appearances with Arsenio Hall, and calmly canned answers to glassy-eyed Generation X questions from MTV "News" moppets -- created a tabloid presidency for a tabloid era.

The challenge will be more daunting in 1996. No longer is Clinton the new kid in town, the fresh face of change. Years of decisions (or, more often, indecision) have left their mark in public opinion. But believing Clinton will fail ignores everything learned about the 1992 campaign, where Clinton survived his darkest hours through sheer and shameless chutzpah. At moments where men of lesser ambition would have folded their tents in embarrassment and surrender, Clinton and his campaign minions browbeat reporters and pundits mercilessly, asking them: Did they really want to destroy what they all believed was the chance for a great presidency?

Professional responsibilities can become the least of priorities to a journalist swooning in political infatuation. In an October 17, 1994 appearance on CNBC's *Tim Russert* show, CBS reporter Lesley Stahl celebrated a new documentary on Franklin Delano Roosevelt, and mourned the passing of a time when a President's personal life was not a media concern. When Russert asked if the media should return to that protective code, Stahl replied: "In my personal opinion, yes. I think it has almost nothing to do with leadership....I was watching FDR. Here was a man who was cheating on his wife, someone in the show said he lied constantly, he was a great liar. He was a great poker player. He had all these flaws. He was a brilliant leader of this country. He took us, he saved us from the Depression, he brought us into that war. And even I wanted to follow him after watching him just a couple of hours."

Then there's PBS omnipresence Bill Moyers, who can't stop talking about his love for Democratic icons. In an April 11, 1995 NBC commentary, Moyers remembered: "FDR was the only President we had for the first 11 years of my life and when he died, 50 years ago tomorrow, our people in East Texas were not sure the sun would rise the next day...The man was flawed, crafty, conniving, dissembling, didn't seem to matter. We didn't even know about the wheelchair and braces, or hear whispers about other women. What we heard on the radio was the cheerful aristocrat speaking up for common people. The message is what mattered. Class and power were not fixed by nature, inequality was wrong and unemployment humiliating, runaway capitalism could be tamed, privilege checked, monopolies broken up, an end put to government by organized money."

One can't watch these starry-eyed tributes and not understand how this depth of feeling carried over into a bitter journalistic hostility against Ronald Reagan, the only President to threaten the persistent statist experimentation of Roosevelt and his successors; or, for that matter, the current animus against Newt Gingrich and his band of revolutionaries in the House. These comments also explain why reporters will circle the wagons and make excuses in defense of a leader they admire, and why the media were so outraged that conservatives would focus on such trite matters as Whitewater, cattle futures, and Paula Jones when the Clintons were valiantly attempting to make socialized health care the law of the land, a move that would have made FDR very proud indeed.

The media's protective cordon around President Clinton proved that impartiality is not the goal of today's journalists: changing society for the better is. A generation of reporters who were taught in journalism school to "afflict the comfortable and comfort the afflicted" feel the daily temptation to stick it to those who disagree with their politics, to denounce those who obstruct the liberal crusade, to condemn those who will not agree that an ever-expanding activist government would improve American life.

Oh, Bill Clinton presented himself as a different kind of Democrat, one who would supposedly temper the party's impulse to make the government the first resort for any problem. But reporters knew that Clinton held the "right" position on the issues they cared about, and they knew they wanted an end to the long Republican hold on the White House. If Bill Clinton had a tendency to lie about his past, to skate over the difficult issues of infidelity to family and country, or to downplay his financial benefit from moneyed friends, the media would simply downplay those disadvantages as cynical mudslinging against an idealistic leader.

Tim Graham has taken the many strands of news media misbehavior the Media Research Center staff has collected in the Clinton years and woven them into a powerful narrative of a promotional press. No one would argue that the Clinton presidency has drawn a uniformly "easy" press, but this book is a handy howitzer against those critics who maintain the national media are in any way, shape, or form out to "get" this President. At the top of that list of critics of journalistic harshness, is, of course, Bill Clinton himself -- but anything less than that would be out of character for this man.

INTRODUCTION

The Most Talented Candidate

"The group of people I'll call The Press -- by which I mean several dozen political journalists of my acquaintance, many of whom the [Patrick] Buchanan administration may someday round up on suspicion of having Democratic or even liberal sympathies -- was of one mind as the season's first primary campaign shuddered toward its finish. I asked each of them, one after another, this question: If you were a New Hampshire Democrat, whom would you vote for? The answer was always the same; and the answer was always Clinton. In this group, in my experience, such unanimity is unprecedented....

"Almost none is due to calculations about Clinton being 'electable'....and none at all is due to belief in Clinton's denials in the Flowers business, because no one believes these denials. No, the real reason members of The Press like Clinton is simple, and surprisingly uncynical: they think he would make a very good, perhaps a great, President. Several told me they were convinced that Clinton is the most talented presidential candidate they have ever encountered, JFK included." -- New Republic Senior Editor Hendrik Hertzberg, March 9, 1992 issue.

Despite the well-worn myth of reporters as cynical, ink-stained wretches who abhor manipulation by politicians, many reporters have allowed themselves to be manipulated by a candidate (or even President) on their beat. Bill Clinton's idol, John Kennedy, benefited from a reporting corps that cooperated in hiding the sordid details of his private life. In 1992, reporters once again huddled protectively around a Democratic candidate they hoped would be a great President.

As the election year unfolded, Bill Clinton had not one problem with scandal, but many. Clinton had an extramarital sex life that sometimes relied on state jobs to procure silence and, as was later discovered, sometimes depended on state police officers to procure conquests; a record of draft avoidance with excuses that changed with each new revelation; a tricky tangle of business deals with the owner of an insolvent savings and loan. Each of these stories, with the potential to doom most presidential campaigns, would be aggressively ignored or downplayed by a protective news media with its desire to end twelve years of Republican control of the White House.

Does the charge of liberal bias imply a dastardly conspiracy, perhaps a four-network conference call over coffee in the morning? Hardly. Bias emerges as a tendency, a reflex. The inside skinny on journalistic motives for overcovering or undercovering a story can be illuminating. For example, the media jumped on the accuracy of George Bush's commercials in part because the Clinton campaign strongly urged them to do it. But the media's intentions matter less than the content of the actual product -- what the voters see, hear, or read. Even if the media had decided it would not cover a story like Gennifer Flowers because they didn't want the responsibility of single-handedly destroying presidential candidacies, the tone and amount of that coverage had the effect of aiding Bill Clinton. Despite their competition for readers and viewers, media outlets often conducted what media scholars Robert Lichter and Larry Sabato have called a "race to be second" on damaging stories about a vulnerable candidate who could serve as a promising vehicle for their beliefs.[1]

Did the media elect Bill Clinton? No, but the tenor of their coverage (or lack of it) had an impact, at least on television. Consider a study by the Center for Political Studies at the University of Michigan on how the voters used the media in the 1992 campaign. Asked how much attention they paid to newspaper articles about the campaign, 50 percent of respondents said "none," and 77 percent said they paid no attention to magazine articles. Sixty-four percent said they hadn't listened to speeches or discussions on the radio. But the numbers for television were much higher: 31 percent said they watched a "good many" TV programs on the campaign; 39 percent said "several."[2] The network newscasts still played a powerful role in setting the agenda, and in the case of some potential Clinton embarrassments, keeping things off the agenda.

The 1992 campaign is perhaps the best demonstration in modern times of a liberal bias in the news media, and of the damage that bias can do -- by leaving the public uninformed about the person it elects to the nation's highest office. George Bush charged Clinton with engaging in a "pattern of deception" about his personal and political life in Arkansas. But the pattern of deception wasn't simply Clinton's, but the media's as well. The image of Bill Clinton reporters sold to the country in 1992 would in no way resemble the fuller, much less flattering picture of Clinton's past that emerged month by month throughout his presidency.

As the nation gravitated toward conservatism in the elections of Ronald Reagan and George Bush over liberal Democrats, the views of news reporters moved in the opposite direction. After the 1992 election, the Freedom Forum released a survey of 1,400 journalists by Indiana University professors David Weaver and G. Cleveland Wilhoit. The study found 44 percent of reporters surveyed considered themselves Democrats in 1992, up from 38 percent in 1983 and 35 percent in 1971. By contrast, the number of Republican reporters fell from 25 percent in 1971 to 16 percent in 1992. Compared to the general population, reporters were 5 to 10 points more likely to be Democrats and 10 to 15 points less likely to be Republicans.[3]

Some reporters now admit their profession is predominantly liberal, but insist that it doesn't affect coverage. Some won't even admit that much. "My own view, for what it's worth, is that there is not enough ideology in most reporters to fill a teaspoon or a thimble," claimed *Washington Post* reporter/columnist David Broder in June 1994.[4] But many reporters covering the 1992 campaign openly suggested their coverage hurt the Republicans. In a post-campaign survey of 250 reporters and media executives, the Times Mirror Center for the People and the Press reported: "A substantial majority (55 percent) of the American journalists who followed the 1992 presidential campaign believe that George Bush's candidacy was damaged by the way the press covered him. Only 11 percent feel that Gov. Bill Clinton's campaign was harmed by the way the press covered his drive."[5]

Interestingly, that didn't mean reporters felt coverage was unfair. In fact, 80 percent graded election coverage as good or excellent in the Times Mirror Center survey. That feeling was even stronger among a more powerful subset of 48 news executives, producers, anchors, and political reporters labeled "the powers that be" -- 84 percent of them felt that coverage was good or excellent. Of the minority who didn't believe Bush was hurt by the press, fully 45 percent of reporters and 61 percent of the "powers that be" felt that negative coverage of Bush was due to Bush's sorry record, not due to reporters.[6] Reporters were just doing their job.

Like Hendrik Hertzberg's informal gut check, the Times Mirror Center poll showed that in 1992, reporters clearly felt their professional role laid not in old-school notions of objectivity and fairness to each campaign, but in exposing the failure of George Bush's presidency and hailing the possibility of a new era under Bill Clinton.

This book documents how "objective" national media sympathy toward the Clinton campaign translated into a dramatically biased election portrait. Month after month, on issue after issue, the media made it easier for Clinton to march toward victory in 1992. Once the Clinton presidency had begun, reporting became more skeptical, but the national media still often served to promote Clinton and his policies as superior to the Republicans. The media's role in the campaign and presidency of Bill Clinton will be explored in seven sections:

■ *THE PRIMARY SEASON:* Despite subsequent network breast-beating that they had hammered Clinton with a one-two punch of Gennifer Flowers and draft dodging, TV reporters actually worked hard to bury both issues. Only 14 evening news stories in a six-day period focused on Flowers. The draft story elicited only 13 evening news stories in its first ten days, compared to 51 in the first ten days of Dan Quayle's 1988 National Guard controversy.[7] Network reporters did even less on Whitewater. After Jeff Gerth's March 8 *New York Times* article first broke the scandal, instead of launching new investigative reports, the four networks did only five full stories on the Clinton finances in March, and then dropped the story for the rest of the year.[8] Would Clinton have survived if what is now known on the Whitewater scandal had come out in 1992?

■ *CONTRASTING CONVENTIONS:* When the Democrats convened in New York City, reporters saw an inspiring array of speeches that spelled out a new moderate vision for America, with none of the networks using the word "liberal" to describe Bill Clinton, Al Gore, or the Democratic platform. CNN's Candy Crowley declared: "Bill Clinton, of course, is a conservative Democrat, he is a moderate Democrat." But the media found that Republicans gathering in Houston suffered from apocalyptic right-wing extremist rhetoric sure to strike a chord of fear or disgust in the average voter. CNN's Frank Sesno called convention speakers Pat Buchanan and William Bennett "very hard, far-right conservatives." On 70 occasions, network reporters suggested an unduly harsh and negative tone at the Republican convention, which they never did once to the Democrats in New York.[9]

■ *THE FALL CAMPAIGN:* While the media found Democrats offering hope and solutions, they portrayed the Republicans as tired, desperate mudslingers. CBS prompted an advertising writer to describe the Bush campaign's ad technique: "I think it's lying."[10] When George Bush asked Bill Clinton to explain his Vietnam-era trip to Moscow, *CBS This Morning's* Harry Smith exclaimed: "Clearly that red-baiting junk didn't work for the President last night. What's he going to try next?"[11] When third-quarter economic growth rose to 2.7 percent (later adjusted to 3.9 percent), ABC's Peter Jennings suggested the public's economic gloom was more telling than mere statistics: "All over the country, millions of people hardly need any statistics to tell them what is happening."[12] On all of these issues -- the advertising, the draft, the economy -- the benefit went to the Democratic ticket.

■ *THE NEW ADMINISTRATION:* The Clintons' arrival in the White House caused a frenzy of celebration. Despite a rocky start, reporters supported the Clintons and their appointments. In fact, some reporters, like *Time's* Strobe Talbott, became Clinton appointees: in the first two years of the Clinton administration, more than twice as many reporters jumped on board than in the entire four years of the Bush administration.[13] Reporters like Martha Sherrill of *The Washington Post* and Margaret Carlson of *Time* celebrated

Hillary Clinton as "our leading cult figure," and an "icon of American womanhood."[14] Despite criticism of the White House's strategic bungling, reporters became part of the publicity team on the Clintons' major initiatives. CBS regularly described the Clinton "stimulus" package as a "job creation plan." On the Clinton economic plan, which contained a dramatic tax increase, reporters repeatedly echoed *Newsweek*'s Eleanor Clift: "It's the first serious attempt to cut the deficit in this country."[15] *New York Times* reporter Thomas Friedman proclaimed: "Bill Clinton is trying to lasso the moon. I think we have to give him credit for that. He's trying to lasso the moon on health care, the economy."[16] When the Clinton health plan was introduced, ABC's Jim Angle claimed: "Though many analysts are skeptical of the administration's numbers, they say universal health care will save the government money."[17]

■ *THE TRAVAILS OF 1994:* Despite the media's best efforts, uninvestigated stories surrounding Clinton's personal life and financial affairs returned home to roost, from the revelations of Troopergate and Paula Jones to criminal referrals mentioning the Clintons' Whitewater connections. Following their 1992 pattern, network and news magazine reporters moved quickly to take these stories off the front burner or off the stove entirely. Stories about Clinton's sex life were kept to a minimum compared to other sexual allegations made against conservatives. For example, the total evening news coverage of Gennifer Flowers (14 stories), Troopergate (22) and the first month of Paula Jones coverage (21) still didn't add up to the first five days of Anita Hill's charges against Bush Supreme Court nominee Clarence Thomas in 1991 -- before the Hill-Thomas hearings even began.[18] Despite the reemergence of scandal, often prodded by a conservative alternative media, liberal reporters continued to promote Clinton's initiatives on health care and crime. NBC took $3.5 million from the liberal Robert Wood Johnson Foundation to air a two-hour commercial-free special on health care starring the First Lady in which two-thirds of the panelists and floor speakers were liberals.[19] On the crime bill, soundbites from supporters on the evening news outnumbered opponents by two to one.[20]

■ *THE COLLAPSE OF THE OLD ORDER:* As the 1994 elections neared, the media doubted they had given Clinton enough credit, and sought to sell the public on his list of accomplishments. Newt Gingrich's idea to unite Republican House candidates behind a Contract with America drew explicit criticism from the press as a cheap trick that would be economically and politically disastrous. Gingrich himself drew almost universally negative remarks from journalists, who called him, among other things, "bombastic and ruthless," "less intellectual than obnoxious," and a "radical geek."[21] When the Republicans took the House and Senate by storm, media pundits claimed the results were not a vote for the Contract with America or a desire to restrain government growth. When Republican success sank in, some media figures grew bitter. Peter Jennings complained in a radio commentary about an American electorate in need of government's parenting: "Imagine a nation full of uncontrolled two-year-old rage. The voters had a temper tantrum last week."[22]

■ *CLINTON VS. GINGRICH:* When the Republicans took over the House of Representatives for the first time in forty years, the same reporters who downplayed Whitewater played up ethical allegations against new Speaker Newt Gingrich, including a book advance he rejected after controversy. Ethical problems for Democrats drew much less attention. The media saw mostly negative consequences in the enactment of the Contract with America, and thought conservative rhetoric helped explain the bombing of a federal building in Oklahoma City. As Republican candidates announced their intentions in 1995 to run for the White House, network reporters were much more investigative and hostile than they were when Clinton announced in 1991. Reporting on the budget continued the recent historical pattern of presenting the odd picture of a federal government suffering from fiscal starvation, even as it grew well beyond the rate of inflation. The GOP's planned reduction in the double-digit annual growth of Medicare and Medicaid was presented as "deep cuts." As the Senate Whitewater hearings uncovered new evidence of a coverup, the networks downplayed new disclosures and suggested nothing new was being uncovered.

Far more common than admissions of a pro-Clinton slant among reporters was the assertion that the media didn't have a liberal bias, just a very professional interest in a good story. As *Newsweek*'s Jonathan Alter put it, "They will go for a good story before an ideological story 99 times out of 100."[23] Unfortunately for voters, the actual record of news content ignored the "good story" -- the myriad of unanswered questions about Clinton's peccadilloes, pocketbook, and policies -- for the ideological story: the man from Hope, coming to Washington to do good and overturn the Reagan-Bush years.

When the news turned sour, Clinton tried, with some success, to blunt damaging media coverage by complaining of historically unfair treatment. His complaints stirred apologies from two network anchors for bringing up the Gennifer Flowers story, and provoked a *Nightline* special about overcovering Whitewater. When a damaging draft story broke in September 1992, he told *USA Today:* "Nobody's had a tougher press than I have. No candidate in history has."[24] This book will demonstrate that contention is nonsense.

I. THE PRIMARY SEASON

1

Regaining Control

"The foremost lessons in the mind of everyone were the failures of 1988. We were determined to regain control of our senses, regain control of the process of press coverage. In 1988 there was a kind of consensus that we had surrendered too much of our judgment and had been manipulated too skillfully by the handlers in the two campaigns." -- NBC anchor Tom Brokaw on covering the 1992 campaign in the book Talking Politics: Choosing the President in the Television Age.

"My reaction to that button ['Rather Biased'] and others, in part, is a button I bought yesterday that says 'Yeah, I'm In the Media, Screw You!'....I do understand why a lot of people are upset with us, why we rank somewhere between terrorists and bank robbers on the approval scale. We do criticize. That's part of our role. Our role is not just to parrot what people say, it's to make people think. I think that sometimes I just want to say to the electorate 'Grow up!'" -- Newsweek reporter Ginny Carroll on C-SPAN, August 21, 1992.

In decades past, reporters suggested the best approach to journalism was to report the truth and let the chips fall where they may. In the 1992 campaign, reporters did the opposite, suppressing damaging stories about the Democrats and if the stories broke, catching the chips as they fell. The media did not act as if they wished to merely watch the news unfold and describe it as it happened. Their approach suggested they wanted their opinions, their critique, to help shape the election. Reporters did not see themselves, as they often try to present themselves, as neutral providers of information. Instead, they saw themselves controlling the campaign, and criticizing it from above. As the 1992 campaign approached, media bigwigs consciously decided to make the elections run on their agenda, on what they felt was important, not on what the candidates wanted to talk about.

As ABC political reporter Jeff Greenfield explained: "What happened in 1988 was all the networks looked up and said 'We can't do this anymore.' And I know there was a very conscious decision here. We said, 'We cannot cover campaigns the way we have been covering campaigns. We're prisoners of the campaign trail; we're prisoners of the thought of the day, of the canned comment -- we've got to figure out a different way to cover campaigns.' And all of the networks in 1992 did very different kinds of work, quite deliberately."[1]

Greenfield echoed what NBC Washington Bureau Chief Tim Russert had said in *The Wall Street Journal* in early 1992: "After the 1988 election, there were endless post-mortem conferences at all the networks. And the sense of them all was, 'Never again.' We could no longer be slaves to photo opportunities; we had to use them as a peg to tell a more substantive story. We had to dissect the political ads. We really had to do a better job of trying to distinguish the issue differences between the candidates."[2]

The networks might have based these complaints on how they felt they had failed the Democrats: that the Bush campaign had held photo opportunities at flag factories, that Bush campaign ads and Willie Horton ads too effectively damaged Democratic nominee Michael Dukakis, and that the delineation of ideological differences between Bush and Dukakis left the Democrat painted as an effete Massachusetts liberal, quick to tax, soft on crime and defense. In 1992, reporters trying to make up for the 1988 campaign suggested they did not want to see the Democrats suffer from what they considered cheap scandals or be painted into an ideological corner by the Republicans.

Democrats and media figures alike looked for a candidate to present a more moderate image in the 1992 campaign, someone to whom the damaging label "liberal" would not stick. Bill Clinton impressed them as that kind of candidate. From the beginning, reporters touted Clinton's moderation and proclaimed that 1988-style attacks on Democratic liberalism would not work. Reporters did not see liberalism in Clinton's evolving proposals to raise taxes to fund greater government involvement in health care and job training. Nor did they emphasize that Clinton would favor openly gay soldiers in the military. They did not dwell on how Clinton would need to please the liberal wing of his party, not to mention the Democratic leadership of Congress. Without a single exception, the news magazines uniformly presented him before the primaries as a moderate or conservative, not as a liberal.[3]

U.S. News & World Report correspondent Matthew Cooper thought Clinton might be too conservative for the Democrats, writing in the July 22, 1991 issue: "Clinton has youth and vigor but a minimal Democratic base -- and he sounds too much like a Republican to be nominated."[4] *U.S. News* writer Donald Baer, who joined the Clinton White House as a speechwriter in 1994, added on October 14, 1991: "Once, he was a liberal who became the nation's youngest Governor; now at 45, Clinton is the innovative darling of disaffected moderates."[5]

In *Newsweek,* reporter Ginny Carroll announced on September 30: "Clinton's expected entry into the race next week gives Democrats a chance to break the liberal lock on the party." On November 25, *Newsweek* contrasted Clinton with old-time liberal New York Governor Mario Cuomo: "Aides to Arkansas Gov. Bill Clinton called Cuomo 'the ultimate Big Government liberal' and the perfect foil for Clinton's 'New Paradigm' candidacy." Two weeks later, they repeated the same thought: "Aides to Arkansas Gov. Bill Clinton have already begun referring to Cuomo as 'the last of the Great Society candidates.'"[6] Little did the public know that this "moderate" candidate would become the liberal President who sold his plan to nationalize health care as the next logical extension of the New Deal and the Great Society.

At *Time,* Senior Political Correspondent Michael Kramer reported on October 14, 1991 that "Many of Clinton's ideas [like national service]...are viewed by liberal Democrats as neo-Republican." In the December 30 issue, Deputy Washington Bureau Chief Margaret Carlson suggested on welfare policy, "Clinton, the moderate Southerner, is yin to Cuomo's northeastern liberal yang."[7]

In two *Nightly News* reports, NBC's Lisa Myers touted Clinton as if she had internalized the mantra of the last Democratic nominee: competence, not ideology. On September 12, she claimed: "Clinton has racked up a fairly strong record in 11 years as Governor. This year fellow Governors voted him the most effective Governor in the nation. His claim to fame: education...Clinton increased school attendance requirements, raised accreditation standards, and required teachers to pass competency tests, over the vehement objections of the teachers' union. Then he raised taxes to pay for it all, including higher salaries for teachers. It worked." On October 3, Myers repeated the theme: "His prescription: an ambitious agenda to make government work and help the forgotten middle class...A star since being elected Governor at age 32, Clinton is less driven by ideology than what works...Name a problem, Clinton probably has a solution."[8]

Almost four years later, liberal columnist Mark Shields wrote of a *New York Times* editorial campaigning for mother-killer Gina Grant's admission to Harvard as the year's preeminent example of "elitist press bias," and then turned to coverage of Bill Clinton: "A milder, calmer, less virulent strain of this same bias in favor of the Truly Smart infects many of us in the political press. The literature of the 1992 campaign provides abundant evidence of the press's general veneration of knowledge and intelligence over all other qualities of candor, courage, compassion, or strength."[9] From the beginning of his national ascent, reporters played down Clinton the corner-cutting abuser of power and played up Clinton the policy wonk -- the intellectually insatiable student of politics -- presenting that side of Clinton as an obvious contrast to George Bush, the uncurious been-there, done-that President.

2

Regretting Gennifer Flowers

"If the public is going to behave like an idiot on the subject of sex, the candidate will naturally do almost anything to avoid telling the truth about any behavior less than impeccable...Given the size of the job that needs to be done, it is time for America to get serious. At the very least, turn off the television set. And grow up about sex." -- Time essayist Lance Morrow on the Gennifer Flowers controversy, February 3, 1992.

"While George Bush -- all whiteness -- talks about 'family values,' the Clintons demonstrate them by confessing to adultery." -- Former Washington Post reporter Sidney Blumenthal in the February 17, 1992 New Republic.

The media's first episode of rescuing the Clinton campaign from sudden death began on January 23, 1992, when the tabloid *The Star* released a story quoting Gennifer Flowers alleging a 12-year affair with Bill Clinton. The Flowers scandal would be the one-week story reporters regretted all year long. Five months after the January disclosures, at a luncheon before the Democratic Convention held for top Democratic donors, NBC anchor Tom Brokaw complained about the Flowers spectacle: "I think we've made it almost unbearable [for candidates] to enter the public arena." ABC anchor Peter Jennings called coverage of Flowers a mistake and a "a bad beginning to the year that probably alienated a public already critical of news media."[1] ABC's *World News Tonight* had aired three stories on Flowers, *NBC Nightly News* five.[2]

No one in the media wanted to be the first on the story. The Clintons planned to go on ABC's *Nightline* or *Prime Time Live,* but after amazement at the network blackout on the Flowers story, they backed out. They claimed logistical difficulties, but *Newsweek's*

Eleanor Clift explained two months later: "The real reason was that the Flowers story didn't make the evening news. The Clintons won some valuable time to prepare a response."[3]

Expecting an interview with the Clintons as late as 9 p.m., *Nightline* devoted its show on Thursday night, January 23, to the Flowers story, casting it as a debate about journalism rather than an investigation of the charges. But a one-sided panel -- Clinton aide Mandy Grunwald, *Newsweek*'s Jonathan Alter, and professor Larry Sabato -- agreed the story didn't deserve air time. As Jeff Greenfield remembered it, "We were left at nine o'clock at night with that story, whereupon Clinton's aide, Mandy Grunwald, being a very smart woman, beat the living daylights out of Koppel for doing the story. She basically excoriated us for 'slipping into the gutter.' But she made a quite powerful point that 'why aren't we talking about health care, crime, the economy, foreign policy?' And for one of the few times I can ever remember, in the years I was on *Nightline,* Koppel was clearly on the defensive about this...And that was, from a political point of view, very effective."[4]

Only *NBC Nightly News* mentioned Flowers the next day, in a few sentences in the middle of a Lisa Myers story. The other networks waited until after the Clintons appeared on *60 Minutes* Sunday night and Flowers held her press conference Monday afternoon before doing their first stories Monday night -- a full four-day wait.

Reporters claimed to care not about the adultery, but whether Clinton was telling the truth or not. But Hendrik Hertzberg's poll of journalists suggested they really didn't care, that the search for a great President mattered more. After all, as *Newsweek*'s post-election book noted about the campaign trail, the truth was not Clinton's approach to quashing the story: "Clinton began with what had become his rote reply -- that the rumors were fictions made up by the Republican opposition in his last gubernatorial campaign."[5]

The fuss was quickly buried in a week. The four networks did a grand total of 14 stories between them on the evening news. Instead of longer investigative pieces by reporters, eight of them were brief anchor-read stories, often highlighting the money Flowers received from *The Star.*[6] The weekly news magazines touched on the allegations in only one issue, with headlines in the February 3 issues reading "Money for Mischief" (*U.S. News & World Report*), "We're Voting for President, Not Pope" (*Newsweek*), and "Who Cares, Anyway?" (*Time*). *Time*'s Michael Kramer began his story: "Let it never be said that Bill Clinton does not understand the game and how to win it. As a strategist and tactician, the Arkansas Governor is as thoughtful a student of politics as has ever held office."[7] The news magazines were not used to dismissing scandal stories, especially about Republicans. Consider the *Newsweek* headline when Bush Chief of Staff John Sununu was accused of excessive use of military aircraft: "Headed for the Exit," without a question mark, months before his actual resignation.[8]

One crucial part of Clinton's success in using the networks to perform damage control was Rick Kaplan, who served in 1992 as executive producer of ABC's *Prime Time Live* after a long stint in charge of *Nightline*. (In 1993, he became executive producer of *World News Tonight*.) Kaplan worked behind the scenes to aid candidate Clinton. He did not deny *Spy* magazine's 1992 report that he attended Clinton campaign staff meetings and helped set up the campaign's press office.[9]

When the Gennifer Flowers story broke in January, "Kaplan called Clinton adviser Susan Thomases, a mutual friend," *Los Angeles Times* reporter Tom Rosenstiel recounted in his book *Strange Bedfellows*. "'Bill has to come out and do something about this,' he told her...Soon Clinton called Kaplan for advice...'Do the toughest interview you can, Kaplan advised Clinton. On the road to the airport, Clinton used the cellular phone to again talk with Kaplan, and the night ended for Kaplan at 4 a.m., when Clinton called one last time."

Rosenstiel wrote that Clinton "was considering doing *60 Minutes*. If you do, Kaplan said, it should be with Mike Wallace or Morley Safer or Ed Bradley. Otherwise tell them forget it. People aren't going to be impressed with somebody whose name they couldn't recall. They are going to remember that you stood up to Mike Wallace. It was advice Clinton ignored." (Younger *60 Minutes* correspondent Steve Kroft did the interview.) Kaplan told Rosenstiel he'd been friends with Clinton for more than a decade: "I knew that he was not

'Slick Willie' and not a scourge, and really a terrific, terrific person."[10]

Left in the dust of the one-week-and-punt coverage were the actual tapes Flowers made of conversations with Clinton, which aired only in small snippets on *Nightline* and in one *CBS Evening News* story. Bill Clinton personally apologized to New York Gov. Mario Cuomo for suggesting on the tapes that he "acts like" a Mafioso (the Cuomo segment was one of the snippets CBS aired). But reporters continued to question the authenticity of the tapes. None of the reporters found it important to emphasize that Clinton told Flowers to lie about her state job: "If they ever ask if you've talked to me about it, you can just say no."[11]

Reporters also ignored an important story that showed that Governor Clinton used the powers of his office to secure a state job for Gennifer Flowers. State employee Charlette Perry, a black woman, was due a promotion, and it had been recommended by her supervisor. But that job's description was changed and given to Flowers. A grievance panel found that Perry was unfairly denied the promotion. Then a Clinton appointee overruled the grievance panel's finding. The issue was not sex, but Clinton using state office to help friends (or potential squealing enemies). The entire media (with the exception of *USA Today* and *Newsday*) have ignored Charlette Perry's story -- for four years and counting.[12] On CNN's *Crossfire* two weeks after the election, Fred Barnes asked *Newsweek*'s Jonathan Alter why the Perry story wasn't covered. Alter replied: "I think that's a good question. I think there should have been more scrutiny of that. I actually at one point, in *Newsweek,* suggested that more people look into it." But the words "Charlette Perry" have never appeared in *Newsweek,* then or since.[13]

Reporters did not ignore *The New York Post* when they ran a story on August 11, 1992 publicizing rumors from a new book that President Bush had an affair with aide Jennifer Fitzgerald. CNN's Mary Tillotson put the question to Bush in a press conference with Israeli Prime Minister Yitzhak Rabin. NBC's Stone Phillips asked the President about the charges in a *Dateline* interview. Some reporters questioned the reliability of the source used by Susan Trento, author of the book *The Power House,* and her husband, Joe Trento, a former CNN reporter who had an interview with the supposed source of the rumor, Ambassador Louis Fields, who died in 1986. But the networks actually took this story more seriously than the Flowers story. In January, neither Flowers nor anyone from *The Star* was invited on any morning or evening interview show. But, the appearance of sleaze be damned, ABC's *Good Morning America* interviewed both Trentos and *CBS This Morning* brought on Susan Trento on August 12.[14]

On the August 15 *Inside Washington, Newsweek*'s Evan Thomas told a different tale: "Actually, we've heard the tape of this old Ambassador Fields, who's now dead, talking to one of the reporters, and the tape makes it pretty clear that he thinks it's just gossip."[15] His magazine used exactly that tone in publicizing the rumor in the August 24 issue. But rejecting the "race to be second" on this story, *Newsweek* had published the rumors in the June 15 issue by playing up a *Spy* magazine story that Bush had three affairs: "Numerous sources are quoted in the story, but none of them goes on the record. Still, combined with Hillary Clinton's quote in *Vanity Fair* about an alleged Bush affair, the *Spy* article may force into the open a topic that until now has been the subject mostly of unsubstantiated whispering among journalists and political insiders."[16]

While associating the Republicans with dirty politics was a media mantra, network reporters defended the Democrats against charges that they spread the Bush infidelity rumors. Ignoring Hillary Clinton's suggestions in *Vanity Fair* that reporters investigate Bush's sex life, NBC reporter Andrea Mitchell proclaimed on the August 12 *Today:* "I see no evidence that this was promoted by the Democrats, and the Republicans have been throwing around a lot of mud, the surrogates." *Wall Street Journal* Washington Bureau Chief Al Hunt agreed: "I don't think the Democrats had anything to do with this."

Then NBC reporter Jim Miklaszewski suggested: "I've talked to some reporters who have personally received faxes from the Clinton campaign. This story, according to these reporters, was in fact pushed by the Clinton campaign as early as a month ago."[17] On *Inside Washington, Newsweek*'s Evan Thomas concurred: "It's true that Clinton's folks faxed around copies of the book to people. That's true."[18]

Clinton campaign manager James Carville stumbled through the most interesting interview on the August 13 *Today* show. When Bryant Gumbel asked if the Democrats helped spread the Fitzgerald rumor, Carville responded: "Governor Clinton said that was not a thing for discussion and I'm not going to discuss it, because, frankly, I don't want to get fired." When asked for an answer again, Carville repeated: "Nobody in our campaign's pushing this and I don't want to talk about it anymore because I don't want to get fired. It may be the easy way but it's the only way for me to keep my job."[19] But reporters didn't push for a real answer, or a real controversy.

Carville was frustrated at the lack of information the Clintons had given him, the senior strategist of their campaign. *Newsweek* reporter Mark Miller held a journalistically envious position as an insider within the Clinton campaign, with the understanding that much of what he learned would not be published until after the election. In 1994, Miller's work finally surfaced: "As scandals kept popping, aides complained about how little the Clintons had told them about their private lives and personal finances. 'We stand a chance of losing the presidency because of our research on ourselves,' Carville said during one flap. 'It sucks,' Hillary's chief aide, Richard Mintz, agreed. 'It worse than sucks,' Carville said. 'Sucks can be put in a positive light. This is a disaster.'" In this case, Miller referred to Mrs. Clinton's claim that she "never, ever" profited from the Rose Law Firm's business with the state government in Arkansas. The staff discovered that was not true, but "the staff ended up sitting on the memo -- which, fortunately for Clinton, never leaked." *Newsweek* did not jump on this story when Miller's agreement expired: it just sat there in a 1994 story on Mrs. Clinton's commodities profits.

In Miller's account, Carville also complained: "I've had blind dates with women I've known more about than I know about Clinton." Another senior aide said that night: "The arrogance! The arrogance that they -- because they are smarter than most people -- can talk their way out of any problem."[20] But reporters, who have often prided themselves on pricking the balloons of egotism in politicians, allowed some damaging stories to fade away unnoticed.

3

Maintaining His Political Viability

"I think the more people read the letter, the actual draft letter, the more people will come back to Clinton...One of the sentences in the letter he gets blasted for is that he wanted to keep his political viability. Well, he was, what, in his early twenties? He was running for Congress when he was 25. What happened to the notion 'I want to grow up to be President?' That's a good thing." -- Time Deputy Washington Bureau Chief Margaret Carlson on Inside Washington, February 15, 1992.

"It would have been outrageous if he [Clinton] had been done in by the draft thing because that was a bum rap. The word 'draft-dodging' does not belong in any sentence with Bill Clinton's name in it." -- Time Editor-at-Large Strobe Talbott, who Clinton later named Deputy Secretary of State, on Inside Washington, March 7, 1992.

Two weeks after the Flowers outburst, *Wall Street Journal* reporter Jeffrey Birnbaum uncovered another intriguing story: that to avoid the draft, Bill Clinton had promised to serve in the ROTC at the University of Arkansas. The February 6 story raised obvious similarities to the feeding frenzy of 1988, when reporters quickly suggested Dan Quayle had improperly gained entry into the Indiana National Guard to avoid the draft. But in February, as well as with new revelations in April and September, the media quickly glossed over the Clinton allegations, if they mentioned them at all, a very stark contrast to the feeding frenzy surrounding the Quayle story.

On the night of Birnbaum's story, the networks were less than impressed. ABC made it story number five. CBS and NBC aired nothing, as if it hadn't happened. In his book *Strange Bedfellows,* Tom Rosenstiel explained that "at ABC, too, many wanted to let it pass.

It smelled of a leak, perhaps by Republicans, at a time when Clinton was vulnerable." Rosenstiel quoted *World News Tonight* Executive Producer Paul Friedman proclaiming: "Now look, we climbed all over this fella named Dan Quayle because of the draft thing. We have to look at this as hard as we looked at that."[1]

Two days later on the *CBS Evening News,* reporter Bruce Morton declared: "They [the public] may not care whether Governor Clinton has had affairs, or what his draft status was on any given day. But they will almost certainly care a lot if they discover he has lied to them about these things, or that he really in fact did dodge the draft. My point is not to judge Clinton. It is simply to say that character of Presidents and presidential candidates does matter. And when attacks are made on character, the press ought to report them and then let the voters decide who's right and who's wrong."[2] Wasn't Morton watching the absence of reporting on his own network?

Then, one of Clinton's ROTC officers, Clinton Jones, released a 1969 letter from Clinton he had kept for years thanking ROTC commander Eugene Holmes: "I want to thank you, not just for saving me from the draft, but for being so kind and decent to me last summer, when I was as low as I have ever been."[3] The response was again protective. ABC producer Mark Halperin handed Clinton aide George Stephanopoulos the Jones letter on February 10. Rosenstiel recalled the discussions within ABC: Friedman did not want to go with the story yet, and Peter Jennings worried about ABC "piling on" and "manipulating the process." Friedman and Jennings thought "the letter was simply too complicated for the nightly news. How much of this dense three-page letter would you have to put on the air to be fair, or for it even to make sense to viewers?"[4]

ABC reporter Jim Wooten had interviewed Clinton on February 10, but the network sat on the story. Ted Koppel also obtained the letter and asked Clinton to appear on *Nightline.* But Clinton, not the media, appeared to be in the driver's seat. Rosenstiel reported: "After sleeping on it, Clinton agreed to release the letter...By their clumsiness, ABC had allowed Clinton to steal their scoop and obscure the meaning of the story."[5] But ABC wasn't as clumsy as it was oddly reluctant to be the first to seize the story and beat the competition.

The network claimed to worry about "manipulating the process," but by sitting on the story, that's just what it did: it again had allowed Clinton time to make his own decisions.

Clinton released the letter in a press conference February 12. None of the evening newscasts began with it, and each aired only one story. CBS did the most inaccurate story, referring to Clinton blaming the Republicans for leaking the letter four times, in addition to allowing Clinton four soundbites to accuse the GOP. Anchor Dan Rather began: "Democrat Bill Clinton says Bush-Quayle re-election forces are using a smear campaign to constantly raise questions about his past."[6] The other three networks correctly reported the same night that Jones sent the letter to ABC News, not to GOP officials. CBS News never corrected its mistake.

Late on the night of the 12th, just a few weeks after assembling a panel to unanimously dismiss the Gennifer Flowers story, Ted Koppel again played a role in defusing a damaging story for the Clinton campaign. According to the *Spy* story he didn't deny, Rick Kaplan, formerly executive producer of *Nightline,* coordinated arrangements between the campaign and ABC. Koppel interviewed Clinton about the letter he wrote in 1969 about avoiding the draft, announcing at the outset: "It is, as Governor Clinton himself described it today, the account of a conflicted and thoughtful young man. It is quite a remarkable letter, actually, eloquent and revealing."

After reading the entire letter for the audience, Koppel never charged Clinton with hypocrisy or dishonesty. In fact, Koppel appeared to absolve Clinton, suggesting that his actions at the time were no longer relevant: "And indeed, if we were electing that 23-year-old man, what he said and thought and felt at that time would be germane. Now, however, it is what the 45- or 46-year-old Bill Clinton thinks." Despite his reputation for tough questioning, Koppel began with three questions about Clinton's "feelings" about conscientious objection and what Clinton would have done as President if America had a draft during the Gulf War. He did not challenge Clinton when he asserted "All I've been asked about by the press are a woman I didn't sleep with and a draft I didn't dodge."[7]

In retrospect, despite Eleanor Clift's subsequent evaluation that Clinton seemed "earnest and sincere,"[8] Clinton lied repeatedly on the show that he didn't know whether he'd be called for the draft in December 1969, when it was later revealed he received an induction notice in the spring of that year. In a moment that looks ironic in retrospect, Koppel asked near the end of the program: "When Dan Quayle, when the story about his National Guard service came out, it was in the media for weeks, probably for months, I think it's fair to say. You think you're going to be able to put this one behind you now?" Clinton responded: "I'd just like to point out what I said about that at the time. I said, Dan Quayle oughta just tell the truth, get the facts out, and let it go."[9]

Clinton's advisers were ecstatic over the show. In Jack Germond and Jules Witcover's book *Mad as Hell,* adviser Paul Begala added: "I know that show got us out of the woods with the press." Begala said Koppel had treated the interview "the way it ought to be treated. It wasn't just a sort of ambush, gotcha, chicken s--t journalism."[10] In Tom Rosenstiel reported in his book *Strange Bedfellows* that after Koppel read the letter and hailed its eloquence, campaign manager James Carville "leapt out of his seat, shot a fist into the air, and turned to the others. 'He was f--king great to us! We got no complaints!'" Soon other news outlets dropped the draft story. As Rosenstiel noted: "*Nightline* would prove a turning point in saving Bill Clinton as a viable political figure...When *The New York Times* followed with a story probing more deeply into the ROTC questions, some reporters even argued with Howell Raines, the paper's Washington bureau chief, that he was piling on."[11] Reporters worked to pressure editors into dropping the story.

This kid-gloves approach did not match ABC's treatment of Sen. Dan Quayle on August 18, 1988, when the GOP nominee for Vice President was charged with draft evasion through the National Guard. Reporter Judd Rose introduced *Nightline* viewers to the controversy by suggesting (inaccurately) that Quayle's National Guard unit had no vacancies when he joined. Koppel then questioned Bush campaign operative Craig Fuller, loading his interview with long, accusatory speeches: "Jeff Greenfield used the term 'elitism.' Let me use another term. How about hypocrisy? Here's a man who has really, since the age of 17, when he was an unabashed Barry Goldwater supporter, very early, precocious young man, politically active, he has been a hawk. He was very much in favor of the war in Vietnam and yet, as Jeff has just put it, leaves this image now of having said, 'Here, I'll hold your coat, you go and fight in Vietnam, I'm going to join in the National Guard,' which is a perfectly acceptable thing to do, but is also something that you do because you know you probably won't have to go to Vietnam and fight."

After Fuller tried to answer, Koppel followed up with another speech: "I'm suggesting that Dan Quayle, the man who is now a vice presidential candidate, and who has been a hawk all his life, whose main issue, until you folks started talking about the job training program, has been that he is so pro-militaristic, that this man in particular, who for his entire political career, has been emphasizing that issue of militarism, now turns out to have been a fellow who wanted to stay behind in the National Guard rather than go over and fight, as indeed he admits his brother did, that may smack just a little bit of hypocrisy."[12]

ABC reporters seemed apologetic for having to report the controversial aspects of Clinton's record. On February 14, Chris Bury reported: "In the campaign's final crunch, questions of Clinton's character, his personal life, and the draft are pursued daily, almost always by the press. And that is the trouble for Clinton: the press hounds him about his character; voters seem more worried about other things."[13] Like Bruce Morton at CBS, Bury must not have watched his own newscast, which did just four stories in ten days.

The other networks weren't blameless. On February 15, CNN replaced its 10-11 PM (ET) *World News* with a special titled *The Battle to Lead*. Political reporter Ken Bode (who now hosts *Washington Week in Review* on PBS) narrated an eight-minute profile of Clinton. Though Bode reviewed Clinton's personal history, he completely omitted the draft scandal.[14]

In the ten days following the first revelations about the two candidates, 1988 Quayle stories outnumbered 1992 Clinton stories by a margin of almost four to one. In the first ten days of Quayle's

National Guard controversy (August 18-27, 1988), the four net-works did 51 news stories solely on Quayle's National Guard service. (This counts only evening news, not any of the 158 times the networks raised questions about Quayle's controversies during prime time coverage of the 1988 Republican Convention.) By contrast, in the first ten days of Clinton's draft flap (February 6-15, 1992), the four networks aired only 13 stories. If the disparity is broken down by network it looks worse -- ABC 15-4, CBS 18-2, CNN 18-3, and NBC 13-4.[15]

On August 18, 1988, the first night of the Quayle draft story, the four networks aired 15 stories on Quayle. CNN did two stories, ABC did three, and CBS and NBC each broadcast five. The Quayle news led all four evening newscasts. In other words, the networks did more stories on the first night of Quayle's draft flap than in the entire ten days following the Clinton revelations.[16]

All the networks failed to do any investigative work of their own on Clinton, and offered viewers few new details. But in 1988, the networks not only reported on Paula Parkinson's allegations of sharing an apartment for a weekend with Quayle and two other congressmen, but also questioned the truth of Quayle's resume and whether personal influence helped his admission to law school. These investigations caused another 13 stories on Quayle's personal life during the first ten days of his draft scandal.[17]

The press had developed an interesting formula for its differing approaches to Quayle and Clinton. Quayle's failure to serve in Vietnam made a compelling story because of his support for the war; Clinton's opposition to U.S. policy made it reasonable, even courageously logical, for him to avoid it. This is not a standard of hypocrisy journalists would apply to Clinton when it came to Whitewater -- the social conscience against the Decade of Greed, the man who claimed to represent people who played by the rules and didn't get ahead, making special real estate deals with contributors, and then performing government favors in return.

4

The Induction Notice Fizzle

"Bill Clinton did not do anything illegal. There were, most young Americans at that time that were in his income and educational background did exactly what he did. They tried to find some way to avoid service." -- *Wall Street Journal Washington Bureau Chief Al Hunt on CNN's Capital Gang, February 8, 1992.*

"His academic record is mediocre, his memory (just how did he get into the National Guard?) is mediocre, his honesty (he fudged his resumé) is mediocre, and his judgment (who would go off on a golfing weekend, however innocent, with two pals and a female lobbyist?) is mediocre." -- *NBC News President Michael Gartner on Dan Quayle in The Wall Street Journal, September 1, 1988.*

On April 6, a second shoe dropped on the draft story. Former Clinton friend and fellow Rhodes Scholar Cliff Jackson released a letter he had written from England dated May 8, 1969 telling a friend back in America that Clinton "received his induction notice this week."[1] Clinton had indeed received a draft induction notice in the spring of 1969, contradicting years of statements that he'd gotten lucky and never been called. CNN's *World News* made no mention of the story. The other networks buried this startling revelation in the middle of their stories on the next day's primary in New York, the last obstacle in Clinton's soon-to-be-clear path to the nomination. In other words, the presumptive Democratic nominee had been exposed with documentary evidence of telling a blatant lie about his draft status for years, and the networks didn't feel it deserved a single complete story.

The news magazines weren't much better in their April 13, 1992 issues and beyond: *U.S. News & World Report* wrote nothing in the midst of covering Clinton's positions on welfare and other issues; *Newsweek*'s Eleanor Clift mentioned the story in one paragraph. *Time* ignored the revelation on April 13, but included three paragraphs in its April 20 cover story featuring a photographic negative and the headline "Why Voters Don't Trust Clinton."[2]

Perhaps the cover should have read: "Why Voters Can't Trust *Time*." This was an especially embarrassing revelation for *Time* Editor-at-Large Strobe Talbott, an Oxford roommate of Clinton, who had put his credibility on the line supporting his friend's version of events. People reading or hearing Talbott's defenses of Clinton knew little of their friendship. For example, he contributed $300 to Clinton's first campaign in 1974 for Congress, and perhaps engineered $250 contributions to Clinton's presidential campaign through his sons, Devin, 15, and Adrian, 11. Talbott explained his sons were using "discretionary money." Readers might not have known that future Labor Secretary Robert Reich wrote of his and Talbott's feelings in *The American Oxonian,* the Oxford alumni publication: "America will survive the next four years the same way it survived the last 20 since we set sail for England: waiting for Clinton to become President."[3]

Talbott had risen through the ranks at *Time* to Washington Bureau Chief, and by 1992, he had assumed an Editor-at-Large position, which allowed him to draft opinion pieces and appear as a pundit on television. From his position of influence, Talbott first defended his Oxford classmate by calling reports of Clinton's attempts to manipulate his draft status a political dirty trick. On the talk show *Inside Washington* March 7, Talbott declared: "It would have been outrageous if he had been done in by the draft thing because that was a bum rap. The word 'draft-dodging' does not belong in any sentence with Bill Clinton's name in it."[4]

Talbott then took advantage of his power at *Time* to try to help Clinton smother the draft issue with a dramatic apologia for his friend in the April 6 issue of the magazine, issued just days before the induction revelations. Declaring the time had come for "full disclosure," he claimed his Oxford roommate Bill Clinton came to London in the fall of 1969 unsure whether he would be drafted.

Talbott took the offensive, hurling this grenade at the media: "I've been disappointed to see how many of my colleagues in the press, in their coverage of Clinton, have referred to the matter as though draft dodging were proved. Well, it's not, and it can't be, because it's not true." He continued: "At issue here is what lawyers call state of mind: How real was Clinton's concern that he might be drafted? The surmise that Clinton had nothing to worry about is based on more than 20 years' hindsight. It's a perfect example of how a partial recitation of the facts can lie."

The Talbott article also contained a large black box quoting a letter Clinton wrote to his friend Richard Stearns in September 1969: "I am about resolved to go to England come hell or high water and take my chances." Talbott added: "He is not referring to the risk of being run over by a double-deck bus on the Oxford High Street."

Near the end of the article, Talbott lobbied again: "In the spring of 1970, the Rhodes administrators circulated a questionnaire to determine which scholars were planning to return for a third year. Clinton's answer: 'Perhaps. If not, will be entering Yale Law School, or getting drafted.'"[5]

So when Cliff Jackson proved Clinton had indeed received an induction letter, Talbott's credibility had been shot. Was Talbott duped by Clinton? Perhaps, but that would fly in the face of Talbott's own article, where he claimed he "sat in on many long, intense discussions" with Clinton and roommate Frank Aller about resisting the draft. If Talbott was unaware of Clinton's real draft status, how could he authoritatively claim "full disclosure" on the issue and call draft dodging charges false? Asked by *Washington Times* writer John Elvin if he would revise his apologia, Talbott said "No."[6]

In the fall of 1992, Cliff Jackson wrote *Time* Managing Editor Henry Muller, demanding space to challenge Talbott's historical memory. Jackson claimed that Talbott not only knew about Clinton's draft dodging, but actively helped Clinton: "I know that Strobe was one of the chief architects of Bill Clinton's scheme to void his draft notice, avoid reporting on his scheduled (postponed) July 28 induction date and to secure a 1-D deferment, yet nowhere in his personal testimony does Strobe mention his involvement." Jackson continued: "I have a crystal clear recollection of Strobe and Bill standing in my office door at Republican State headquarters in the summer of 1969 and discussing the plan, devised by Bill with the able assistance of friends, to kill his draft notice and secure a deferment." Jackson received no reply from *Time*. Repeated calls to Muller went unreturned before a secretary told him the magazine was "not interested" in an article challenging Talbott's credibility.[7]

For his part, Talbott stonewalled, refusing to talk to anyone in the press about his role. Reporters never put Talbott on the spot about his story, even after Clinton appointed him as ambassador to the Russian republics and then promoted him to Deputy Secretary of State. Not a single journalist raised the question of a friendly quid pro quo between Talbott and Clinton.

5

The First Leaks of Whitewater

"At no time during his presidency has George Bush been subjected to a comparable barrage of scandal-type stories, the kind that can alter forever how the public views a politician." -- Washington Post media reporter Howard Kurtz, March 27, 1992.

"Little Rock is a corporate plantation, but there is no evidence that the Clintons profited personally from hobnobbing with business people or political backers." -- Washington reporter Eleanor Clift in Newsweek, April 13, 1992.

Perhaps the biggest journalistic failure of the 1992 campaign came and went in the Whitewater story in the month of March. While independent counsels Robert Fiske and then Kenneth Starr would be appointed later to investigate whether Clinton's campaigns benefited financially from draining a failing savings and loan, reporters in 1992 responded with a collective yawn.

The story first surfaced on March 8, when *New York Times* reporter Jeff Gerth disclosed the Clintons' peculiar partnership with James McDougal, and his then-wife, Susan. Together, they formed Whitewater Development, which planned to sell a patch of vacation properties perched on the hills above the White River in northern Arkansas. Gerth reported that the Clintons had invested less money in Whitewater Development than the McDougals, and raised questions about state regulatory decisions made on behalf of McDougal's eventually failed Madison Guaranty Savings and Loan. (McDougal became owner of Madison after going into business with the Clintons.) One week later, *The Washington Post* reported on Hillary's work at the Rose Law Firm and questioned how it handled cases before state agencies run by her husband's appointees. After the *Post* story, Democratic opponent Jerry Brown accused Clinton of "funneling money through his wife's law firm" with state business. But in both cases, the networks aired only snippets of arguments, doing nothing to investigate the claims independently. From March 8 to 31, the four networks did only five full stories and mentioned the financial questions in only four others.

NBC aired only one story, on the 16th. CBS made a brief mention of the *New York Times* story on the 8th, and then dismissed financial questions on the 16th. Reporter Richard Threlkeld portrayed questions into Mrs. Clinton's representation of Madison as an invasion of privacy: "And now, as Hillary Clinton is asking, must a wife sacrifice her career if it might interfere with her husband's? Not the sort of campaign issue the voters were expecting." The news magazines were even less interested. In their March 23 editions, *Newsweek* devoted one clause; *Time* reported nothing; and *U.S. News & World Report,* which did a big report on the foreign oil dealings of presidential son George W. Bush the week before, left the Clintons alone.[1]

On March 20, *The Washington Times* reported that contrary to Hillary Clinton's claim that she never got "one dime" from state business, she received $2,000 a month in legal fees for at least 15 months for defending McDougal's Madison S&L before a state agency. The charge, now a standard element of the Whitewater story, was totally ignored. Instead, *Time* and *Newsweek* wrote apologetic articles about unfair scrutiny of working political wives. Echoing the Democratic line, *Newsweek*'s Ginny Carroll argued: "The core issue, arguably, is whether America is really ready for a self-confident, politically active woman like Hillary Clinton as First Lady."[2]

Time's Margaret Carlson, then the magazine's Deputy Washington Bureau Chief, wrote: "The political wife that scares people most is usually a super success like Hillary Clinton, who ranks among the nation's most powerful lawyers and got better law-school grades than her husband. Perhaps she would be better off just trailing behind her husband, holding the Nancy Reagan gaze. Instead she is out speaking, spinning, and strategizing with as much force as the candidate."[3]

Carlson used the same promotional tone in introducing the First-Lady-in-Waiting to the country in January, in the same issue of *Time* that dismissed the Flowers story. Her hosannas included calling Hillary "an amalgam of Betty Crocker, Mother Teresa, and Oliver Wendell Holmes," and a woman who "discusses educational reform...then hops into her fuel-efficient car with her perfectly behaved daughter for a day of good works."

Only a week before that rave review, *Time* displayed a stunning contrast in a pointed assault on Marilyn Quayle by Associate Editor Priscilla Painton. Painton included only one quote from a mostly positive *Washington Post* series on the Quayles, from an unnamed "Quayle associate" who sneered that "Nancy [Reagan] would be considered a woman of the people" compared to Mrs. Quayle. Painton alleged that should she ever become First Lady, Marilyn Quayle "would make Americans long for Nancy Reagan -- taffetas, tyrannies, and all," and called Mrs. Quayle a "controlling" woman, a "grudge-bearing campaigner" and a "watchdog of a wife with an ambition as long as her enemies list."[4] All of these evaluations -- controlling, grudge-bearing, armed with ambition and an enemies list -- were a fitting description of some of Mrs. Clinton's attributes.

Other media figures turned on Hillary's critics. As primary returns came in March 17, NBC commentator John Chancellor took sides: "Jerry Brown's inaccurate attack on Hillary Clinton's legal fees did not work." On March 23, ABC's Chris Bury asserted: "Brown repeated claims that Clinton made money by directing state business to his wife's law firm. Those claims have never been proven."[5] This was a convenient argument for reporters and pundits to make -- charge Brown and Republicans with making unsubstantiated claims, especially when you don't intend to make any effort to substantiate them. Senate Whitewater hearings discovered in the last days of 1995 that contrary to her claims in the 1992 campaign and in her 1994 press conference on the cattle futures issue, Hillary did extensive work for Madison Guaranty and did most of the billing.[6]

But even media reporters, the very journalists who might have been expected to wonder about the media's lack of investigative fervor toward the Democrats, ignored the *Washington Times* story of a $2,000-a-month Madison Guaranty retainer and came to the Clintons' defense. In a March 27 story, *Washington Post* reporter Howard Kurtz complained: "At no time during his presidency has George Bush been subjected to a comparable barrage of scandal-type stories, the kind that can alter forever how the public views a politician." But at that point, Kurtz's own paper had done only five stories on Whitewater, only one on the front page, and would only report two more stories on Whitewater the whole election year.[7]

Near the end of his plea for Clinton, Kurtz protested: "Other complicated stories also have been reduced to damaging tidbits. Last Sunday [March 22], the *Post* published a lengthy article on Clinton's relationship with Don Tyson, president of a major chicken-process-ing firm in Arkansas...The 24th paragraph noted that the Clintons had accepted nine free trips on Tyson aircraft. Clinton was asked about the airplane rides that day on NBC's *Meet the Press* and headlines the next day focused on the free trips." But Kurtz didn't mention the story his paper developed in 1991 creating the issue of free trips on military aircraft by White House chief of staff John Sununu. In the 70 days after the *Post* first published its Sununu scoop, it wrote 27 stories, 11 of them on the front page. Clinton's relationship with Tyson barely caused a ripple by comparison.[8]

In the April 6 *Newsweek*, media critic Jonathan Alter wrote "Clin-ton's recent treatment sometimes crosses the line from investigation to vivisection...Jerry Brown was grossly wrong about Clinton 'fun-neling money' into his wife's law practice... Hillary Clinton takes no share of state fees, but if she did, it would be peanuts." Alter failed to note the $2,000-a-month fee from McDougal, complaining in-stead that George Bush's sons "make Hillary Clinton's activity look like one of those tea-and-cookies parties she disparages," but "the less convincing Arkansas stories [will continue], because of their daily drip-drip quality and the willingness of Jerry Brown to exploit them."

Alter concluded: "The voters are left more confused. All they know is that Clinton is in trouble again, and that red-meat phrases like 'S&Ls' and 'cocaine dealer' are making their way down the food chain, passing through the New York tabloids en route to Jay Leno's monologue and the files of GOP hit men."[9] This again showed the peculiar new logic of the press in 1992: Don't report the news and let the chips fall where they may if it damages Clinton. Drop the charges if the gatekeeping old media loses control of the story, lest they end up as fodder for jokes and 30-second ads.

Far from being demonized like Mrs. Quayle, Mrs. Clinton benefited from a sexist double standard, insisted neoliberal *Washington Monthly* editor Katherine Boo: male spouses of politicians have their professional activities scrutinized, while female spouses are ignored. Boo pointed out that when Sen. Tom Harkin (D-Iowa) ran for president, reporters ignored wife Ruth Harkin's work for the powerful law firm of Akin Gump, but when Rep. Pat Schroeder (D-Colo.) barely considered running for president in 1988, the newspaper *Legal Times* raked Schroeder's lawyer husband over the coals.[10]

The Whitewater story died before the month of March ended when Denver lawyer and Clinton friend James Lyons released a report performed for the Clinton campaign claiming the Clintons actually lost money on the Whitewater investments. Looking back at campaign coverage, Gannett's John Hanchette told the *American Journalism Review* in May 1994: "All of these spreadsheets came out with all this little tiny print on it that looked like a bank statement for a complicated business. People sort of looked at it and said 'What the heck is that?'" *U.S. News* Assistant Managing Editor Harrison Rainie explained in the same *AJR* story: "For better or worse, [the Lyons report] stopped the story."[11] The story died before it really got started.

Why would the media be so quick to drop the Whitewater story? Why weren't they asking elementary questions about the Clintons' finances -- like their undisclosed 1979 and 1980 tax returns, which were revealed in 1994 as holding the secrets of Mrs. Clinton's $100,000 fortune in cattle trading? The Times Mirror Center's post-primary poll of journalists suggested that a majority of national reporters had a viscerally hostile reaction to news of the Clintons' S&L scandal. Reporters were asked their initial journalistic impressions to some stories about the presidential candidates. First, the pollsters explored Andrew Rosenthal's infamous *New York Times* story about Bush's reaction at the demonstration of an automated supermarket checkout scanner. Rosenthal portrayed Bush as out of touch with everyday life by reporting he was amazed by a common supermarket scanner, which was instead a newly developed high-tech scanner. (Rosenthal wasn't even on the scene with Bush, and erred in translating reports from the traveling press pool.) Forty percent of national reporters said they had a positive journalistic reaction to the story -- that it was well-reported and newsworthy -- while 34 percent did not.

The pollsters then asked about the first *New York Times* reports on the Clintons' dealings with McDougal. This time, only 17 percent of national reporters had a positive journalistic impression of the story, while a surprising majority -- 53 percent -- had a negative reaction. Among local reporters in the Times Mirror Center sample, only 29 percent responded negatively.

The reasons for their disapproval were also fascinating. Of the national press, 16 percent felt the issue was "exaggerated," or "no big deal." Another 10 percent called it "irrelevant." Keep in mind this story dealt directly with possible financial conflicts of interest in a savings and loan that cost taxpayers more than $50 million to bail out. By contrast, only five percent thought the misreported Bush Supermarket Scandal was overblown, and only one percent called it unimportant.[12]

This revulsion to the story may be better explained by a 1995 column by *Washington Post* Editorial Page Editor Meg Greenfield about the media: "We have a tiny attention span. 'It will be a two-day story,' we say hopefully, when some ghastly crime or impropriety perpetrated by someone that we care about is uncovered. We don't understand that for others a certified reality doesn't cease to exist just because it is no longer the focus of our reporting."[13]

Another mostly unreported scandal surfaced on June 2, when *Dateline NBC* ran a very tough (and for the networks, very rare) investigative piece on Clinton, questioning whether he used his influence to cover up a mistake made by his mother, Virginia Kelley, that may have cost a young woman her life. Reporter Brian Ross and producer Mark Hosenball discovered that in 1981, a car of drunk young whites yelled racial epithets and obscenities at blacks in Kelley's hometown of Hot Springs, Arkansas. A black man threw a piece of concrete at the car, striking 17-year-old Susan Deer in the face and damaging her mouth and nose. Although the surgery was routine, Clinton's mother, then named Virginia Dwire, struggled in moving the tube supplying the girl's air from her nose to her mouth. She died on the operating table.

What happened next smelled of politics. Ross and Hosenball reported that the state medical examiner, Dr. Fahmy Malak, appointed by Clinton in 1979, took Mrs. Kelley off the hook by ruling the death a "homicide," resulting in six months in jail for Deer's black assailant, Billy Ray Washington. The Malak report made no mention of a breathing tube, or of the doctors' concern about the professionalism of Clinton's mother. The case also signaled Clinton's political clout, even at a time when he was temporarily out of office, when his mother obtained the official autopsy report, because the state crime lab normally only released such reports to prosecutors in homicide cases.

Questions about the report died down until a public campaign began to oust Dr. Malak, whom some found so incompetent that a group of families formed a group named VOMIT (Victims of Malak's Incredible Testimony) to pressure Clinton to remove him. Clinton eventually removed Dr. Malak by promoting him to a higher-paying job in the state Department of Health and Human Services.[14]

Ross pointed out that Mrs. Kelley claimed to be willing to talk about the incident, but only if the Clinton campaign assented -- and they said no. On the July 16 *Today*, Katie Couric's scheduled interview with Mrs. Kelley provided an obvious opportunity to ask about the Susan Deer controversy, but she chose to ask Kelley comfortable questions: "I also read in the many things that have been written about your son and his childhood that he used to walk to church alone with a Bible under his arm." Couric followed up with more softballs: "There have been things though in more recent memory that have been very difficult, I know, for you. He, of course, has been the target of a lot of controversy involving allegations of marital infidelity, draft dodging, not inhaling. Are these legitimate campaign issues, in your view?...How tough has it been for you, Ms. Kelley, to witness this, to see these, in many ways, character assassinations, and negative comments made about your son?"[15] No national news outlet except *Dateline* touched the Susan Deer story.

The Clinton campaign had learned a valuable lesson from media coverage of the primaries: for all the liberal hand-wringing about a tabloid-dominated national press, the Clintonites could kill any damaging news story within a few days, if the story surfaced at all. While that served the Clinton campaign, would it serve the public?

At a Columbia University seminar in February 1992, CBS reporter Betsy Aaron explained the dangers of bias by omission: "We're always going to have this argument between 'do we have an opinion, don't we have an opinion' -- we have an opinion because we're breathing, and the largest opinion we have is what we leave out. I mean, it sounds simplistic, but I always say, worry about what you're not seeing. What you are seeing you can really criticize because you are smart and you have opinions. But if we don't tell you anything, and we leave whole areas uncovered, that's the danger."[16]

The public would learn it had a President it felt it could not trust -- and a media that could not be trusted to even investigate, let alone report, charges that voters might have found important at the ballot box in 1992.

6

The Gold Dust Twins

"I think Gore and Clinton could be the all-generational change ticket, and I suppose if they lose they could do cameo appearances on 'Studs' or something." -- Newsweek reporter Eleanor Clift on The McLaughlin Group, July 4, 1992.

"I must say I was struck by the expanse of their chests. They may have to put out their stats." -- Clift on Clinton and Gore on CNN's Inside Politics, July 10, 1992.

"I must say, looking at some of that footage, it looks like the all-beefcake ticket." -- Clift on The McLaughlin Group, July 11, 1992.

As the dog days of summer approached, media junkies could witness the same reliable media method of attacking Republicans and hailing Democrats. Vice President Dan Quayle drew media accusations of insensitivity and right-wing extremism, but vice presidential nominee Al Gore returned to national attention as a squeaky-clean, green-thumbed, handsome family man -- and a "centrist."

Late in May, reporters jumped on Quayle for suggesting in a speech that TV character Murphy Brown's decision to have a child out of wedlock did not represent one of television's highest moments of moral education. "This was not an accident," insisted *U.S. News* Senior Writer Steven Roberts on the PBS show *Washington Week in Review.* "This was not a casual speech. This was a speech very much part of the White House game plan, a very deliberate attempt to use these family values, which are an amorphous collection of ideas, but to use them as a wedge issue to drive divisions in this country along cultural lines, along social lines, and to some extent, along racial lines."[1]

Newsweek reporter Eleanor Clift howled in print: "There they go again. Only this time, instead of Willie Horton, the GOP is making Murphy Brown the symbol of what's wrong with the liberal elites."[2] *Time*'s wiggy essayist Lance Morrow picked up on the same thought: "The racial dimension flows naturally into the political, where the uglier side of Quayle's mission begins to become apparent. One of Quayle's amazing but unlikable feats last week was metaphorically to transform old Willie Horton into a beautiful blond fortyish WASP has-it-all knockout."[3] The media may have believed that a TV character was a trivial issue -- but who turned this one sentence of a speech into a national controversy? The real scandal was that Willie Horton, a man who went to prison in Massachusetts for stabbing a gas station attendant to death, drew a weekend furlough under Gov. Michael Dukakis and raped a woman in Maryland, was, to liberal journalists, as trivial as Murphy Brown, mere shorthand for cheap Republican gimmickry. What moral message were they sending?

CBS reporter Bruce Morton devoted a haughty commentary to Quayle on the June 13 *Evening News:* "If you want to see the problem, visit a housing complex called Clifton Terrace. You could talk to, say, a 15-year-old mother of two who doesn't want her kids; wants instead to be a child herself and play with a doll. She might have been helped by a good sex education course, by readily available condoms, maybe even an abortion. Your administration disapproves of those." Morton's CBS colleague, Bernard Goldberg, offered a minority media viewpoint in *TV Guide:* "Over and over the anchors made the point that Murphy Brown's a fictional character -- as if that's really an issue. Do you think for a moment that if some TV character started saying vicious, ugly things about blacks, would anyone say 'Hey, it's only fiction'?"[4] When the elite consensus shifted to the idea that Dan Quayle was right about the social importance of the two-parent family, reporters did not apologize.

Meanwhile, former *Newsweek* reporter Mickey Kaus reflected on the media's view of the Clinton candidacy in the May 11 issue of *The New Republic:* "I'll vote for Bill Clinton in the District of Columbia primary on May 5. I agree with those who say he could be a very good President. Better than any of his Democratic opponents. Better than Bush or Perot. On the issues, he'll more than 'do' -- he's almost a neoliberal's dream....many pro-Clinton journalists can reasonably hope for something more than glamorous candlelight dinners in the Clinton White House. They can hope for jobs in the Clinton White House. The air is thick with undisclosed ambition....let's just say that the positions of press secretary and speechwriter to President Clinton will be among the more hotly contested job opportunities to come along."[5]

The summer months were unquestionably the best days for the Clinton campaign's media effort. The network morning show stars worked positive mentions into their coverage. *Today*'s Bryant Gumbel asked a panel of political experts on June 3: "Clinton is saying and doing a lot of the correct things. How does he get some attention?" *CBS This Morning* co-host Paula Zahn began the program on June 22: "Making headlines this morning: Bill Clinton comes up with a plan for the economy -- tax the rich, cut the deficit, and help just about everyone else."[6] The more than occasional lack of difference between Clinton commercials and TV coverage sometimes gave a whole new meaning to the campaign phrase "free media."

So it came as no surprise when Clinton's selection of Senator Al Gore as his running mate drew a wave of excitement in the headlines on July 10. "A Well-Groomed Understudy," read *The Washington Post*. "Moderate Who Was Raised to Be President," said *The New York Times*. "Born to Politics, Gore Fits the Ticket's Needs," wrote the *Los Angeles Times*. *Time* magazine headlined their story "Gore: A Hard-Won Sense of Ease," and Walter Shapiro called Clinton and Gore "the new gold dust twins of the Democratic Party."[7] In an otherwise serious article, *Los Angeles Times* reporter Sara Fritz paused to note: "'Prince Albert,' some have called him...Gore, whose handsome good looks have sometimes been compared to those of actor Christopher Reeve, has been on a political fast track all of his life."[8] Reporters touted how Gore's strengths countered Clinton's weaknesses. NBC's Andrea Mitchell said of the Republicans: "They also believe that the Willie Horton of this campaign is family values, and you can't get much more squeaky clean than Al Gore, his four kids, and his wife Tipper."[9]

ABC's Jim Hickey noted Gore's views on the environment, but actually cited liberal environmental groups as proof he was not an extremist: "One of the biggest advantages in choosing Gore as a political partner is the Senator's track record on the environment. He is a best-selling author on the subject. It's a track record the White House tries to paint as extremist. But Gore has already received the endorsement as an outstanding choice by the Sierra Club and other powerful conservation groups."[10] Despite Gore's scorn for man's depredation of the earth, reporters did not note Gore's annual receipt of $20,000 from Occidental Petroleum leases for the right to mine zinc on his family's Carthage, Tennessee farm. In August, *Washington Post* reporter Charles Babcock investigated that story, but no other media outlet followed up on it.[11]

The major media also ignored that "centrist" Al Gore had one of the lowest American Conservative Union ratings in the Senate. In 1988, he rated a cellar-dwelling 9. (Liberal Sen. Howard Metzenbaum had a rating of 4.) The National Taxpayers Union called him a "Big Spender," with ratings of 17 in 1990 and 21 in 1991.[12] But ideological camouflage was all the rage.

On the July 9 *CBS Evening News,* reporter Richard Threlkeld asserted: "Both Gore and Clinton are centrist, some would say conservative Democrats, white and male." On July 13, reporter Susan Spencer went even further: "I think it's fair to say that if you talk to delegates, even liberal Democrats now, they think that Al Gore and Bill Clinton could be a winning ticket. They're willing to swallow their problems that they have with such a conservative pair in hopes of winning."[13] The actual record of these liberal politicians and the actual promises of their platform were obscured in the campaign to avoid the L word at all costs.

II. CONTRASTING
CONVENTIONS

7

The Big Picture

"He's become a little more disciplined, Bill Clinton, but you know he loves a crowd. And he has, don't want to get carried away here, but he has the kind of hands people respond to." -- Peter Jennings during ABC convention coverage, July 15, 1992.

"Bush, the exponent of a 'kinder, gentler' approach to government at the 1988 convention, was presented with a 1992 platform loaded with puritanical, punitive language that not only forbade abortions but attacked public television, gun control, homosexual rights, birth control clinics, and the distribution of clean needles for drug users." -- Boston Globe reporter Curtis Wilkie, August 18, 1992.

In the television age, political conventions have metamorphosed from formal nominating events into four-night public-relations extravaganzas. Both parties in 1992 sought to use their convention time on television to present an inspiring, telegenic event to persuade voters to back their candidates.

Conventions are also political and social occasions for the elite, including the media elite. As previously mentioned, anchors Tom Brokaw and Peter Jennings appeared for a group of Democratic donors just before the Democratic convention in New York. When the National Lesbian and Gay Journalists Association held a reception honoring liberal Democrats -- then-Rep. Barbara Boxer (D-Calif.) Rep. Barney Frank (D-Mass.) and Del. Eleanor Holmes Norton (D-D.C.) -- they counted *Los Angeles Times* Editor Shelby Coffey, CNN President Tom Johnson, and *New York Times* Publisher Arthur Sulzberger Jr. among the attendees. Asked if they would attend a reception honoring Republicans at their Houston convention, Coffey stammered: "What we're doing was, has no political meaning other than signifying equality of opportunity to journalists."[1]

In addition, New York *Daily News* columnist Elizabeth Jensen noted celebrity attendees at *People* magazine Publisher Ann Moore's power lunch for Ellen Malcolm, President of EMILY's List, a fundraising group for liberal Democratic pro-abortion women. Among the guests were NBC's Faith Daniels and Mary Alice Williams, ABC's Lynn Sherr, CBS's Paula Zahn, and National Public Radio's Nina Totenberg.[2]

Major anchors, editors, and reporters did not often contribute to political campaigns, but a Media Research Center study of Federal Election Commission records from 1988 through the summer of 1992 did find contributions from their corporate supervisors. In a blow to the left-wing theory that media corporations are conservative, media executives and a few reporters donated to the Democrats six times more often than the Republicans. One mogul new to the national media business, Time Warner's Steven J. Ross, gave $100,000 to the Democratic National Committee.[3]

Would that care-free approach to the appearance of impartiality carry over to the convention coverage? Yes. As the conventions unfolded as a political mini-series, the networks helped Democrats promote their screenplay, a story of two likable Southern moderates shedding the electoral curse of liberalism with a positive, even conservative, vision of change. In stark contrast, the Republican convention was filtered through the network cameras as a gathering captured by threatening extremists who relied on a negative campaign of fear and hate of people unlike themselves.

In his January 4, 1993 article hailing Bill Clinton as *Time*'s "Man of the Year," essayist Lance Morrow's look back at 1992 distilled the media take on the two conventions. First came the Democrats at Madison Square Garden: "Clinton, whose stepfather's violent alcoholism shaped his early life, and Al Gore, who often borrows recovery language and concepts, turned the Democratic convention last summer into a national therapy session and display case for personal trauma and healing....The subtext of the recovery-and-healing line is that America is a self-abusive binger that must go through recovery. Thus: the nation borrowed and spent recklessly in the 1980s, drank too deeply of Reagan fantasies about 'morning in America' and supply-side economics. And now, on the morning after, the U.S. wakes up at the moment of truth and looks in the mirror. Hence: America needs the 'courage to change' in a national atmosphere of recovery, repentance, and confession."

But Morrow felt the Republicans' stint in Houston's Astrodome had a different character entirely: "The President permitted Buchanan, the man who tried to destroy him, to speak at the Houston convention during prime time. Buchanan delivered a snarling, bigoted attack on minorities, gays, and his other enemies in what he called the 'cultural war' and 'religious war' in America. Buchanan's ugly speech, along with another narrow, sectarian performance by Pat Robertson, set the tone of right-wing intolerance that drove moderate Republicans and Reagan Democrats away from the President's cause in November. If Houston represented the Republican Party, many voters said, they wanted out."[4]

Journalists wield power at conventions with their ability to create a positive or negative impression of the candidate -- as the previously little-known Sen. Dan Quayle drew near-universal media disapproval in 1988. To document the difference in convention coverage, the Media Research Center monitored prime time convention reporting as it unfolded nightly on ABC, CBS, CNN, NBC, and PBS. (Early in prime time, NBC tried to save money by combining its coverage in joint appearances with *The MacNeil-Lehrer NewsHour* staff on PBS while it ran entertainment fare on its own network airwaves). The results were distributed in a daily newsletter both to Democrats in New York and Republicans in Houston. After the conventions ended, prime time coverage, as well as morning show coverage, were evaluated for the following journalistic trends:

■ *Labeling:* Where did Republicans and Democrats land on the political spectrum? Would reporters characterize one party as conservative, the other as liberal? Or would Democrats be placed in the middle and Republicans on the extreme right?

■ *Agenda Questions:* Would reporters ask both sides devil's advocate questions from the other side's point of view? Or would both parties be pressed with liberal concerns?

■ *Controversies:* Would either party suffer from an embarrassing set of gaffes or uncomfortable ethical questions? Would either party suffer from harmful internal divisions?

This methodology duplicates an approach used by a team led by Georgetown Professor William Adams for the 1984 conventions on CBS and NBC. In that year's convention coverage, the Mondale/Ferraro Democrats were labeled "liberal" just 21 times to the Republicans' 113 "conservative" labels. In 1984, Democratic agenda questions were put to Republicans 84 times, but Republican agenda questions were submitted to Democrats only 11 times.[5] In 1988, the Media Research Center completed a similar study using the Adams parameters and found similar results.

What follows is an elaboration of the network trends that surfaced during the two conventions in 1992, as well as a look at the media's reaction to charges of liberal bias, and the surprising difference in approach to interviewing the spouses of the candidates.

8

Look for the Liberal Label

"The views that dominated the party for so long, what was proudly called liberal, are hardly in evidence in Madison Square Garden this week....Mr. Mondale, who in 1984 was the last down-the-line liberal to win the Democratic presidential nomination and who lost 49 states to Ronald Reagan in November, said he was resigned to the change." -- New York Times reporter David Rosenbaum, July 14, 1992.

"When you take a look at the party platform, some of the planks they are going to be talking about today, especially when it comes to business and economic affairs, this a very mainstream, if not in some cases conservative-sounding platform." -- ABC Good Morning America anchor Mike Schneider, same day.

The networks asserted their version of the political spectrum at the beginning of both conventions. ABC reporter Jim Wooten introduced the Democratic convention on the July 13 *World News Tonight:* "Not a liberal in sight, and that's the picture Clinton wants the convention to leave with the country, Democrats happily moving from their liberal past to their centrist future....So Clinton and his moderates have captured the Democratic Party for the moment."[1] CNN's Patrick Greenlaw presaged coverage of the Republican convention on the August 12 *Inside Politics:* "Word from within GOP ranks says the party may be in trouble if it caters too much to the far right."[2]

During the Democratic convention in New York City's Madison Square Garden, reporters used moderate labels more than liberal labels, 51 to 38. Amazingly, neither Bill Clinton nor Al Gore were labeled liberal once, but on 19 occasions they were called "moderate," "centrist," "middle of the road," or even "conservative." Similarly, all 12 prime time references to the Democratic platform described it with moderate or conservative, not liberal, labels.[3]

While this practice did not accurately describe to the public the administration that would follow, it was perhaps less implausible than the insistence in 1988 that Michael Dukakis, even Jesse Jackson, was not a liberal. *Newsweek's* table of contents read: "George Bush wants to convince voters that Michael Dukakis is a big spender who will raise taxes, coddle criminals, and disarm America. In other words, a 'liberal.' But does the dreaded 'L' word stick to Dukakis? Probably not."[4] Dukakis was described as "liberal" during 1988 convention coverage on only 13 occasions, and drew 10 "moderate" labels. Jesse Jackson drew only 9 liberal labels, but during CBS convention coverage, Walter Cronkite insisted that Jackson "succeeded in conducting a brilliant presidential campaign in which he enlisted white support as well as black support...and conducted a mainstream campaign." Overall, 52 percent of the networks' 86 labels at the 1988 Democratic convention were "liberal" to 48 percent "moderate." Republicans drew 214 labels, two and a half times as many descriptions, 85 percent of them "conservative."[5]

In 1992, the networks repeated its quadrennial pattern of submerging the Democrats' natural liberalism. During each of his three July 14 All-Star baseball game break-ins, Dan Rather announced the Democratic center had arrived: "Delegates approved the Clinton-Gore, center-of-the-road Democratic Party platform, trying to move the party closer to voters around the malls in America's suburbs." On CNN the same night, Ken Bode reported that the convention had "passed this moderate platform" and on NBC, Tom Brokaw declared: "This is a centrist platform."[6] The networks did not emphasize where the platform was less than centrist: backing abortion on demand, slashing defense spending, allocating more federal funds to schools, or returning to massive government jobs programs.

Although some network analysts did acknowledge that the convention delegates were more liberal than most of the country, most liberal labels were used to contrast politicians such as Mario Cuomo and Jerry Brown with the "moderate" Democratic nominee. On opening night, CBS reporter Bob Schieffer explained the beneficial side of Brown's 800-number liberalism: "It doesn't hurt to have someone acting kind of goofy off to the left because it leaves the man in the center looking more moderate." Similarly, Peter Jennings wondered: "Doesn't Tom Harkin represent sort of a dilemma here, because he's on the left wing of the party and Bill Clinton and Al Gore are really trying to move this party to the center?"[7]

One month later, Republicans gathering at Houston's Astrodome were tagged with about 40 more ideological labels than were the Democrats, and they were described with various conservative labels over moderate ones by a margin of 9 to 1. In total, viewers could have heard 118 conservative labels and 13 moderate ones. While there's nothing incorrect about describing the Republican party as conservative, the sheer numerical force of the labeling (118 conservative labels for the GOP, to only 38 liberal labels for the Democrats) served as a warning to voters that Republicans were more ideological than Democrats. While no Democrat in New York was ever described as "far left" or "hard left," CBS and CNN each used "hard right" or "far right" on five occasions to describe Republicans.[8]

The difference in the frequency of labeling quickly became apparent. In New York, the networks labeled the Democrats 22 times the first night. In the first night from Houston, however, the networks used about three times as many labels. ABC and CNN used more labels on Monday in Houston than they did in four nights of Democratic coverage.[9]

The networks' ideological estrangement from the GOP came across on all four channels. On ABC Monday night, Peter Jennings mused it was "very much conservatives' night. A very conservative opening prayer." At another point, Cokie Roberts found "an extremely conservative convention." On CBS, reporter Bob Schieffer thought the delegates represented "a very, very conservative group of Republicans."[10]

Dan Rather claimed it was Pat Buchanan's job "to set a frame of reference around a Moral Majority right, heavily influenced party." Rather twice described Buchanan's speech as "hard right." On the last night, August 20, Connie Chung called Dan Quayle's speech "far right" and asked Pat Robertson: "Has the party gone far right enough for you? I mean there's the gay bashing that you brought up. There's some people who think it's gone too far."[11]

In her personal preview of Pat Buchanan's Monday night speech, CNN's Candy Crowley explained: "As for what Buchanan has to say, this is really an appeal to the far right." On the last night, CNN's Charles Bierbauer recalled Buchanan's speech as being "heavy-handed conservative" and Frank Sesno labeled Buchanan and Bill Bennett as "very hard, far-right conservatives."[12]

NBC's Tom Brokaw said the platform "takes a right-hand turn on almost every key issue." That wasn't accurate, since the Republican platform had not taken a "right-hand turn" from previous platforms, but instead came close to a carbon copy, as Brokaw later acknowledged: "They've also put together here a platform that is very conservative...And the explanation is 'It's worked in the last three presidential elections, why shouldn't we try it again?' Well, in part, it is a changed world."[13]

The same divisions emerged in the three network morning shows. Democrats drew 31 "moderate" labels to 16 "liberal" ones. Republicans were described as "conservative" on 54 occasions, and "moderate" on 14. On the August 20 *Today*, NBC reporter Jim Miklaszewski found a positive in First Lady Barbara Bush's convention speech: "She stressed tolerance in an apparent attempt to pull the party back from the conservative hard-right turn it's taken at this convention so far."[14]

The trend grew so explicit that even the liberal *New York Times* noticed the labelmania. Reporter Elizabeth Kolbert wrote: "Ideally at a political convention, the response of the delegates is supposed to cue the television audience....On Monday night...it was hard for those in the television audience to feel that sympathetic bond. This was because every few minutes, commentators broke in to point out just how far to the right the Republican convention was aimed."[15]

9

The Agenda of Questions

"Do the poor and the inner cities get left out with this [Clinton-Gore] ticket?" -- NBC anchor Tom Brokaw to Texas Gov. Ann Richards, July 13, 1992.

"But if you cut taxes, isn't that going to drive the deficit further up, the bond market might collapse?" -- CBS anchor Dan Rather to HUD Secretary Jack Kemp, August 17, 1992.

The public expects reporters to play devil's advocate, making politicians respond to points from their opponents. In 1988, Republicans were challenged with 128 Democratic agenda questions, while the Democrats faced only 49 Republican agenda questions.[1] In 1992, Media Research Center analysts again scrutinized the agenda of the networks' questions. Some are purely informational, but others are more ideological in tone, from the right or the left.

Judging by the queries posed in 1992, reporters considered liberal Democrats just as much, if not more of, an opponent for the Clinton-Gore ticket than were the GOP and conservatives. The networks asked more questions (or raised more points) from the left than from the right, by a count of 46 to 38. But the Republicans were almost exclusively queried from the left, with liberal questions outnumbering conservative ones by a count of 130 to 17.[2] (The question count included statements made by reporters to which other reporters reacted. At the Republican convention, for instance,

NBC's John Cochran asserted: "Some of these [family values] issues have racial overtones, such as Bush's support for welfare reforms which penalize single mothers who continue having children.")

At the Democratic convention, examples of questions from the left came during Monday's joint PBS/NBC airtime, NBC's Andrea Mitchell told House Speaker Tom Foley that Clinton has "been trying to move the party farther to the right. Doesn't that leave you traditional liberals out in the cold?"[3] CNN's Gene Randall asked Sen. Howell Heflin: "You were part of the Anita Hill hearings this year. Will there be some kind of effect from those hearings that will play to the Democrats' advantage?"[4]

One of the smaller sample of questions from the right came from CNN's Catherine Crier, who asked Al Gore: "You are seen as someone with the environment as a major part of your agenda, even at the cost sometimes of an economic recovery. How are you going to avoid the label of being environmentally radical at a time and period when people are so worried about the economy and dollars?"[5] On July 14, NBC's John Cochran asked Arizona delegate Janet Napolitano: "Has the party become too sensitive to the women's movement?" and "Does the party need to do more to reach out to the white male?"[6]

NBC's Maria Shriver, like a true Kennedy, asked liberal questions at both conventions. At the Democratic convention, she asked Rep. Maxine Waters (D-Calif.): "After the L.A. riots, you talked about people needing change, wanting to empower themselves. What specifically should give them a reason to vote for this ticket -- two white boys from the South?...Do you feel that you have to sell out here?" Shriver asked Gov. Mario Cuomo: "Some say this ticket is hard to distinguish from the Republicans. I mean, they've moved so far to the right."

After Elizabeth Glaser's politicized speech to the Democratic faithful on her experience with AIDS contracted through a transfusion, including the sentence "My daughter did not survive the Reagan administration," Shriver asked Glaser to reiterate her rhetoric: "You place responsibility for the death of your daughter squarely at the feet of the Reagan Administration. Do you believe they are responsible for that?"[7]

On Tuesday of the Republican convention, Shriver challenged then-Health and Human Services Secretary Louis Sullivan: "To...one of those 36 million people [without health insurance], and that number is growing every day, to them that is not good enough. They need health insurance now. So are they better off voting for Bill Clinton if the Congress has this in their hands to have a Democratic President?"[8]

Another liberal question came from CNN's Bernard Shaw, who asked President Bush on August 17: "On the economy. President Bush, how would a tax cut help a person without a job?"[9] A number of liberal questions to Republicans addressed the social issues. On August 17, ABC's Lynn Sherr asked: "Peter, one of the deepest divisions in the Party this year has been the issue of abortion. I'm here with Kate Nyegaard, she's an alternate delegate from California, a lifelong Republican. But Mrs. Nyegaard, you're telling me that it is possible you may not vote for George Bush because of his position on abortion?"[10]

The next night, Peter Jennings asked William Bennett: "You said that Pat Buchanan gave a very good speech last night. How did you feel about all those negative references to gays and lesbians?..How good is it for the party?"[11] That same night, CNN's Catherine Crier asked Marilyn Quayle: "Is it fair when discussing family values to level an attack on a woman because she raises a family, child or children, and works? I mean, you worked the first two years after your children was [sic] born."[12]

The evening pattern of bias came through even stronger in the morning programs. Democrats were asked just 11 questions from the conservative agenda, but 26 from the liberal side, while Republicans drew more than 60 questions from the liberal agenda, and only 10 from the conservative side.[13]

CBS This Morning co-host Paula Zahn lobbed questions from the left at liberal Sen. Tom Harkin: "Critics though, even folks within your own party, are a little bit concerned that the ticket seems too narrow to them. Where are the voices of the unions, for example?" She also asked: "There is a feeling, though, Senator, that in reaching to those Reagan Republicans or Reagan Democrats that in fact you're disenfranchising some of your minority voters."[14]

Social issues motivated liberal questions from the morning hosts as well as the evening anchors. On the August 17 *Today,* Katie Couric asked Missouri Gov. John Ashcroft: "Aren't you fearful that this position, this very conservative position, will in fact alienate many women and more moderate Republicans and it will make a difference?"[15] *CBS This Morning* co-host Harry Smith asked Jerry Falwell and Family Research Council head Gary Bauer: "Let's throw some other words out to you and see if these resonate as words that should be included in family values, words like religious tolerance, racial harmony, compassion, empathy. Where are those words and how does that fit into this whole discussion? Because we haven't heard them."[16]

By setting the agenda of the questions, the networks drove the agenda of conversation, and created a very different tone at the two conventions. For all of each party's hope that it could manipulate its convention into a successful public relations presentation, the media had an impressive power in assisting (in New York) or frustrating (in Houston) the drive to gain the voters' support.

10

Covering Controversies

"I thought that the Buchanan speech had ugly elements in it, especially there at the end, take back our culture, take back our country. I think that was an appeal to racism." -- CBS analyst Charles Kuralt in prime time, August 17.

"Some have said they find the tone of this convention, some Republicans, a bit troubling. Abortion rights have been totally ignored in the platform; gay rights not acknowledged in the platform. Recently, Rich Bond said 'We are America, these other people in America are not America.' The 'other people,' presumably are Democrats. Do you think the Republican Party has grown, or become too exclusionary, too intolerant, and that this kind of rhetoric is divisive and counterproductive?" -- Katie Couric to Dan Quayle, August 19 Today.

By focusing on controversies, whether within the conventions or in a candidate's wider record, journalists imply that some actions or stands on the issues could be politically damaging. In some cases, repetitive media suggestions that something's "controversial" are meant to place an issue or action beyond the political pale.

Reporters have often focused more on controversies during Republican conventions than Democratic ones. In 1988, the networks avoided mentioning Michael Dukakis's prisoner furloughs or House Speaker Jim Wright's ethical offenses, which would end his career the next May. But when the 1988 Republican convention began, NBC's Tom Brokaw led off coverage: "In this hall, you'll hear nothing of Iran-Contra, or Meese, or Deaver, or Nofziger, or the tragedy in Beirut." In 1988, network anchors and reporters raised controversies like this on 32 occasions. Out of 898 network questions at the 1988

GOP convention, 125 (14 percent) centered on Dan Quayle's service in the National Guard or rumors about a relationship with lobbyist Paula Parkinson. Another 32 mentions occurred in discussions among the network experts themselves.[1]

The pattern changed in 1992, but the bias did not lessen. Reporters never made any Democrat respond to a question about the draft issue or discuss the political impact of Clinton's draft avoidance. Democrats drew only 15 mentions of controversy, and CNN was responsible for more than half of those. Most mentions were brief references to Clinton's struggles with charges of marijuana use, draft dodging, and infidelity. Reporters vaguely listed them as character tests Clinton faced down during the primaries and put behind him. CNN brought up two additional mentions of another controversy, the Democrats' role in the S&L bailout, which did not include the word "Whitewater."[2]

The networks totally ignored the House Bank and Post Office scandals in prime time. Asked why the story was missing, ABC's Ted Koppel responded: "I think, first of all, you'll find that the House banking scandal will probably get a lot of coverage at the Republican convention, just as the S&L scandal is getting a lot of coverage [at this convention] -- not because reporters are raising it, but because the speakers and delegates are raising it."[3] But the House Bank didn't come up in Houston, either.

Only CNN, outside of the prime time coverage in the study sample, alluded to the *Washington Times* story that Bill and Hillary Clinton purchased stock in 1978 in the South African diamond conglomerate DeBeers and then reported capital gains on their sale in 1980 and 1981, years in which apartheid continued and liberals called for divestment from South African businesses. "If that is true, it constitutes an outrage," left-wing TransAfrica activist Randall Robinson told the *Times*. "It goes beyond uninformed insensitivity."[4]

At the Republican convention, the networks surprisingly avoided highlighting controversies involving the Bush administration, such as Neil Bush's S&L problem, which was raised once on CBS and once on the joint NBC/PBS broadcast. Instead, the dramatic difference in controversy coverage came from within the conventions, especially on the following themes:

Accuracy: None of the Democratic addresses drew the network truth squads, even the Rev. Jesse Jackson's claim that the Virgin Mary was a single mother, somehow forgetting her marriage to Joseph. By contrast, the networks deemed Republican claims inaccurate three times in prime time. For instance, after Pat Buchanan's speech noted that Hillary Clinton compared marriage to slavery in a 1982 *Harvard Educational Review* article, Peter Jennings claimed: "Took a number of shots at Hillary Clinton. Didn't get that altogether accurate, but that'll come out in the debate as time goes on."[5]

The same questions of accuracy came up on the evening news. Days before the convention, on the August 12 *World News Tonight,* ABC's Cokie Roberts disdained Republican National Committee chairman Rich Bond for distributing the Harvard article, which clearly stated in illustrating the legal view that "certain individuals are undeserving of the right to take care of themselves," that "past and present examples of such arrangements include marriage, slavery, and the Indian reservation system." Roberts could have explored the article with context and nuance, explaining that Mrs. Clinton meant that in the past, some legal codes did use marriage to place women beneath their husbands in legal status. Instead, without spending more than 15 seconds on the essay, Roberts simply declared the opposite of the obvious: "She did not equate marriage with slavery. [The TV screen read: "DID NOT EQUATE MARRIAGE WITH SLAVERY."] Still, Republicans have seized on the article as evidence that Bill Clinton cannot be a moderate; not if he listens to his liberal wife. There's a concerted Republican effort to portray Hillary Clinton as an out-of-the-mainstream radical."

Roberts concluded: "In responding to stories about his personal life yesterday, President Bush said, 'It's ugly to go after your family and children and I don't want any part of it.' Republicans who report to the president seem ready to do the job instead."[6] ABC's gut-punching ending not only misled the viewer (had Bond attacked Chelsea?), but made no distinction between "going after" a candidate's family and debating the political views of a family member who would be assigned major political responsibilities if the Clintons won the White House. The language of the report suggested that its intention was not to educate the voter about Mrs. Clinton's beliefs, but to shame the Bush campaign out of trying this line of argument.

Exclusion: In New York, the Democrats excluded pro-life Pennsylvania Gov. Robert Casey, denying him permission to address the convention to express his opposition to the Party's abortion-on-demand stance. Instead, the Democratic National Committee permitted six Republican women to declare they would not vote for Bush because of his pro-life stance. But only CNN and NBC interviewed Casey in the four days of prime time convention coverage. CNN made another four mentions of the controversy in prime time. Even NBC anchor Tom Brokaw told *Dallas Morning News* TV writer Ed Bark after the convention he felt Casey's story "was underplayed." Bark quoted Brokaw: "During the course of the convention, it just kind of got lost in a lot of stuff. I think he should have gotten more attention for not getting attention."[7] But NBC never returned to the subject of Casey or the Democrats' position on abortion during the Republican convention.

But in Houston, on more than 20 occasions, network analysts charged the Republicans with trying to exclude people from their party. For example, Tom Brokaw told Buchanan on Tuesday night: "You gave the impression that if you're not a white, heterosexual, Christian, anti-abortion, anti-environment, you're somehow not welcome in the Republican Party."[8] CBS totally ignored Gov. Casey in New York, but in Houston Connie Chung asked Rep. Connie Morella (R-Md.): "Do you think the pro-choice voice has been stifled?"[9] Chung ignored that Labor Secretary Lynn Martin and Massachusetts Gov. William Weld were allowed to address the GOP delegates with their pro-abortion positions.

Chung went even further in an interview with Maine Gov. John McKernan, who explained that pro-abortion Republicans had only four of the six states required to force a floor fight on the platform's abortion plank. Chung sounded like an abortion advocate: "You are such a strong supporter of abortion rights but you gave up, you succumbed to the pressure....You know, it seems like such a small number. Good heavens, all you needed was six state delegations to try and bring it on the floor, then obviously two-thirds of the delegations, but I don't think you were organized, sir."[10]

Negativity: None of the networks called Democratic oratory at Madison Square Garden mean or personal, despite Elizabeth Glaser's charge that her daughter did not survive the Reagan administration, or in another Bible-mangling metaphor, Jesse Jackson's comparison of Dan Quayle to baby-killing legend King Herod. Instead, Dan Rather hailed Jackson as "one American politician who consistently speaks for the poor and downtrodden." On CNN, Bill Moyers oohed and aahed over Jackson: "You know a speech like this reaches me...I love the vibrations and the rhythms and cadences he puts behind lost causes."[11]

But the networks thumped a steady drumbeat of disapproval of Republican political rhetoric. From Willie Horton to Hillary Clinton, the networks suggested to Republicans on 70 occasions that they had been too negative with the Democrats in the four nights of prime time coverage.[12] That's 70 compared to zero occasions during the Democratic convention.

CNN's John Holliman asked a roundtable of voters on August 19: "You know, there's been a lot of criticism that the Republicans have been bashing the Democrats fairly big time in this campaign...Have the Republicans been too heavy-handed in being critical of the Democrats?" After Vice President Quayle's speech that night, CNN anchor Bernard Shaw took exception: "Very frankly, I am very puzzled by one paragraph, one sentence in the Vice President's speech on page six. In a very petulant voice, and listen to the words: he said, 'To Governor Clinton I say this: America is the greatest nation in the world and that's one thing you're not going to change.' Implying that Clinton is some kind of guerrilla, saboteur, or what have you. That's my reaction to that line, Ken Bode, I don't know about you. It implies something that, it seems that he's saying you're not as American as I am, your blood is not as red as mine."[13]

The same theme of Republican nastiness presented itself in the morning shows. On the August 21, 1992 *Today*, NBC reporter Andrea Mitchell not only complained of "really gross inaccuracies" about Governor Clinton's tax-and-spend record in Bush's acceptance speech, but added: "The meanest thing that he did, though, was trying to -- calling Bill Clinton's economics plan 'Elvis economics' and all of the Elvis references, because Elvis, of course, is Bill Clinton's patron saint, and that was really a low blow."[14]

Reviewing the media coverage, *Wall Street Journal* TV critic Dorothy Rabinowitz compared the real convention in Houston to what she called the "Reporters' Convention" on television. Rabinowitz took special notice of the difference between coverage of Democratic and Republican attacks: "The [Democratic] convention which saw a major address, delivered -- and much celebrated -- which flat out claimed that if George Bush were re-elected 'We are all at risk for AIDS.' This diatribe was, as we know, followed by another -- a mother with AIDS who charged that her child did not survive the Reagan administration and who told us she and her son would not survive another Bush administration. Did journalists come forward *en masse* to object that to make such charges so self-evidently preposterous -- and so brutal -- was unheard of, and pushed back the boundaries of fair play? On the contrary, most reporters seemed to see nothing remarkable -- or in need of correction in that rhetoric."[15]

11

Twisting the Tenets of Feminism

"Ever since the Clarence Thomas hearings last fall, the Republican Party has been struggling to overcome the perception that its regard for women is only a notch or two higher than that of the Navy Tailhook Association." -- *Time reporter Michael Duffy, August 24, 1992 issue.*

"Do you think the American people are not ready for someone who is as accomplished and career-oriented as Hillary Clinton?" -- *Katie Couric to Hillary Clinton, August 24, 1992 Today.*

In true Democratic "gender gap" form, media coverage of women gave the impression that Democrats were for women, and the Republicans were not. During the week of the Houston convention, Ted Koppel hosted a *Nightline* on the role of Hillary in the campaign. (The Clinton campaign sent George Stephanopoulos instead of Hillary.) Koppel began the program on what he probably thought was a generous note: "Let us not for a moment be confused into believing that this is only a conservative Republican thing, this business of some people feeling threatened by smart, assertive, professional women...Women who speak their minds in public are still swimming upstream in this country."[1]

In the same story in which he compared the GOP's record on women to the sexually harassing Navy airmen at Tailhook, *Time's* Michael Duffy protested that "no sooner had Bush been accused of infidelity than GOP chairman Rich Bond attacked Mrs. Clinton for likening marriage to slavery -- a gross distortion." Duffy did not explain how Bond was wrong. Duffy did rush to criticize Mrs. Quayle: "While the First Lady's image is cuddly and grandmotherly, Marilyn Quayle can seem hard, intolerant, and combative...Ever since a *Washington Post* series on her husband last winter depicted her as a power-mad spouse who once kicked to shreds a framed picture of her husband playing golf, Mrs. Quayle has been trying to soften her Cruella DeVil [*sic*] nature."[2]

But the media's soft spot for Democratic women became most apparent in the networks' wildly divergent approach to interviews with the two tickets' spouses. Mrs. Clinton and Mrs. Gore were puffed and promoted and asked to decry Republican attacks, while Mrs. Bush and Mrs. Quayle were poked and prodded about the inappropriate nature of Republican tactics.

The *Today* show first made it comfortable for Hillary Clinton and Tipper Gore on July 20. Bryant Gumbel added to the post-convention bounce with a set of light and favorable questions, uncharacteristically letting them speak for 60 to 90 seconds before interrupting. Gumbel began: "How are you? How's the trip going?...What's fun about jumping on a bus and wandering around through over 1,000 miles? Mrs. Gore?" Gumbel also asked: "You two, this comes as no bulletin, you two have surely seen the widespread speculation that one campaign isn't big enough for two women as strong-willed, independent-minded, outspoken as each of you are. You're laughing. How's that speculation strike you?" Gumbel stuck to the theme of Republican nastiness: "Mrs. Clinton, in an interview with PBS, you said you thought that the Republicans had made a calculated political decision to, in your words, go after you. How big an issue do you think you're yet going to be in this campaign?" After 73 seconds, Gumbel asked: ""You think it's going to get pretty nasty?"[3]

The "interview with PBS" came from Judy Woodruff, then with *The MacNeil-Lehrer NewsHour,* which provided an eye-opening demonstration of the double standard. During PBS convention coverage on July 14, Woodruff pitched softballs to Hillary Clinton, asking questions like: "You've been at this now for nine or ten months. What does this nomination mean to you and to your husband?....How is this different from other conventions for you?....The Clinton campaign has been saying that this is a week that they were trying to tell the American people more about who Bill Clinton really is. What is it that you think the American people should know about your husband that they may not know or may not understand?"

Woodruff especially helped Mrs. Clinton in discussing her role in the campaign: "Many people out there, of course, are still trying to figure out who Hillary Clinton is and one of the images that's been batted around, I guess you would say this year, is 'Well, she's this hard-driving, not only smart, but really pushing mastermind behind her husband who's even more ambitious than he is. What do you, you've obviously had to address that, what do you say?"

When it came to Republican attacks, Woodruff suggested they should not be part of the campaign: "How important do you think it is that Hillary Clinton not become an issue in this campaign, and I ask that, because Republicans, conservatives are already saying, you know about the articles that have been written -- 'She's very liberal, she came into this campaign being the wife of a governor with a strong set of opinions about everything to children's rights to aid to the El Salvador rebels and so on and so on. How important is it that that not enter in, and should it enter in?"[4]

But Woodruff grilled Barbara Bush on August 18: "Republican Party chairman Rich Bond saying the views of the Republicans are America, Democrats' views are not America...Well, I didn't hear a Democrat say that you're not American if you're Republican." Next, she demanded: "Campaign official Charles Black and Pat Buchanan have both said in the past 24 hours those who favor rights for homosexuals have no place in the Republican party...Were you pleased to have that message going out over television?"

The hardballs kept coming: "U.S. Treasurer Mrs. Villalpando, who just said yesterday, who joked that Gov. Clinton is a skirt chaser...Does that have a place in this campaign?" Woodruff went on: "Former Commerce Secretary and campaign chairman Robert Mosbacher..." Cutting her short, the First Lady took Woodruff to task: "Look, you're saying nothing nice...where were you during the Democrat convention defending us?" Woodruff tried to ignore that, returning to her line of inquiry: "But Mosbacher, who said in the last day or so that Gov. Clinton's alleged marital infidelity is a legitimate campaign issue." Mrs. Bush let loose: "You didn't listen to the Democratic convention, I think...I'm not sure you've been to the same political year I've been to, Judy. Now, c'mon, be fair." When the interview ended, Mrs. Bush suggested: "I'm going to listen to your questions. I'm going to monitor you."[5]

If Mrs. Bush was watching two days later on *The MacNeil-Lehrer NewsHour*, she might have uttered the Reagan line "There you go again." Woodruff ran Marilyn Quayle through the same gauntlet about her convention speech: "You also mentioned draft dodgers, another characterization made about some baby boomers. In this campaign, Senator Gore went to Vietnam, served there for a while. Your husband chose to stay here, and join the National Guard, and others. Why did you bring that up? Why is it important to discuss the war in Vietnam?" She continued: "But I guess I still don't understand what bringing up draft dodging and some of the other points you made has to do with this election."

Woodruff then questioned Mrs. Quayle's own campaigning: "You said in some remarks, you've been out speaking to delegations this week at the convention, and I read in an AP wire story that you told a Kentucky delegation and this is a quote, 'Maybe Bill Clinton did inhale, and we didn't notice, maybe he didn't notice.' Why did you bring that up? Is drug use important in this campaign, do you think?"

Woodruff ended by taking exception to Republican portrayals of Mrs. Clinton as liberal: "You have said, at least I saw in an interview that I think ran in *The New York Times* this week, 'Mrs. Clinton's ideas, some of them, are radical.' You used the word liberal, I think you used the word radical a couple of times. What were you referring to?...But I'm sure, as you know, they say these words, these terms, expressions that have been brought out, are taking them out of context, or a distortion of what she was trying to write twenty years ago, or fifteen years ago or something like that."[6]

Woodruff's husband, *Wall Street Journal* Washington Bureau Chief Al Hunt, sang the same song on CNN's *Capital Gang* on July 13. Columnist Mona Charen charged: "Hillary Clinton represents the left wing of the party, and she still has a big faction within the Clinton camp." Hunt replied: "I would point out that that is based on law review pieces she wrote 20 years ago. It's utter, complete nonsense. You don't have anything factual." When Charen noted the

New World Foundation, on whose board Mrs. Clinton had served, gave money to the Committee in Solidarity with the People of El Salvador (CISPES), which supported the Marxist FMLN guerrillas, and radical lawyer William Kunstler, Hunt screamed: "No! That is the far-right *American Spectator* kind of neo-fascist hit nonsense!"[7]

On August 24, both *CBS This Morning* and NBC's *Today* featured taped interviews with the dynamic duo of Democratic spouses, and both offered themselves as eager and willing forums for criticism of the just-completed Republican convention. *CBS This Morning* co-host Paula Zahn asked: "I wanted to ask both of you if you could react to a comment that Mrs. Quayle made during her speech when she basically said liberals are disappointed because most women don't want to be liberated from their essential natures as women. What do you think she was saying to American women?"

Zahn then asked: "I wanted you to respond to another thing Mrs. Quayle's chief of staff said when she was asked to draw a distinction between Mrs. Quayle and yourself, and she said 'Marilyn Quayle is absolutely committed to her family. She makes time for her children, and she always is home for dinner by seven o'clock.'" When Mrs. Clinton refused to address the question, Zahn claimed: "What we've heard, though, from a number of voters, in particular women, is that they wanted to see you swinging back. Why haven't you defended yourself in the last couple of weeks?"[8] Mrs. Clinton was not blind to the political advantages of these interviews: since the morning news women were doing the spin control for her, she chose not to present herself as the snippy revenge-seeker who asked the press to chase George Bush's sex life in *Vanity Fair*, but as the Superwoman next door who could let that awful criticism roll right off her back.

On NBC, *Today* co-host Katie Couric didn't ask questions so much as try to set up speeches: "If you listen to Pat Buchanan, he talked about you, Mrs. Clinton, he talked about you in his speech before the Republican convention. I'd like to give you an opportunity to respond to those charges."

Couric also declared: "One reason, Mrs. Clinton, you came under attack by not only Pat Buchanan, but by Rich Bond, chairman of the Republican National Committee, and to a lesser degree, by

Marilyn Quayle and Barbara Bush, was that they claim that you and your husband have predicted that this will be a co-presidency. You've probably heard that a lot." Then Couric asked a real toughie: "Do you think the American people are not ready for someone who is as accomplished and career-oriented as Hillary Clinton?"[9] Conservative predictions that Mrs. Clinton would be both liberal and powerful in the White House, which came true, were greeted repeatedly with psychoanalysis, that conservatives feared strong women.

Four days earlier, Couric also hammered Mrs. Bush: "Bill Clinton actually says that discussion about Hillary and talk about where she stands on various issues and analysis of some of her previous writings have been really misinterpreted and taken out of context. And he finds it, quote, something like [a] 'pathetic and desperate effort.'"[10]

The pounding of the Republican spouses and the puffing of the Democrats twisted the tenets of feminism in a strange way. The women who feminists reviled for being deferential to their husbands drew the toughest inquiries, while the women who proclaimed the arrival of a new, more powerful woman were given softball questions. Mrs. Clinton and her strongest supporters in the media insisted that she was a "transitional figure," a new sort of First Lady who would chart a new course for the role of women at the center of power. But the actual tenor of coverage was not in any way a reflection of journalistic change: instead, media women provided aid and comfort to the women they agreed with, and demanded that women that in any way disagree with them defend their political incorrectness.

Time's Margaret Carlson, Hillary's most active booster, explained her feelings in a fall Freedom Forum special report on campaign coverage: "There are many women in the press, and you couldn't have fought the battles you have fought to get where you are and not find what the Republicans said about women offensive...It's not possible, you cannot be that objective. When Marilyn Quayle says that I have given up my essential nature as a woman and that I don't take care of my family because I'm working, I cannot help feeling offended by that."[11] Taking offense (not to mention taking Mrs. Quayle out of context) was not something journalists resisted in the name of professionalism. Liberalism trumped professionalism.

III. THE FALL CAMPAIGN

12

Delighting in Double Standards

"There's a huge pool of economic anger in these small towns, and Clinton is trying to exploit it...In the heart of America, Clinton is finding the hurt of America." -- Reporter John Dancy, August 29 NBC Nightly News.

Reporter Tom Pettit: "Quayle also likes working obscure small towns in the South...The Quayle campaign stop begins to resemble Disney World's Main Street -- the crowds predominantly white. But Quayle officials say he has been in many ghetto areas, but says he hasn't been there recently because there aren't many Republican votes there....No dirty cities, no urban decay, no problem...Why is Quayle avoiding big cities?"
Historian Michael Beschloss: "The strategy is to keep him away from places he can do harm."
Pettit: "Right now, he is presenting his vision to the America of the past -- small town America." -- Same newscast, next story.

Campaigns must be much more fun for reporters than they are for politicians. Journalists, unlike politicians, aren't often ridiculed in public for their constantly shifting standards, even within the same newspaper or newscast. From the 1992 conventions until Election Day, one campaign's brilliant tactic could easily be described as the other campaign's attempt to avoid certain disaster.

Reporters were eager to elaborate on the campaign story they began during the summer: an appealing, moderate candidate of change crusading against an old, tired, desperate slinger of mud, embarrassed by his running mate. Reporters on the Clinton bandwagon wrote of jovial candidates and inspiring speeches, while journalists on the Bush trail found a nasty band of attack specialists who said all the wrong things. Any hint of scandal in Clinton's past was quickly spun into another example of Republican negativity. The September 14 *New York Times* provided a succinct demonstration of bias: on one page, the *Times* ran a story headlined "Al Gore Runs with Quips and Pranks on Trail." On the opposite page, the *Times* story on the Republican campaign was headlined "Bush Is Harsh, His Backers Harsher."[1]

The love affair with Clinton and Gore grew most obvious when the Democrats began a cross-country bus trip in the third week of July, right after their convention. In *The Washington Post*'s infamous Style section story headlined "New Heart-throbs of the Heartland," writer Joel Achenbach declared: "Clinton and Gore go together like a flannel lumberjack shirt and blue jeans. They match! They fit together in a photograph the way George Bush and Dan Quayle never could."[2]

In another story, *Post* reporter Edward Walsh proclaimed: "When they appear with their wives, Hillary Clinton and Tipper Gore, they look like two suburban couples, perhaps old college friends, out on the town for a good time. And whether they are playing miniature golf with their wives, tossing a football around or gleefully backslapping each other at campaign rallies, the images and the message are always the same: Youth, vigor, energy. And change."[3] On *The McLaughlin Group*, *Newsweek*'s Eleanor Clift added: "They got more positive coverage on this bus tour than the Beatles got on their first tour of America. More reporters were oohing and aahing. It was almost embarrassing. I'm sorry I didn't get a chance to do it until now."[4]

A couple of weeks later, *Post* reporter David Maraniss promoted the foursome again: "Delighted Democrats like to say of Clinton and Gore that theirs is a partnership where 1 plus 1 equals 5, and when Hillary Clinton and Tipper Gore are added to the equation, 2 plus 2 equals 10. And the power of their numbers does seem to multiply exponentially at times such as this afternoon, when the eight-bus caravan made a semi-impromptu stop at a rest area in Bowling Green, Mo."[5] Brookings Institution analyst Stephen Hess told *The Washington Post*: "You read the papers and you'd think it was going to be a runaway election for Bill Clinton."[6]

Even as the bus trip idea lost its novelty in August, *Newsweek's* Joe Klein celebrated the magic of the campaign: "Clinton and Gore had once again transcended the traditional rites and cliches of politics...The crowds this time wouldn't be so large or enthusiastic, the candidates wouldn't be quite so eloquent -- but something was happening out there on Highway 61, an emotional connection that mocked and then demolished the industrial-strength cynicism of the 150 journalists tagging along." Two weeks later, this same writer summarized the Republican convention this way: "The whole week was double-ply, wall-to-wall ugly....the Republican Party reached an unimaginably slouchy, and brazen, and constant level of mendacity last week....[Bush] is in campaign mode now, which means mendacity doesn't matter, aggression is all and wall-to-wall ugly is the order of battle for the duration."[7]

Klein's bald advocacy in favor of Clinton apparently didn't stop in print. Howell Raines, then-Washington Bureau Chief of *The New York Times,* told the *Columbia Journalism Review* that "he made it a main job to warn against and protect his younger reporters from the 'Conformity Cops,' specifically [former *Washington Post* reporter Sidney] Blumenthal and Joe Klein of *New York* magazine and since the spring, of *Newsweek.*" Raines said: "When reporters go around campaign planes criticizing reporters who refuse to cheerlead, that's unhealthy. That's part of what we've seen this year."[8]

A similar story appeared in *The New Republic,* where writer Jonathan Rauch told a "prominent political reporter" that the Clinton economic plan had a "rich larding of sham and evasion," and the reporter responded: "You economic people aren't happy unless a candidate puts a gun in his mouth and pulls the trigger."[9] The term "political reporter" acquired another meaning: not only did they report on politics, but these anecdotes suggested their news coverage was driven more by their political views than by a sense of fair play.

As the fall campaign began, the networks rededicated themselves to avoiding what they felt were the mistakes of the 1988 campaign, the feeling of being manipulated into the stories the campaigns staged and selected. ABC anchor Peter Jennings even announced it on the air on September 17: "We'll give you the day's headlines, and we'll only devote more time to a candidate's daily routine if it is more than routine. There'll be less attention to staged appearances and soundbites designed exclusively for TV."[10]

ABC led the networks, then, in refusing to cover the actual campaign -- the speeches, the rallies, the face-to-face meetings with voters -- in favor of "the issues" as they decided to define them. Liberal writer Mickey Kaus wrote an article in *The New Republic* noting that on September 17 (the day of Jennings' pious announcement), a Bush campaign speech that Kaus called a "fine demagogic effort" did not receive one syllable of coverage on the evening news. Bush accused Clinton of studying "social engineering," declaring "my opponents are cranking up their models, ready to test them on you." (That's not very demagogic, considering the 1,300-page Ira Magaziner model that became the Clinton health plan.)

Kaus decried the networks' power grab: "The things the networks have given us in place of the campaign -- endless analyses and repetitive interviews with ordinary voters -- don't illuminate the electorate's mindset as much as threaten to embalm it. How can any candidate make a fresh point or change anyone's mind when newscasts are shaped almost entirely by elaborate celebrations of what the voters already think?"[11] Changing minds away from the pro-Clinton wave they helped generate was not exactly the media's first priority.

13

The Draft and The Trip

"There is no evidence that Bill Clinton has lied. He's done nothing illegal. He has what I would call the politician's disease. He has tailored the truth to adapt to the reality of running in a conservative southern state." -- Newsweek reporter Eleanor Clift on The McLaughlin Group, September 12.

"What are your expectations? How nasty do you expect George Bush to try to be?" -- Bryant Gumbel to John Chancellor, October 9 Today.

Few reporters dug into Bill Clinton's draft history the way the entire press corps clawed over Dan Quayle's record in the summer of 1988. One exception was William Rempel of the *Los Angeles Times,* who uncovered an entirely new angle on Bill Clinton's draft history on September 2. Rempel found a new character, Clinton's Uncle Raymond, whose machinations with the local draft board delayed the future President's physical for an unusually long ten and a half months, and secured an unopen slot in the Naval Reserve. Robert Corrado, the last surviving member of the Hot Springs draft board, complained that an aide to Sen. William Fulbright (D-Ark.) also pressured Clinton's draft board. (Clinton interned for Fulbright when he attended Georgetown University.) Rempel added allegations that Sen. Fulbright met with Clinton's Uncle Raymond in July 1968.[1]

In short, not only had the public learned in February that Clinton not fulfilled his obligation with the ROTC at the University of Arkansas as promised; or learned in April that Clinton had lied for more than a decade about receiving a draft induction notice; now, the story deepened to Clinton's use of the influence of relatives and powerful politicians to secure an otherwise unavailable Naval Reserve slot and to delay his military physical. Each of these stories peeled away another layer of deception like the skins of an onion. Writ large, the media reaction in every case was not embarrassment or outrage, but apathy.

Despite the story's increasing resemblance to the allegations that triggered the Quayle feeding frenzy, once again, none of the networks led with Rempel's bombshell that night. ABC, CBS, and CNN did only one story on their evening newscasts. NBC reported nothing. The next week's newsmagazines also downplayed the story. *Time* dedicated four paragraphs, *U.S News* just two paragraphs, and *Newsweek* gave it the second-to-last paragraph in a campaign roundup under the heading "The Character Caricature."[2]

In an effort to once again crush a damaging story, Clinton responded by trashing the media, charging "You've got a feeding frenzy on about something that even if it's true, it doesn't amount to a hill of beans," and, "Nobody's had a tougher press than I have. No candidate in history has."[3] Not only did the story trigger no feeding frenzy, the media's tone remained defensive despite being deceived by Clinton. The September 9 *USA Today* did finally put the story on the front page, but declared: "Democrats can also counter with accusations that Quayle used family influence to land a spot in the Indiana National Guard."[4]

Reporters spent weeks feeding on Quayle in 1988, reporting (inaccurately) that there were no vacancies in the Indiana National Guard and decrying the unfair use of family influence. Now, when a reporter uncovered that Clinton received a Naval Reserve slot that was created especially for him and gained an unprecedented, nearly year-long delay on his physical, this story received a dramatically weaker emphasis than the Quayle story.

Quayle's opposite number, Al Gore, never faced any journalistic investigation of his Vietnam service and the possibility of Senate influence. Why did Gore only spend six months in Vietnam instead of the usual 13-month tour? Did Gore get special assignments due to the influence of his father, Senator Al Gore Sr.? Since Gore served as a journalist with *Stars and Stripes,* why did he release in 1987 a presidential campaign brochure with a Vietnam-era picture of him holding a rifle? No one in the media except *The Washington Times* raised these questions.[5]

Reporters saved their outrage for another story. On October 5, *The Washington Times* reported Bill Clinton had traveled to Moscow in the middle of the Vietnam War.[6] On CNN's *Larry King Live* two days later, Bush responded to a question by calling for Bill Clinton to "level with the American people"[7] about his activities during the Vietnam War, including his student trip to Moscow. Bush simply challenged Clinton to tell the voters what he was doing in Europe in 1969 and 1970, organizing demonstrations abroad while misleading the ROTC at home.

Republicans thought they had found a way to identify Clinton as a liberal for organizing anti-war protests, as well as put the focus of attention on Clinton's ever-changing life story. In an October 9 column in *USA Today,* former President Gerald Ford noted that Clinton told Phil Donahue "I didn't have anything to do with" the Vietnam Moratorium Committee. But in his 1969 letter to his ROTC commander, Eugene Holmes, Clinton wrote: "After I left Arkansas last summer, I went to Washington to work in the national headquarters of the Moratorium, then to England to organize the Americans here for demonstrations." Clinton also claimed on *Donahue* that "I was not a big organizer of anti-war activities."[8]

Reporters didn't ask Clinton for an explanation. They wanted Bush's hide. On *The McLaughlin Group, Newsweek* reporter Eleanor Clift protested: "This is in the finest McCarthy tradition, to suggest there was something suspicious with no evidence...I don't see how George Bush sleeps at night after stooping this low."[9] On *CBS This Morning* October 12, co-host Harry Smith declared after the first debate: "Clearly, that red-baiting junk didn't work last night." Smith tried the same line on Pat Buchanan on October 19: "Why is it the White House, though, has insisted on this sort of campaign to discredit Bill Clinton, which has clearly not worked in the least?" To radio and television talk show host Rush Limbaugh on October 21, Smith again insisted that "none of this red-baiting, none of this stuff, none of it works."[10]

Instead of asking Clinton about the substance of the question (Why can't you tell a straight story about your role in the anti-war movement?), reporters simply asked for reaction (Isn't this tactic desperate and sad?). *Time* headlined its story "Anatomy of a Smear." *Newsweek* media critic Jonathan Alter's column was titled "The Smear Heard 'Round the World."[11] In the same issue, *Newsweek*'s Joe Klein wrote an article titled "Bush's Desperate Game." After the subhead "Sewer patrol," Klein wrote: "Never before has a candidate for President been so directly, *personally* mean-spirited and derogatory toward his opponents, so willing to indulge in demagogic innuendo." (Italics his.)[12]

Reporters also downplayed the October 27 news that Ross Perot's running mate, Admiral James Stockdale, blasted Clinton's involvement in protests against the Vietnam War. Stockdale, who spent eight years in Vietnamese prison camps, declared: "Those comrades of mine who died, the extra 10, 15, 20 thousand, that blood is on your hands, you war protesters." Stockdale added: "Every time in prison we would hear that they had one of these big galas of the sort Clinton was arranging here and there in the world, 'Huh,' we'd say. 'Another year in this place.'" While *The Washington Times* put the story on the front page and *USA Today* spotlighted it on page 2, *The Washington Post* buried it in the 23rd paragraph of a Perot story on Page A-11. *The New York Times* buried it at the very end of a Perot story on Page A-17. CBS and NBC read brief stories late in their newscasts. ABC totally ignored it.[13]

While Clinton would eventually blame the Cold War's demise as one reason for his unpopularity -- after all, he was denied the role of leader of the Free World, which might have added to his stature -- the end of the Soviet Union and its client states drained all the shock value out of his Vietnam organizing activities. Had Clinton been the Democratic nominee in 1988, his resistance against the American war effort might still have been clearly identified as appeasement in the face of tyranny.

14

Where Was Whitewater?

"In essence the platform, like this convention, is beckoning the disaffected Democrat back home. It's telling them this party will protect the interests of the people who, in Bill Clinton's words, played by the rules and got the shaft."
-- ABC reporter Jeff Greenfield, August 14, 1992 convention coverage.

"For Bush it is more of the same, a laissez-faire embrace of the free markets, a scarcely subtle survival-of-the-fittest signal. The Republicans, it is clear, see nothing wrong with extending the Me Decade indefinitely....But the core of Clinton's vision is distinguishable from the President's and is perhaps best described as the call for a We Decade; not the old I-am-my-brother's-keeper brand of traditional Democratic liberalism, but an acknowledgment that the interconnectedness of global economics requires that many prosper, or no one will." -- Time Special Correspondent Michael Kramer, October 19, 1992.

While reporters continued to ignore Whitewater, the double standard in covering the first family and the aspiring first family continued. On September 15, *Dateline NBC* aired a hard-hitting investigative segment on the financial dealings of George Bush's son Neil. Co-host Jane Pauley introduced the story: "New controversy about his failed oil business...Government-backed loans financed his company. The wells were dry, but he led the good life. Will taxpayers be stuck with the $200 million bill? Brian Ross confronts Neil Bush. Tonight, the facts, the figures, and a most fortunate son."

In a clip from an earlier interview, Neil Bush claimed it was hard to explain complicated transactions. NBC investigative reporter Brian Ross insisted: "It's really not that complicated: quite simply, while his father has been in the White House, American taxpayers have been stuck with millions of dollars in bills from failed business ventures involving Neil Bush, including one deal that only now is fully coming to light, and all the while, the President's son has been living a life that some people say is like that of an American prince." Ross pointed out that Bush paid himself salaries of $120,000 and $160,000 as his ventures failed. The President's son manipulated for personal gain not only a taxpayer-defrauding Colorado savings and loan, but government agencies like the Small Business Administration.[1]

Ross demonstrated the confidence of a good investigative reporter, taking complex investigations and boiling them down for the viewer. He did investigate some stories on the Democratic side, including the June 2 feature on Virginia Kelley's actions as a nurse, and an October 9 story on Al Gore taking campaign contributions in 1988 from junk-bond dealers who were later indicted. His story on Neil Bush very effectively presented the President's son as a dilettante investor trading on his name for personal profit. Ross brought in a small business owner from the Denver area who was denied an SBA loan the same year Neil Bush's application was accepted. To add to the temper-raising impact of the piece, Ross and his camera crew attempted "ambush interviews" of Neil Bush and SBA administrator Patricia Saiki on the floor of the Republican convention, adding to the feel of corruption.

But if NBC raised the Bush family's S&L connections, balance demanded a look at the Clintons' actions as well. In the years before Clinton ascended to the White House, Hillary Clinton made more than $200,000 a year, more than Neil Bush's self-declared salaries, as a lawyer and corporate board member, opportunities at least partially realized due to her marriage to the Governor. She not only served as an owner of Whitewater Development, but represented Madison Guaranty Savings & Loan before state agency heads appointed by her husband. But the week before the Neil Bush report, *Dateline* anchor Jane Pauley interviewed Hillary Clinton -- and asked her not one question about her role in representing Madison, which paid her for legal services at the same time it was defrauding the taxpayers of more than $50 million.

Pauley's interview with Mrs. Clinton, very politely taped and edited, with no ambushing camera crews, focused instead on GOP nastiness: "When you hear yourself held up, as you were at the Republican convention, some people have used the word 'demonized,' does it make you hurt or make you mad?" Pauley also asked Hillary: "What was the worst things you've heard said about you?" and "What was the grossest distortion of your record?"

Pauley asked three more questions on the same theme: "What is it about you that pushes people's hot buttons?...At the Republican convention, there seemed to be an attitude that Marilyn Quayle had the moral high ground, because she gave up her law career to raise a family and be supportive of her husband. Will you cede her the moral high ground?...Before Governor Clinton declared for the Presidency, you prepared Chelsea. Bad things may be said about Daddy. Was Chelsea at all prepared for bad things being said about Mommy?"[2]

Female reporters continued to lavish praise on Mrs. Clinton. On October 20, *Chicago Tribune* writer Jessica Seigel swooned: "The women whom Republicans tried to smear as a cookie-hating Lady Macbeth is being greeted more like an Eleanor Roosevelt. Like Roosevelt, she has overcome criticism from those who resent her independence, earning widespread affection and respect for doing just that." Ten days later, *Washington Post* society writer Donnie Radcliffe added: "It hasn't been easy being Woman of the Year in this Year of the Woman, everybody's favorite target for all that's dangerous about being independent, smart, impatient, articulate, outspoken, ambitious -- and while she's at it, a three-fer: wife, mother, and successful corporate lawyer. By any standard Hillary Clinton has been a handful for America to deal with."[3] Mrs. Clinton's journalistic allies celebrated her law career, but never considered the ethics of what she did as a lawyer.

Reporters kept on ignoring Whitewater, despite major Democratic campaign speeches against the Republicans' profit from and management of the S&L bailout. Candidate Clinton proclaimed in his 1991 announcement speech that "When the ripoff artists looted our S&Ls, the President was silent. In a Clinton Administration, when people sell their companies and their workers and their country down the river, they'll get called on the carpet."[4] Mario Cuomo's nominating speech for Clinton at the Democratic convention taunted: "Americans discovered that wealthy bankers -- educated in the most exquisite forms of conservative Republican banking -- through their incompetence and thievery and the government's neglect had stolen or squandered everything in sight!"[5] Reporters wouldn't turn Cuomo's words on Clinton, but reporters kept the "family values" theme of the Republican convention in the news for weeks in an effort to disparage the Bush campaign. Weeks after the convention, print reporters still quoted unnamed Bush campaign officials claiming they knew the family values focus alienated voters.

If the hot rhetoric of the summer didn't justify another look, the serious decision being made in the fall certainly did. When the *Forbes Media Critic* asked in 1994 to explain why the press did not continue or revisit reporting on the Whitewater story, reporters and editors assigned to the Clinton campaign listed a number of time limitations. When the story first broke in early March, reporters were in the middle of a 28-day period of 28 primary elections, forcing a focus on each race. By late spring, they said, Ross Perot's entry into the race gave the media a new story that required an investment of journalistic resources.[6] But a media that wished to avoid what they felt were the mistakes of 1988 -- unserious PR froth and endless horse-race handicapping -- would have demonstrated media seriousness, instead of the media bias they displayed, by devoting serious attention and resources to the Whitewater story.

As one of Clinton's biggest media boosters, *Newsweek*'s Joe Klein, told *Media Critic* editor Terry Eastland in 1994, the Clintons were guilty of "very clear hypocrisy" for running against "the forces of greed who made out like bandits" while representing themselves "as the defenders of those who worked harder and harder for less and less during the 1980s."[7]

15

Ad Police Brutality

"Feel-bad ads trying to drag down Bill Clinton are regarded as the only hope. In a multi-million dollar assault, Clinton is being portrayed as a duplicitous blobhead who governs a Hee Haw backwater where only the taxes soar." -- CBS Evening News reporter Eric Engberg, October 5, 1992.

"Negative campaigning is a time-honored exercise in trying to avoid responsibility and shifting blame and fears onto the other guy. The fact that the Clinton camp has responded so quickly is a testament to how well this sort of campaigning has worked in the past." -- CBS reporter Mark Phillips, same night.

Having decried any focus on Clinton's personal dealings as out of bounds, reporters moved to declare any attack on Clinton's political career or proposals as equally malicious and false. On the issue where reporters and Democrats alike feared Bush would be most effective -- Clinton's stated intention to raise taxes -- the networks rushed to blunt Bush's attack by labeling it dishonest.

Critiques of the GOP's anti-tax rhetoric started early. On July 21, as the Clinton-Gore bus trips were getting raves, NBC reporter John Cochran attacked Sen. Robert Dole's claim that Clinton's plan called for tax increases twice as large as those of candidates Michael Dukakis and Walter Mondale combined. Cochran pronounced: "Well, not quite. Walter Mondale proposed $85 billion in new taxes in 1984. But Michael Dukakis proposed no new taxes in 1988. Double $85 billion and you get $170 billion. Bill Clinton calls for $150 billion in new taxes on corporations and the rich."[1]

Cochran was wrong. First, Michael Dukakis may not have proposed any new taxes, but he made no "read my lips" pledge -- he only suggested they'd be a "last resort," and they were never a "last resort" in Massachusetts. It was hardly fair to treat Dukakis as a no-new-taxes candidate when he failed, unlike Clinton, to produce a detailed plan of action with revenue estimates. Second, and much more important, Clinton's economic plan may have claimed only $150 billion in new taxes, but that figure did not include any increased revenues for, among other things, ambitious new job training or health care programs. Clinton had proposed a 1.5 percent payroll tax for job training and loosely endorsed a "play or pay" health plan with a payroll tax of seven to nine percent. (The Clinton health plan later proposed a 7.5 percent "employer mandate.") Those two taxes, added to the rest of Clinton's plan, would have easily made Clinton American history's highest tax raiser.

On the August 27 *Nightly News,* NBC aired footage of Bush charging that Clinton's plan included "$220 billion in new spending, plus the largest tax increase in history, $150 billion." With a big red graphic screaming "WRONG," John Cochran declared: "In 1982, Ronald Reagan and his Vice President, George Bush, presided over the largest projected tax increase in history -- $152 billion."[2] The Bush campaign tried to note that the 1982 tax increase took place over five years, not four. Reporters didn't find it odd to argue Clinton wasn't a liberal while insisting he proposed only the second largest tax increase in history. Once in office, Clinton actually proposed a tax increase almost twice the size of the original campaign claims. But the networks never reran their old report with a big red "WRONG" placed over their own reporting.

Meanwhile, Clinton's ads were usually ignored by the "truth squads." On August 30, the Clinton campaign released an ad claiming that under its economic plan: "Those making over $200,000 will pay more. The rest of us get a break." None of the Big Three networks critiqued the ad for accuracy, asking how Clinton could pay for all the programs he promised by only raising taxes on a tiny fragment of taxpayers. The Bush campaign released a detailed rebuttal of the ad, but the networks didn't care to run more than a few seconds of campaign manager Bob Teeter's press conference.

Nine days later, ABC reporter Jeff Greenfield was still perturbed with Bush's claim that Clinton approved 128 tax increases in Arkansas: "Campaigns are not supposed to be exercises in objectivity. We expect them to put their own spin on facts and figures. But even in politics, some facts are more suspect than others...Where did that number [128 Clinton tax hikes] come from? The Bush campaign says it simply looked in the Arkansas legislative handbook and added up every tax and fee hike during Bill Clinton's governorship. But every independent examination of that statistic has called the Bush figures misleading, distorted, or false." But Clinton's campaign listed 127 tax and fee hikes, less than a "New Democrat" fiscal record.[3]

On September 24, the Bush campaign released a humorous banjo-picking ad charging Clinton with raising sales taxes in Arkansas. That day, CNN's Brooks Jackson echoed the Clinton campaign's claims: "The total Arkansas tax burden is still low. In fact, it ranks 46 out of 50." CNN listed its source as Citizens for Tax Justice (CTJ), but didn't mention that the group is a union-funded liberal group favoring tax hikes on the rich, and that David Wilhelm, the Clinton campaign manager, had been a leader of CTJ before the campaign.[4]

Two days later, Dan Rather picked up the attack: "The Clinton-Gore campaign began running new advertising today. The ads, airing in Texas, blame Mr. Bush for the loss of 160,000 jobs in the energy industry." CBS did not evaluate the accuracy of the Clinton ad. Instead, they turned to reporter Eric Engberg, who counted the errors he felt Bush made in a campaign swing in the South. Engberg's corrections sounded like Clinton campaign rhetoric: "It is true that the Arkansas sales tax has gone from 3 to 4.5 cents. Clinton had little choice, given a state constitution that effectively blocks income tax hikes. Bush didn't mention that Arkansas taxes are among the lowest in the nation."[5]

That same night on the *NBC Nightly News,* anchor Garrick Utley tried to correct the Bush claim that Clinton raised the sales tax by 33 percent. Utley declared: "In fact, the increase was only from 3 to 4.25 percent. And Arkansas is still a low-tax state. Third lowest in the nation." Utley not only erred about the increase (to 4.5 percent), he erred about Arkansas.

Later, on October 3, Utley was forced to correct himself: "In our report last week, we showed how campaigns use selective numbers to score political points. And one example was the Bush TV commercial saying that Governor Clinton had raised the sales tax in Arkansas by 33 percent from 3 cents on a dollar to 4.25 cents. However, we incorrectly labeled that a 1.25 percent increase. Indeed, some of you, pocket calculators at the ready, noted that the real increase was 41.6 percent. The Bush campaign got its own numbers wrong."[6] But Utley's math still goofed up about the 4.5 percent sales tax, which the Bush campaign did underestimate -- the increase amounted to half the previous rate, or 50 percent. The "fact checkers" did not inspire confidence.

Clinton's camp claimed Arkansas had the 49th lowest tax burden, but that was cleverly measured on a per capita basis, meaning only that Arkansas is poor, so its tax revenues are necessarily low. However, most economists measure the tax burden by studying the percentage of family income devoted to taxes. By that standard, Arkansas was firmly in the middle of the 50 states, and rising. Stephen Moore of the Cato Institute reported that from 1983 to 1990, Arkansas state taxes as a share of family income grew from 6.4 percent to 6.8 percent, in a decade when family income was also growing. In a 45-state study of governors, Moore gave Democrats like Colorado's Roy Romer and Indiana's Evan Bayh a B grade, but he gave Clinton's performance a dismal D, an evaluation never noted by reporters.[7]

The ads the Clinton campaign feared most came at the start of October, when the Bush campaign began airing an ad with the theme "Here's What Clinton Economics Could Mean to You." Over pictures of steamfitters and salesmen, the ad used specific estimates of how much in new taxes middle-class Americans "could" pay under a President Clinton. All four networks denounced the ad as misleading on their evening news shows.

On ABC's *World News Tonight* October 2, Jeff Greenfield pronounced: "The numbers don't come from Clinton's plan at all. They come from the Bush campaign's very questionable assumptions about Clinton's plan." That same night, NBC's Lisa Myers called the ad "misleading. In fact, Clinton has proposed cutting taxes for the sort of people in this ad. The tax increase that the ad claims could result under Clinton is based on leaps of logic about how he'd pay for his promises." Both these reporters also critiqued bits of Clinton ads for the first time: Myers charged a Clinton radio ad about Medicare and Social Security cuts contained "skillful distortions," and Greenfield quibbled briefly with the Clinton campaign's response ad to Bush.[8]

But crusty CBS reporter Eric Engberg stuck to lambasting the Bush campaign: "Feel-bad ads trying to drag down Bill Clinton are regarded as the only hope. In a multi-million dollar assault, Clinton is being portrayed as a duplicitous blobhead who governs a *Hee Haw* backwater where only the taxes soar. The ads are cleverly worded to suggest Clinton means more taxes....The tax figures jump from the screen with fact-like exactness. They were provided not by Clinton, but by the Bush staff, which admits they are based on assumptions. They assume Clinton will fail to get his program [a middle class tax cut, a line-item veto] through Congress, that his proposal to tax the wealthy won't raise enough money, and that he will then tax the middle class, which he says he won't." Engberg asked *Advertising Age* writer Steven Colford: "The stacking up of assumptions like this, there's a word we use for that." "I think it's lying," answered Colford on cue.[9]

Within the same story, Engberg showed Clinton's response ad, which claimed Bush had "the worst economic record of any President in fifty years." Engberg didn't review that for accuracy: how did Bush's record compare to Jimmy Carter, on whose watch inflation and unemployment rose dramatically? He just talked over it.

At CNN, Brooks Jackson took a different angle, questioning the Bush campaign's charge that nationalized health care would require higher taxes: "Clinton says his proposed controls on health costs will save enough to pay for gradually extending health insurance to all 35 million uninsured Americans. No taxes required." Jackson then pronounced: "A nonpartisan group that did study both the Bush and Clinton health plans sides with Clinton."

Jackson's "nonpartisan" expert was Ron Pollack of Families USA, who claimed: "I don't ever like to call someone a liar, but whoever prepared that advertisement for Bush has a wonderful future in fiction writing." Jackson concluded: "So the Bush ad is misleading, misrepresenting Clinton's position on health care."[10]

A year later, in the September 20, 1993 edition of *Time* magazine, reporters Michael Duffy and Dick Thompson detailed how the "nonpartisan" Pollack met with Clinton on September 22, 1992, and told the candidate he should hit Bush with the weapon of managed competition. "Pollack told Clinton that his group would soon release a 'bipartisan' report detailing managed competition's effect on the budget. Why not, Pollack said, let his group put numbers out?"[11] Jackson presented a very partisan Clinton campaign adviser as an "nonpartisan" observer, and took the "bipartisan" bait Pollack told Clinton he'd offer to the public. So much for truth in advertising.

So how accurate were these reporters' defenses of Clinton? Compare the Bush campaign's five assumptions for the commercial's claim that taxes would go up, as reported by Howard Kurtz of *The Washington Post* (who also found the ad "misleading")[12] with what actually happened:

■ *"That Clinton will raise just $1 billion, not $45 billion, by improving tax collection from foreign countries operating in this country."* Clinton's incoming budget director, Leon Panetta, told *Time* they'd be lucky to get $3 billion.[13] The tax was not enacted.

■ *"That Clinton will not enact the $60 billion in tax relief he has promised for families earning less than $90,000."* Clinton did not return to proposing a middle class tax cut until the Republicans won with the issue in 1994.

■ *"That Clinton's plan to raise $150 billion in new revenue over four years will fall short, forcing him to raise taxes on individuals with taxable incomes above $36,000."* On February 18, 1993 *USA Today* noted: "Looks like Dan Quayle was right. Last year's vice presidential debate...produced an accurate prediction from Quayle about the Clinton budget plan...The final plan, according to Clinton officials, will hit those making $30,000 and above."[14]

■ *"That Clinton has proposed $58 billion in 'phony' spending cuts."* Among those cuts: $9.8 billion in savings over four years from enacting the line-item veto, which was quickly abandoned. Clinton also listed savings from Congressional staff cuts (that wouldn't happen until the GOP took over in 1995) and White House staff cuts, which never materialized in the form of a lowered White House budget.

■ *"That Clinton's health care plan will cost $117 billion more than what he says."* Actually, the Bush campaign claimed that Clinton would have to raise taxes $117 billion to pay for his health care reform plan. The Democrats' own Congressional Budget Office actually estimated the Clinton health plan would cost $748 billion over seven years, to be financed by a large employer tax, but it did not pass.[15] Did anyone ever believe that Clinton could insure 35 million uninsured Americans without raising taxes? Reporters did. "No taxes required," deadpanned Brooks Jackson on CNN.

The Bush campaign attempted to explain, sentence by sentence, the factual basis or statistical projections behind their claims. Campaign officials would hold press conferences and appear on news forums with pages of detail on the Clinton record. But these careful preparations accomplished nothing with a media eager to demonstrate that George Bush had abandoned his nice-guy persona for anything-goes attack politics. In his book *Strange Bedfellows,* Tom Rosenstiel explained why the media joined the ad watch with such vigor. They were flacked into it: "The Clinton team was embarked on an intricate plan to undermine what it feared would have been Bush's most devastating commercial -- and to use the press to do it. In the process, Clinton's team helped damage the credibility of the Bush advertising effort in general and exploit the newest innovation in media coverage, the so-called truth squads. The plot amounted to the most sophisticated use of the press perhaps ever in presidential campaign advertising."[16]

What made this strategy more fascinating was the raging indeterminacy of the Clinton health plan numbers. Arriving at estimates became the subject of heated debates within the campaign, led by Clinton health care guru Ira Magaziner's insistence that nationalizing health care would reduce the deficit. While reporters like Brooks Jackson skewered the math of the Bush ad, Bob Woodward later explained the seat-of-the-pants finish of the Clinton campaign's *Putting People First* estimates in his 1994 tome *The Agenda:* "Health care remained a question mark. Magaziner still hoped to claim savings from reform; the others maintained it was impossible. In the end, they threw in arbitrary numbers they essentially made up."[17]

The ad watches displayed the media's arrogant belief in their self-appointed role as referees of truth. But these were the same journalists who regularly declared as "fact" claims which they had not worked to prove: that America contained three million homeless people, that eight million children were in danger of starving, that Alar-treated apples would give children cancer, that the Gulf War would produce massive American casualties, that the planet would be flooded by global warming. The networks portrayed political commercials as factually challenged attempts to drive up the negatives of an opponent in an unforgettably catchy production. But the networks often scored their Nielsen ratings by driving up the negatives of American society, from the dirtiness of its politics to the decline of its economy to the decay of its moral fabric.

Reporters hoped that the ad watch would suggest to political consultants that they could not get away with statistical malpractice in the heat of political battle. But political consultants could have easily taken an opposite lesson: keep any debatable assumptions out of your ads. Stress style over substance. Reporters hated Ronald Reagan's 1984 ads trumpeting morning in America, and comparing the Soviet Union to a bear loose in the woods. These were powerful symbols and metaphors that did not submit easily to factual scrutiny. In a year that marked a new attention to substance as well as style, the media's truth squads may have suggested that content-free advertising might be a better bet for the next campaign.

16

Quayle's Turn in the Penalty Box

"Quayle was passionate, well-informed? No, I think at times he appeared to be almost raging out of control." -- Detroit Free Press Deputy City Editor Ron Dzwonkowski on CNN's post-debate analysis, October 13, 1992.

"I think Al Gore wins by default, because he didn't set the tone. I think Dan Quayle came across like a Ken doll on steroids...No matter how flimsy your facts are, deliver them with great force and fire." -- Newsweek reporter Eleanor Clift, October 19, 1992 McLaughlin Group.

While Republican ads and speeches drew media boos and hisses, reporters often ignored the daily errors and distortions of the Democratic ticket. The October 21, 1992 *Wall Street Journal* included an editorial by economist Alan Reynolds titled "The Worst Lying About the Economy in the Past 50 Years," detailing distortions in Clinton's statements in stump speeches and the debates.

Reynolds noted that in the first presidential debate on October 13, Clinton said we are suffering "the first decline in industrial production, ever." Reynolds pointed out industrial production rose by 2.1 percent from May 1991 to the fall of 1992. Clinton also charged that U.S. wages have slipped to 13th in the world. Reynolds asserted: "All these figures show is that high German interest rates pushed European exchange rates up. That did indeed make European wages look high when converted to dollars, but it also makes European *prices* look even higher. The real purchasing power of foreign wages is a great deal lower than implied by converting them into dollars." (Italics his.)[1]

In the third debate, Clinton said "I defy you" to find where he supported higher fuel economy standards for cars. *Newsweek* economics columnist Robert Samuelson wrote in the October 28 *Washington Post:* "Please, give me a hard one. Page 98 of *Putting People First* (the Clinton-Gore manifesto) says that a Clinton administration would 'raise the Corporate Average Fuel Efficiency (CAFE) standards for automakers to 40 miles per gallon by the year 2000 and 45 miles per gallon by the year 2015.'"[2]

In fact, the networks did not devote one evening news story to assessing the accuracy of the presidential debates. But on October 14, the evening after the vice presidential debate, ABC and CNN both charged Vice President Dan Quayle with distorting the Clinton-Gore record. Quayle asserted that raising the CAFE standards to 45 miles per gallon would cost 300,000 jobs. On ABC's *World News Tonight,* reporter Jim Wooten asserted: "That estimate is based on an unlikely worst-case scenario that all workers now building cars which do not meet that standard would eventually lose their jobs."

Wooten took exception to Quayle's claim that Gore favored a $100 billion environmental Marshall Plan, as proposed in Gore's book *Earth In The Balance:* "That is not true. Gore's book proposes a global plan financed by several countries, not the U.S. alone. And it does not specify a total cost or America's share."[3] On CNN's *Inside Politics,* reporter Brooks Jackson agreed: "Dan Quayle was flat wrong about that. The $100 billion figure on Page 304 of Gore's book refers to the cost in today's dollars of the post-war Marshall Plan, not what Quayle said."[4]

But Gore's book contained a whole chapter using the Marshall Plan as a model for a global assistance plan led by the United States. A Marshall Plan analogy for any problem means a massive financial commitment of foreign aid. Instead of following up with Gore on the charge (If not $100 billion, how much?), reporters hit Quayle for bringing it up. When ABC's Diane Sawyer interrupted a folksy interview with the Gores on the July 30 *Prime Time Live* to ask that question, long before the debate, Gore was evasive: "I think it will save us money. I think that we'll create millions of jobs." Sawyer replied: "But initially, initially, how much will it cost?" Gore ducked again: "I think that saves us money." Gore called Quayle's reading of the $100 billion figure "totally fictitious" (although it was right there in his nonfiction book), causing Sawyer to ask again: "What is the right figure?" Gore would only say: "Our share of it is small."[5]

Brooks Jackson's CNN story did point out that contrary to Gore's assertion, Clinton's policies did not create a lot of high-wage jobs in Arkansas, since the state's average hourly wage was $2.38 below the national average. But Jackson quickly turned back to the Vice President: "Quayle misrepresented Clinton's economic plan, which calls for a net tax increase of only $46 billion spread over four years -- the $150 billion Quayle mentioned, minus $104 billion in cuts he neglected to mention." But the conservative weekly *Human Events* discovered the $104 billion figure was nowhere to be found in the Clinton-Gore book *Putting People First*.[6]

Gore's errors were mostly missed. None of the networks followed up on Gore's charge that through a foreign aid program called the Caribbean Basin Initiative (CBI), the Agency for International Development (AID) was supporting the export of American jobs to Latin America. Gore specifically charged that a plant in Decaturville, Tennessee was closed and its jobs moved to El Salvador.

Only conservative columnist Mona Charen corrected Gore: "The plant in Decaturville was closed because the company went bankrupt, not because it moved to El Salvador. In fact, the only connection between the two plants (which made different items) is that the same holding company at separate times owned both of them." Charen added: "The 40-year-old American company that opened the plant in El Salvador was able to increase its U.S. employment by 20 percent since expanding its operations to Latin America in 1984. It has never closed a U.S. plant."[7]

But Quayle's assertion that Gore voted for the Caribbean Basin Initiative drew media hoots. Jackson claimed: "Once again, Quayle was wrong. The record shows Gore voted against final passage of the initiative in 1983." But ABC's Wooten took a different take than CNN: "[Gore] did vote against it, twice, but also voted for it once as part of a larger legislative package." Charen added what the networks ignored: "In 1991, Mr. Gore voted for the [CBI] program in stand-alone legislation."

Jackson concluded: "It was Quayle who repeatedly twisted and misstated the facts...The political reality is that voters don't score campaign debates on the basis of who gets the facts straight. But if they did, Dan Quayle would have lost Tuesday night's debate hands down."[8] ABC's Wooten seconded that emotion: "The blue ribbon for factual flexibility goes to the Vice President. More often than Senator Gore, Mr. Quayle was either mistaken or misinformed."[9]

Wooten and Jackson easily slipped into choosing sides in their post-debate stories, calling Quayle "wrong" on estimates of future policy decisions that were too amorphous to know their accuracy. Quayle couldn't give a precise number for Gore's environmental Marshall Plan, because Gore wouldn't commit to one, but it would cost billions. No one could give a precise estimate of job losses with more regulations on automobile production, but it would cost jobs. No one knew how much Clinton would raise taxes and spending, but he had declared that he would raise both. Throughout the year, Clinton's economic plan changed repeatedly. By the time he sent a plan to Congress, it changed again. And then Congress changed the proposal again before it passed. With this fluidity of policy proposals and their cost estimates, how could reporters declare with certainty what guesses about the future were "wrong"?

Exploring the details of candidates' claims is a laudable practice that brings voters more of the statistical nuts and bolts of governing that the networks don't always have the time (or take the time) to explain. But singling out one candidate over another for "ribbons of factual flexibility" in these debates, especially when the Democrats could just as easily, if not more easily, be skewered for that "flexibil-ity," served less as an informational service and more as a political tool -- handing the debate win to Gore and damaging Republican chances for a comeback. Republicans would not be allowed to predict that the Democrats' reign could be costly without a "truth squad" rebuttal.

17

Nails in the Coffin

"Most economists agree that the U.S. recovery is far weaker than the recent 2.7 percent GDP growth spurt indicates. 'That was a nice number, but not sustainable,' says Lea Tyler, manager of U.S. economic forecasting for Oxford Economics in Pennsylvania. The results included a temporary bulge in defense orders and a consumer shopping spree that blossomed in July but quickly faded in August." -- *Time* Senior Writer John Greenwald, November 23 issue.

"Gross domestic product leaped up at an annual rate of 3.9 percent in the third quarter, returning total output of goods and services to the pre-recession pace of mid-1990. Strong increases were registered by consumer spending, business investment, orders for durable goods, sales of existing houses and consumer confidence..." -- *Time's* "The Week" section, two weeks later.

After months of projecting the approaching defeat of George Bush, some media outlets turned up the negativity in the campaign's last week as economic news began to buoy last-minute hopes for the Bush camp. The comeback gained steam on Tuesday, October 27, when the Commerce Department announced a strong 2.7 percent growth rate in the nation's gross domestic product. That evening, ABC *World News Tonight* anchor Peter Jennings was quick to throw cold water on the good news: "That is more than economists had projected, but in many cases, less than meets the eye."

ABC reporter Bob Jamieson continued the spin: "Many economists say the report is not proof the economy is taking a sharp turn for the better." Jamieson added other excuses to downplay the numbers, and concluded with gloomy anecdotal evidence: "All of this adds up to little or no job growth, underscored by Zenith's announcement in Chicago today that it would lay off 15 percent of its salaried employees. For workers at Zenith and other companies, fear about losing their jobs will have a depressing effect on consumer spending."[1]

The next morning, *The Washington Post* rushed out with naysaying economists: "But many independent economists, who had expected about a 1.5 percent growth rate, said the U.S. economy cannot keep up such a pace. They said the figure was inflated by Americans dipping into their already meager savings to cover new purchases, by a temporary boost in military spending and by increases in unsold stocks of goods at the factory and wholesale levels."[2]

That night, Jennings returned to painting a bad economic picture, announcing: "The President may complain about the news media, but the economic growth figures which he is so pleased about are not that definitive, according to a great many independent economic analysts." For effect, Jennings suggested the people really knew the economy was still rotten: "And all over the country, millions of people hardly need any statistics to tell them what is happening."

Jennings then turned to reporter Jim Wooten in New Hampshire, one of the states hardest hit by the recession. Wooten declared: "The President's problem is that his view of the new economic figures often doesn't tell the whole story of what's happened or hasn't happened to thousands of voters who watched his State of the Union address last February."

Wooten found several former Bush voters announcing their vote for Clinton, and concluded: "Mr. Bush would have a tough time reclaiming the Smiths and thousands of other New Hampshire voters for whom the grim reality of recession has not changed since the candidates left here last winter."[3]

Media bigwigs were embarrassed on November 25, when the Commerce Department announced its final estimate for economic growth in the third quarter (July to September) had been revised upward from 2.7 percent to a strong 3.9 percent. On *World News Tonight* that evening, Jennings announced: "Timing may not be everything, but it certainly is crucial in politics. Three weeks after

President Bush lost the election, and several months after insisting the economy was on the verge of an outstanding recovery, President Bush finally got the numbers he was waiting for."[4] Like Jennings, none of the outlets admitted error or made any reference to their own politicized reaction to the pre-election economic numbers.

The bright new economic numbers under Bush actually led some news outlets to promote Clinton further. At the top of the front page on November 30, *The New York Times* published an article by reporter Sylvia Nasar accentuating the positive statistics from July forward and suggesting anecdotally that Clinton's rise had an effect. The article was headlined "Is the Clinton Expansion Here?"[5]

Media outlets found other ways to ruin any momentum the Bush campaign may have generated in the campaign's last month. *The Washington Post* found a new investigative crusade: the involvement of Elizabeth Tamposi, an old New Hampshire ally of John Sununu, a previous *Post* target, in a politically motivated search of State Department passport records of Bill Clinton. Nothing was released, but the *Post* dedicated 12 front page stories to the Tamposi tempest from October 14 to November 19, poking and prodding the rest of the national media to get involved in the frenzy. On November 14, the *Post* published as front page news the small detail that Tamposi had taken passport files home.[6]

The *Post* did not show the same interest in anti-Bush conspiracies. They did only one front page post-election story on Iran-Contra independent counsel Lawrence Walsh's obviously political election-eve reindictment of Reagan Defense Secretary Caspar Weinberger. The *Post* never launched its own investigation into Walsh's last-minute gambit. The *Post* also downplayed the General Accounting Office's (GAO) report on Walsh's financial practices earlier in 1992, including his dual offices in Oklahoma and Washington and his large expense-account tab. Special prosecutors are supposed to be audited annually by the GAO, but somehow Walsh proceeded for five years without GAO oversight. Reporters yawned while they eagerly awaited the GAO report on the Tamposi passport scandal.[7]

If the passport story caused reporters to be outraged over the federal government being used for "partisan politics," why didn't any of them cast that critical eye on Hillary Clinton's actual record as a federal official? As chairman of the government's Legal Services Corporation, a supposedly nonpartisan corporation providing legal aid to the poor, Mrs. Clinton funneled taxpayer money into defeating a 1980 California ballot initiative (Proposition 9) to cut state income taxes in half. In 1983, that same General Accounting Office cited Mrs. Clinton's LSC for violating statutory bars against encouraging partisan political activity.[8] Despite the long campaign, no one cared to cover this story.

18

Bias? What Bias?

"'You do your job,' she said, 'and you remember that bias is in the eye of the beholder.' She said she is impressed that during eight years of covering the Reagan White House, 'they never hanged that allegation on us.'" -- NBC reporter Andrea Mitchell quoted by Houston Chronicle writer Mike McDaniel, August 22, 1992.

"I am shocked when people say that [the media were pro-Clinton], I really am. I mean, people forget January and February, when the media was on Clinton's case with Gennifer Flowers, all the draft stuff. I'm amazed at the public's selective memory." -- ABC reporter Carole Simpson on C-SPAN, November 10, 1992.

Reporters may have given anonymously honest answers to the Times Mirror Center that they knew their coverage slanted in favor of Bill Clinton, but throughout the election year, most reporters fiercely denied any suggestion of liberal media bias. Reporters were used to batting down the question with facile dismissals on talk shows, and often worked harder to deny it on the rare occasion when the issue made its way into news coverage.

The first media reaction to the issue was disbelief. Four days before the GOP convention began, Republican National Committee Chairman Rich Bond made the front page of *The Washington Post* with the charge: "I think we know who the media want to win this election -- and I don't think it's George Bush." Reporters did not take charges of bias in campaign coverage lying down. On CNN's *Newsmaker Saturday* August 15 host Frank Sesno quizzed Bond, who had also poked at *The Washington Post* for dubbing the Democratic ticket "heart-throbs of the heart land." Asked Sesno: "The President's surrogates, many of them, said that they believe the media want to see Bill Clinton win. You said something like that. That's a remarkable statement. What do you base that on?"[1]

Another reaction was contempt. On CNN's *Inside Politics* August 19, *Newsweek* reporter Eleanor Clift worried that reporters might be reflecting on whether they're biased. "There is an effort at intimidation here...I think people are backing off a little and asking themselves 'Am I being fair'?" *Washington Post* reporter/columnist David Broder exclaimed: "It's not wrong to ask yourself 'Am I being fair?'" Clift replied: "Well, do you ask yourself three or four times a night? I think there's more self-examination by the media as a result of the Bush assault."[2]

Clift's *Newsweek* colleague, media critic Jonathan Alter, dismissed the issue of bias: "There hasn't been an unfair number of negative stories on Bush....turning his blundering political campaign into a 'positive' story -- now, that would be biased."[3] Alter did not address the many damaging stories on Clinton that were ignored or squashed within a few days. On *Inside Washington,* liberal reporter Nina Totenberg of National Public Radio tittered and said: "There's certain amount of self-flagellation that's really kind of silly. Most of us are professionals."[4] *Newsweek* Washington Bureau Chief Evan Thomas disagreed: "The Republicans are going to whack away at the press for the next couple of months as being pro-Clinton. And you know what? They're right. The press is pro-Clinton -- not 80-20, but I think at least 60-40. There are a lot of formerly liberal reporters out there who'd like to see the Democrats win."[5]

Reporters on the campaign trail cynically regurgitated the charges, then dismissed them as politically motivated. On August 14, CBS reporter Wyatt Andrews concluded: "Voters will judge if all this press-bashing is the legitimate cry of a party deeply wronged or a desperate effort by a campaign 19 points down to shine the spotlight somewhere else."[6]

Andrews would not have needed to look far to see that the Bush campaign had a point. On his own network, Dan Rather's interview with Bill Clinton on the July 15 *CBS Evening News* defined media softness. Rather was more facilitator than interviewer. After Clinton declared, "If you look at my record, I have consistently fought with a passion for certain things that are constant, that are magnets in my life," Rather asked: "What are those things?" Rather followed up: "It's reliably reported that the Bush-Quayle committee plans to use your own state's statistics to criticize your ability to lead." He ended the interview: "Give me a sentence that tells me what your theme is, what your message is."[7] This kind of questioning allowed Clinton to fill in the blanks any way he liked. Its toughness didn't exactly match Rather's Iran-Contra ambush interview of George Bush in 1988.

Print journalists were also asked about their bias. During the CNN journalism review show *Reliable Sources* on September 5, host Bernard Kalb asked *Newsweek* reporter Howard Fineman about the magazine's post-convention issue, which included an article titled "A Feast of Hate and Fear" by left-wing humorist Molly Ivins: "Is *Newsweek* a magazine of objective reporting or an anthology of partisan columns?" Fineman answered: "I think in retrospect to be honest about it, we could have used a little more of a steady hand, in terms of weeding out the steady procession of stories....We overdid it a bit, and it would be silly to say otherwise."[8]

U.S. News & World Report assistant managing editor Harrison Rainie, a former aide to Democratic Sen. Pat Moynihan, would not be so forthcoming with a C-SPAN caller on September 25: "The press has been, if anything, much more vigilant about fairness and objectivity and sort of explaining issues front to back this year than it ever was."[9] Richard Berke of *The New York Times* echoed Rainie on CNN's *Larry King Live* October 16: "I don't think there is [a bias] at all. I think anyone who accuses the press of bias is acting in desperation, I think. I think the press has been much more aggressive and fair, in being, in going after both sides, and looking, than ever before."[10]

Two weeks later on *Larry King Live*, PBS omnipresence Bill Moyers added to the notion of "the media" the whole realm of opinion journalism, and presented the claims of far-left media critics who actually contended the system favored conservatives: "I think there are reporters around Clinton who are baby boomers who are drawn to him. I think there are a lot of reporters in Washington who just wish for a new story. But I watch probably as many talk shows, and as many interview shows, what George Bush calls the professional talking heads on Sundays, as anybody else. I actually think the bias in the overall system is from the center to the right."[11]

The most surprising exploration of bias came months later. On March 11, 1993, ABC's *Prime Time Live* did an unprecedented story on the media's own biases. In November, Diane Sawyer asked viewers to submit examples of media bias during 1992, which resulted in a deluge: 8,000 people flooded the network with examples, and nine of ten letter writers thought election coverage was slanted against the Republicans.[12]

"We found no grand conspiracy, but we did find some surprising examples of what seemed to be some less-than-objective journalism," declared reporter Judd Rose. He embarrassed *Chicago Tribune* associate managing editor George Langford, who defended the selection of a front-page photo from Associated Press that showed President Bush with his back to the camera standing next to a sign that read "Danger -- Keep Away." It was the only decent photo made available by AP that day, Langford claimed. Not so, demonstrated Rose, showing him four very positive AP photos of Bush that were available the same day.

Viewers also complained to ABC about Clinton flack George Stephanopoulos' manipulated call-in to President Bush on CNN's *Larry King Live* on the Friday night before the election as a political dirty trick. The call allowed Stephanopoulos to underline the news of that day: that Iran-Contra independent counsel Lawrence Walsh indicted Reagan defense secretary Caspar Weinberger just four days before Americans went to the polls. King explained it away to ABC as a "random" call. Not so, Rose pointed out: Stephanopoulos had called the CNN control room to get special access, and producers made sure he got on the program to challenge Bush's honesty.

Rose asked *60 Minutes* executive producer Don Hewitt why CBS ran with Ross Perot's crazy charges on the eve of the election that the Bush campaign tried to sabotage his daughter's wedding. Hewitt claimed: "If Perot had wanted to admit it back when he dropped out last summer, it was a story then....This is a major political candidate who's making a charge." Did Hewitt actually believe Perot's story?

He should have admitted his reason for running that story -- the sensationalism of a Perot exclusive. And whatever happened to the promise that 1992 would be the year where the media wouldn't simply forward unproven charges? Rose did not point out Hewitt's earlier enthusiasm for Perot, as quoted in the May 20 *Boston Globe:* "The only two candidates who appeal to me as someone who could lead the country are Ross Perot and [Democratic Texas Governor] Ann Richards."[13]

The program also illustrated the pomposity of some media figures, like *New York Times* reporter Andrew Rosenthal, who told ABC: "What were we supposed to write? That the 'Message: I Care' in New Hampshire was some kind of a religious epiphany? That the Houston convention was a masterpiece of balance and inclusion? That the breaking of the tax pledge was a brilliant political masterstroke?" Also, for the first time on network TV, ABC reported both that the Freedom Forum found Democratic reporters outnumber Republicans by almost 3 to 1, and the Times Mirror Center found 55 percent of reporters agreed that press coverage hurt Bush.

Rose even critiqued *Prime Time* itself. In interviews with candidates the week before the election, Sam Donaldson told viewers to watch for Bush backing off any tax pledge. He concluded a segment on Clinton: "They're talking about a whirlwind trip around the country. That's commitment." According to Rose, "Sam says he added that remark after our executive producer expressed concern that the tone of the Clinton interview was too hostile."[14]

This suggests a plausible reason for ABC's extraordinary story: it served as penance for *Prime Time* executive producer Rick Kaplan's blatant assistance to the Clinton campaign. In *The Washington Post Magazine,* Kaplan was quoted watching Donaldson's interview with Clinton, claiming Donaldson was too tough. "I'd just like to do this one over again...I'm getting angry watching this...You're making fun of him....You didn't treat Bush this way."[15]

Watching the networks in 1992 could easily lead the average American to believe that the Democratic Party had a monopoly on the positive reflexes of politics: idealism, hope, vision, energy, mainstream values, caring. By contrast, the Republicans were the party of cynicism, despair, anger, small-mindedness, stinginess, extremism, and hate. A viewer that expected of network analysts and reporters a sense of political sophistication would have been disappointed, often left with stick-figure caricatures of political reality. Idealism and cynicism, love and hate, fear and hope could be ascribed to both campaigns, depending on your political point of view. But with their apparent ideological uniformity, the "objective" media failed in its professional obligation to preserve at least the appearance of neutrality in serving as referees of the campaign. As the election season drew to a close, the pattern of bias would extend to interpreting the meaning of the election results.

19

The Post-Game Show

"[The electorate] has grown weary of 12 years of Republican rule, symbolized by a President who seemed insensitive to their bread-and-butter concerns. They were angry at a GOP that ignored, even resented, the rise of a multiracial society and a new social mainstream that includes working women, single-parent families, and gays and lesbians seeking equal rights."
-- Newsweek reporter Howard Fineman in the magazine's post-election issue.

"Bill Clinton hugs other men. It's not a bearhug, usually -- more like a Full Shoulder Squeeze. Women get it, too, but the gesture is more striking in its generational freshness when applied to the same sex. He softens the old-fashioned backslap into something more sensitive. These guys are touching each other! It's unself-conscious, gender-neutral, very '90s." -- Newsweek Senior Editor Jonathan Alter, November 16.

Even before Bush lost, the networks were perfecting their post-election spin, blaming the debacle on the unpopularity of conservatism. Ending the October 17 *NBC Nightly News* with a commentary, anchorman Garrick Utley proclaimed that Bush would lose for being too loyal to Reaganomics: "For eight years, [Bush] supported policies which, it is now widely acknowledged, contributed mightily to our excesses then and our economic problems now; above all, America being held hostage to debt. George Bush went along to get ahead, and it worked. He became President. Now, the painful irony. Now, Ronald Reagan is in happy retirement in California, and President Bush is left to pay the price. The price for supporting something he did not believe in to begin with. He knows it -- knows it is now too late to do anything about that fateful bargain he entered into twelve years ago. Going along to get ahead made George Bush President. Now it may unmake him. The ancient

Greeks wrote about this sort of thing. They called it tragedy."[1]

If Reaganomics didn't beat Bush, then it was the "festival of hate" in Houston. On election night, as state after state fell behind Bill Clinton, the networks asserted that George Bush lost not because of his failed promise to hold the line on taxes or his inherent suspicion of "the vision thing," but because of intolerant social conservatives and their speeches at the Republican convention.

CNN anchor Catherine Crier suggested: "You may have to move to the far right or the far left during a primary to pull those voters to support you during a primary, but you've got to move back and moderate for the general election. We remember the convention in Houston, the Patrick Buchanans and the very conservative movement that took over -- looks like it may have hurt the President."[2]

On NBC's election night coverage, Tom Brokaw asked Pat Robertson: "There are many people in the Republican Party who believe that the Republican National Convention in Houston, at which you were a prominent part, was simply too extreme, too strident in its positions, and they cite your speech and Pat Buchanan's as well." NBC's John Chancellor also promoted the theme: "I think that the convention -- and certainly all the polling data indicates this -- offended a lot of women, offended a lot of people in the country who thought it was too religious and too hard-edged."[3]

Chancellor ignored the exit poll commissioned by all the networks. CBS reporter Ed Bradley explained the exit poll on election night: "We gave the voters a list of things to choose from, Dan, things that helped them make up their minds. I think in past years, the conventions were very important, how they played on television, television ads. This year, they fell at the bottom of the list. The single most important thing that helped them decide were the debates between the candidates -- 64 percent said that was number one."

But when Rather asked: "Did people talk about the Buchanan speech at the Republican convention? Jerry Falwell, Pat Robertson at the President's side? Was that mentioned very often?" Instead of repeating the poll results, Bradley ignored them: "Well, I don't have it in this survey, but my recollection of talking to people, in an informal survey, and particularly among Republicans, there were a number of Republicans who said that they felt let down by their convention, watching it on TV, that what Pat Buchanan had to say, that some of the positions of the religious right, did not represent the way they felt."[4]

The networks' exit poll did not indicate conservatism killed the Bush-Quayle ticket. CNN analyst William Schneider reviewed a network exit poll question: "We asked them which would you favor -- 'A government that provides more services but costs more in taxes,' only 37 percent said that, and even though a Democrat was elected today, most voters said they favored 'a government which would have lower taxes and fewer services.'" An on-screen graphic showed 55 percent for "Lower Taxes." Schneider concluded that "the consensus of the Reagan era, for less government, appears not to be entirely gone." The exit poll was completed by Voter Research and Surveys for all the networks, but this answer never got mentioned in the days after the election by ABC, CBS, or NBC, not to mention *The New York Times*, *Washington Post* or *USA Today*.[5]

Reporters moved from their unsupported scapegoating of conservatism to a celebration of the Democrats' new power. *Boston Globe* reporter Curtis Wilkie's electoral post-mortem declared the dawning of a new era of Democratic politics. In a front page "news analysis" the morning after Clinton won with 43 percent to Bush's 38 percent, Wilkie declared a landslide: "Bill Clinton called for change, but he never dared ask for a mandate as sweeping as the one he received last night. The magnitude of the Democratic triumph was so enormous that it ensures Clinton a strong alliance with Congress and an incentive to move quickly on his domestic programs....He piled up a popular vote nationwide that transcended predictions, while his party strengthened its hold on Congress." But Republicans had gained ten House seats, and within weeks, added a Senate seat.

Wilkie rhapsodized: "The overwhelming margin of his election gives Clinton an opportunity to create a new Democratic epoch, in the same way that Lyndon B. Johnson's 44-state majority in 1964 produced a Great Society....It has been a long, barren period for the Democrats, but Clinton is in a position to lead a restoration."[6]

Time Senior Writer Walter Shapiro found the President-elect inspired more than political enthusiasm: "At a moment when the American libido seems to oscillate between Puritanism and rampant exhibitionism, how significant is it that for the first time in more than 30 years the nation has elected a President with sex appeal?....Cheryl Russell, Editor of *The Boomer Report,* a monthly newsletter on consumer trends, captures a new dimension in the national psyche when she confides, 'Every woman I know is having sex dreams about Bill Clinton.'"[7]

In the November 23 *U.S. News & World Report,* writer Matthew Cooper cooed: "The President-elect's unique trait is a mix of cunning and kindness; he uses both to learn from others in order to make his own decisions...One presidential precedent that Clinton -- and perhaps the country -- can take comfort in is the fact that the last Democratic challenger to win by a healthy margin shared these traits of ideological expediency and diffuse authority. In his day, Franklin Roosevelt had what might be called a Slick Frank reputation."[8]

The puff pieces trickled down to Clinton's staff in the weeks after the election, especially spokesman George Stephanopoulos, whom reporters expected to be named Press Secretary. In the November 30 *Time,* Deputy Washington Bureau Chief Margaret Carlson oozed: "This brooding, dark presence has a quiet authority. His power whisper makes people lean in to him, like plants reaching toward the sun."[9] Cooper of *U.S. News* swooned: "Like the President he will serve, Stephanopoulos is the ultimate political meritocrat....Those who know him best cherish his decency and thoughtfulness."[10]

Washington Post reporter David Maraniss betrayed the reporters' selfishly syrupy desire for access to key sources in the new White House: "Of all the aides surrounding Clinton, Stephanopoulos is the one everybody seems eager to learn more about these days, partly because of his newfound power and attractiveness, but also because he seems to have more depth and complexity. Here is the student of theology making a living in the spiritual void of inside politics. Here is the cheerful countenance with the brooding soul. Here is a fellow who looks so young and dresses so hip yet behaves with such maturity."[11] The Clinton era had begun.

IV. THE NEW
ADMINISTRATION

20

The Great Liberal Hope

"In 1978, Newsweek introduced its readers to a young man with a dream. On Friday, Newsweek will be the only newsweekly to mark the culmination of that dream, with a special newsstand issue on his inauguration. An issue that's sure to be a collector's item because it covers the most important inauguration of our lifetime." -- Newsweek TV commercial, January 1993.

"If we could be one-hundredth as great as you and Hillary Rodham Clinton have been in the White House, we'd take it right now and walk away winners...Thank you very much and tell Mrs. Clinton we respect her and we're pulling for her." -- Dan Rather in a satellite interview with Clinton at a CBS affiliates meeting, May 27, 1993.

The inauguration of President Bill Clinton, a candidate anointed by the media in the primaries, celebrated by the media during the conventions, and defended in the fall elections, sent a current of hope and excitement through the liberal Washington press corps. After twelve years of hostility to the White House's inhabitants, reporters had escorted to power a progressive, baby-boomer President and a working-woman First Lady, a demographic reproduction of themselves. Now the press corps faced a new challenge: could they simply transform overnight from presidential prosecutor to defense attorney? Now that Clinton had become President, reporters tried to strike a more traditional adversary pose, but they would occasionally stop and ask whether they'd been too tough on the President, a question rarely -- if ever -- asked during a Republican presidency.

While Bill and Hillary Clinton were deeply suspicious and even hostile toward the press, the slings and arrows of White House press coverage now rained less on the new administration than it did upon their opponents. Empowered by a liberal President, reporters attempted to aid Clinton in passing liberal proposals. On the central projects of the Clinton presidency, from a new budget plan to a massive nationalization of the health care system, reporters spent 1993 hailing the President's agenda and attacking those who would stand in its way, obscuring by billions (or even trillions) the costs of the Clinton agenda.

For all the pomp and pageantry, for all the traditional journalistic courtesy, the previous three inaugurations had not been true celebrations for reporters. In an essay for *Time* after the 1988 election, Garry Wills captured their mood: "Bush won by default, and by fouls. His 'mandate' is to ignore the threats to our economy, sustain the Reagan heritage of let's pretend, and serve as figurehead for what America has become, a frightened empire hiding problems from itself."[1]

But the Clintons' arrival in Washington made them all aglow. Across the divide of four years, *Time* essayist Lance Morrow declared in one of the magazine's "Man of the Year" stories: "Clinton's campaign, conducted with dignity, with earnest attention to issues and with an impressive display of self-possession under fire, served to rehabilitate and restore the legitimacy of American politics and thus, prospectively, of government itself. He vindicated (at least for a while) the honor of a system that had been sinking fast. A victory by George Bush would, among other things, have given a two-victory presidential validation (1988 and 1992) to hot-button, mad-dog politics -- campaigning on irrelevant or inflammatory issues (Willie Horton, the flag, the Pledge of Allegiance, Murphy Brown's out-of-wedlock nonexistent child) or dirty tricks and innuendo (searching passport files, implying that Clinton was tied up with the KGB as a student)."[2]

Newsweek's Joe Klein proclaimed the Clinton campaign represented "more than just a holy war against the pinched, divisive brand of conservatism that had overtaken Republicans in recent years; there was also a confluence of longstanding aspirations and frustrations -- Democrats, baby boomers, 'new ideas' types all were hoping that their moment had finally come, that it was time to reclaim the idealism of the Kennedy years."[3]

Some reporters were even more swept up in the revelry. *Wall Street Journal* reporter Jill Abramson, later the paper's Deputy Washington Bureau Chief, expressed her enthusiasm in an appearance on C-SPAN: "It's an exciting time to be in Washington. I work near the little store where they're selling the Inaugural commemoration items and there is a line going out the door and around the corner. People are excited. They're happy about change. They're intrigued by Bill Clinton, Al Gore, and their families. And I think you're going to see crowds for these Inaugural events the likes of which we haven't seen in Washington -- ever."[4]

As the Clinton presidency began with a few bumpy controversies, from the illegal alien nanny of Attorney General nominee Zoe Baird to the imposition of a new policy allowing openly gay soldiers in the military, critics of the idea of a liberal press noted that reporters treated President Clinton with more skepticism, more like other Presidents and less like the political savior depicted in campaign coverage. By January 31, eleven days into the Clinton presidency, *Washington Post* media writer Howard Kurtz was touting the media's turn as evidence against the idea of a pro-Clinton bias: "What happened to the liberal media that supposedly gave Bill Clinton every break during the campaign? In the blink of a news cycle, the new President has gone from *Time*'s Man of the Year to punching bag of the week."[5]

Kurtz did not mention the treatment Clinton sometimes received in his own newspaper, as in this profile of the new President's brother Roger by reporter Laura Blumenfeld: "Roger's life is in some ways the story of any younger sibling clobbered by the spectacular success of the one who came before. The presidential brother syndrome. If your brother is Christ, you have a choice: become a disciple, or become an anti-Christ, or find yourself caught somewhere between the two."[6]

Political reporters, often obsessed less with ideas than with the political process and its winners and losers, focused their negative coverage of Clinton on tactical bungling inside the White House: the clumsy handling of Cabinet appoinments or the lack of a centralized decisionmaking process on most issues. But this may not have reflected journalistic toughness as much as it telegraphed the disappointment of fellow liberals in the newsroom: would this White House make their policy wishes come true?

Thomas Friedman, who covered the White House for *The New York Times,* expressed his frustration in describing a briefing with White House spokesman George Stephanopoulos on the May 21, 1993 *Washington Week in Review:* "What he [Clinton] says so often is, it seems to me, right on about where the economy is, what we need to do to create more jobs in this country, what we need to do to tackle the deficit, but something is missing in that White House because it's not delivering on the other end...It was truly depressing. You say to yourself, 'We are at a watershed moment in this country's history and these people are so muffing it.' Yesterday I just wanted to get a hook and pull Stephanopoulos offstage and say 'George, go back, get your ducks in order, and then come out here, because this is too serious!'"

Nine days later, *Boston Globe* columnist and former reporter Tom Oliphant wrote with the same sentiment: "We're talking about someone who with the help of his spouse is making a mess of his presidency, whose obvious talents and worthy agenda make their failings all the more infuriating."[7]

21

Unexpected Beginnings

"Corporations pay public relations firms millions of dollars to contrive the kind of grass-roots response that Falwell or Pat Robertson can galvanize in a televised sermon. Their followers are largely poor, uneducated, and easy to command." -- Washington Post reporter Michael Weisskopf, February 1, 1993 news story.

"If you wear green on Thursday you're a queer, a pansy, a sissy. How many generations of contemporary Americans, particularly American boys, entered grade school and learned homophobia along with their ABCs, long before discovering anything of the fluttering of the birds and the bees?" -- Los Angeles Times reporter John Balzar's front-page story headlined "Why Does America Fear Gays?," February 4, 1993.

The first days of the Clinton presidency were marred by controversy over new appointments and policies. First, Attorney General nominee Zoe Baird was found to have hired an illegal alien as a nanny, and failed to pay Social Security taxes for the nanny's services. Reporters who not only supported Clinton, but led upper-class working-couple lives with nannies, admitted they hadn't thought Zoe Baird would have a problem until a wave of outraged phone calls to Washington made it clear. A *Los Angeles Times* editorial announced Baird's mistake was not disqualifying. A surprised Nancy Gibbs of *Time* called it "another livid lesson in how America really lives."[1] Baird's nomination was killed, but not by reporters.

Trouble intensified around Clinton's pledge to allow openly gay soldiers in the military, a subject almost totally ignored during the campaign. Like the Baird controversy, reporters were blind to the public outrage over gays in the military. *Baltimore Sun* reporter Carl Cannon told how his former editor at Knight-Ridder News Service explained why the gay issue got no airing in 1992: "We're liberal. When Clinton says he'll fight for gay rights or rescind the ban [on gays in the military], we're hearing something that doesn't sound outlandish to us at all. In fact, it sounded reasonable. It sounded fair."[2] It sounded so reasonable that *Washington Post* reporter Michael Weisskopf was openly dismissive of the avalanche of phone calls against it. In an article on the wave of conservative opposition, Weisskopf attributed this supposedly manufactured tide of public opinion to the exhortations of conservative evangelists Jerry Falwell and Pat Robertson: "Their followers are largely poor, uneducated, and easy to command."

The next day's *Post* corrections box apologized: "There is no factual basis for that statement." In a February 6 Howard Kurtz story on reader protests, Weisskopf dug himself a deeper hole. He called the sentence "an honest mistake, not born of any prejudice or malice for the religious right," but then said he should have said that evangelicals were "relatively" poor and uneducated. According to Kurtz, "Weisskopf said he bases the description on interviews with several experts, but didn't attribute it to anyone because 'I try not to have to attribute every point in the story if it appears to be universally accepted. You don't have to say 'It's hot out today, according to the weather man.'" In the next day's *Post,* Ombudsman Joann Byrd wrote: "The most embarrassing mistakes in newspapers are invariably the ones the paper had abundant opportunity to catch. And this was one of those. As the story moved through the editing process, several able editors read it, and still the sentence, sitting out there with no support, did not jump out."[3]

Supporting the new President remained the dominant tendency. On gays in the military, the networks sought to educate a resistant public about the merits of Clinton's position. *MediaWatch* analysts reviewed every evening news story on gays in the military from January 21 to 30, and discovered talking heads favoring gays in the military outnumbered opponents by 70 to 42 on the three broadcast networks. ABC (27-14) and CBS (32-17) both gave nearly twice as much attention to the liberal argument. NBC (11-11) split its head count down the middle, but also aired a Maria Shriver special promoting the gay viewpoint.

That January 26 edition of *First Person* featured 42 soundbites of gays (and one of Clinton) to seven soundbites opposing homosexuality. Shriver explained opposition to the gay agenda: "In the end, it all comes down to fear." Reporters narrated stories from the gay perspective. On the January 29 *World News Tonight*, ABC reporter Beth Nissen explained: "They say they see in all of the switchboards lit with anti-gay calls the crossed wires lit with intolerance and bigotry. Yet many gays are hopeful that laws and attitudes will change, that there will be less hatred."[4] Reporters did not allow that opposition to homosexuality could be based in something other than fear or hatred. Despite the media support, Clinton's pro-gay politics led to an increase in the number of voters who described him as liberal, presaging one cause of Democratic defeat at the 1994 polls.[5]

Reporters strained not to "pile on" the White House. *Time* reporter Nancy Traver explained on C-SPAN: "This cover [of *Time* featuring Zoe Baird] that you held up hits him pretty hard on the whole issue of his nomination of Zoe Baird. Then this week, we considered running another really tough cover story on Clinton about gays in the military, and we decided no, that was too tough, that's too much, that's piling on. So we'll move that story inside. We just didn't want to come across as beating up on the President."[6] They rooted for the President to get better organized, as National Public Radio's Phyllis Crockett explained on CNN's *Inside Politics:* "I think he is really trying to do some decent things....I don't think the program has been the problem. I think the execution has been the problem."[7]

Technical "appearances of impropriety" may have driven news coverage in the Reagan and Bush years, but scandal would continue to be downplayed as Clinton arrived at the White House. *National Review* noted that the Ethics in Government Act "prohibits senior congressional staff from dealing with former employers for one year after their departure. Mr. Stephanopoulos was a senior aide to Rep. Richard Gephardt in 1991 and spent 1992 with the Clinton campaign, on at least one occasion acting as a liaison with congressional Democratic leaders." Sam Donaldson asked Stephanopoulos to respond to the charge on *This Week with David Brinkley* January 24, but the issue never made the network morning or evening shows.

Five days later, *The Washington Times* reported that the Clintons' health care task force met in secret, violating the Federal Advisory Committee Act, which the *Times* said "requires that any presidentially appointed advisory task force which includes non-governmental employees or outside advisers must keep all events and meetings public." The task force obviously included Mrs. Clinton and Mrs. Gore, who were not government employees. But with the exception of the *Times,* the media reported nothing, even after the ranking Republican on the House Government Operations Committee, Rep. Bill Clinger, demanded the closed meetings stop.[8]

When the White House press corps questioned Clinton's bumbling too much for his liking, the President returned to attacking them, as when Clinton attacked Brit Hume after the ABC reporter asked about his zig-zag approach to the nomination of Ruth Bader Ginsburg for the Supreme Court. Clinton's persecution complex missed the elementary difference between the media coverage of his presidency and Ronald Reagan's. Reagan's first days also got bogged down in mini-scandals of less-than-planetary significance (White House china, National Security Adviser Richard Allen's watches), but the media also deplored the central projects of his presidency: tax cuts, spending restraint, the defense buildup. Clinton, on the other hand, received more gushing acclaim than skeptical evaluation of his primary goals: one of the largest tax increases in American history, not to mention the approaching "no new taxes" promise of a nationalized health care system. Compared to recent Republican presidencies, Clinton had no right to complain of unfair treatment.

22

Working for the White House

"There's no doubting that the nation is about to be led by its first sensitive male chief executive. He's the first President to have attended both Lamaze classes and family therapy (as part of his brother's drug rehabilitation). He can speak in the rhythms and rhetoric of pop psychology and self-actualization. He can search for the inner self while seeking connectedness with the greater whole." -- Newsweek reporter Howard Fineman, January 25, 1993.

"Some days I say 'Why is he [Clinton] doing that?' or 'Gosh, can he do it a little better'? But it may be time to, sort of as you say, chill. We know when it comes to politics and governing, whatever you think of this President, whether you voted for him or not, he can hang -- which is to say, he can do it." -- Dan Rather on The Arsenio Hall Show, January 28, 1993.

In addition to their obliviousness to the Zoe Baird controversy, reporters marked the new promotional attitude toward the White House most obviously in the coverage of the new President's nominees. Suddenly reporters defended presidential appointees against the opposing party's criticism instead of burying them in it, as some Reagan and Bush nominees had experienced. One of the strangest defenses came from *Wall Street Journal* Washington Bureau Chief Al Hunt, who denied Health and Human Services nominee Donna Shalala, despite years of left-wing activism, was any kind of ideologue: "All I can tell you is that the football coach at the University of Wisconsin didn't want her to leave. I don't think she's any lefty."[1]

Time allowed its own Editor-at-Large Strobe Talbott to join the Clinton State Department ("Our loss will be the country's gain")[2], and thereafter defended Clinton's diplomatic nominees such as Morton Halperin and Sam Brown, who were both well-known activists of the radical left. The nomination of Halperin to a newly created peacekeeping position at the Pentagon drew support in *Time* from reporter Kevin Fedarko: "How did Halperin manage to get himself caught between the cross hairs of a confirmation hearing so savage it resembled a drive-by shooting?" Fedarko claimed Halperin's "liberal views...in defense policy" were offset by working for the American Civil Liberties Union, which defended the rights of "Oliver North, Lyn Nofziger, and the conservative student writers at the *Dartmouth Review.*"[3]

Fedarko ignored what sparked conservative opposition: Halperin's role as an accomplice in the release of the Pentagon Papers, his relationship with traitorous ex-CIA agent Philip Agee, and his belief that "covert operations are incompatible with constitutional government and should be abolished." To *Time*'s chagrin, Halperin's nomination died and he was appointed to a position not requiring confirmation.

In a June 6, 1994 article on the appointment of Sam Brown to be ambassador to the Conference on Security and Cooperation in Europe (CSCE), *Time* columnist Margaret Carlson began: "Why are good people reluctant to serve in government? All the civics student needs to know can be found in the saga of the nomination of Sam Brown." Carlson said of Colorado's Republican Senator: "No one understands why Hank Brown has decided to make Sam Brown his personal nemesis..Some think Hank Brown simply wants to zing the President, refight the Vietnam War and triumph over an old rival."

Carlson and other reporters ignored what *The Washington Times* termed "some very vociferous and anti-American comments and actions of Mr. Brown's over the years." Among the quotes the *Times* cited was Brown's 1970 admission: "Part of me wanted to blow up buildings, and I decided that those who have waged this war really should be treated as war criminals." In 1977, while a Carter administration official, he proclaimed: "I take second place to no one in my hatred of the intelligence agencies." That same year he participated in a New York rally staged by the communist rulers of Vietnam. Yet

Carlson claimed Brown "was at the suit-and-tie end of the antiwar movement and was inside the convention handling Senator Eugene McCarthy's delegates, nowhere near the Yippies."[4] Brown was eventually sent to Vienna to head the CSCE delegation but without the rank of ambassador, which required Senate confirmation.

Some reporters' commitment to the Clinton administration extended beyond supporting them in print or on the air. A number of national reporters jumped ship to work in the Clinton administration, to make policy or explain policy for the liberal Democrats in the White House. In *The New Republic,* Jacob Weisberg described the closeness between the White House and segments of the media, as well as government and academia, as "Clincest."

Weisberg noted *Time* writer Michael Kramer's reported attempts to get Clinton to nominate his wife, Judge Kimba Wood, as Attorney General. (Wood was publicly rumored for the job and was then publicly dumped for Baird-like problems with a domestic employee). *Newsweek* reporter Howard Fineman urged the Clintons to send their daughter Chelsea to the trendy private Sidwell Friends school -- since his own child was attending the school. When the Clintons did so, sparking criticism for avoiding the D.C. public schools, they were defended by *Wall Street Journal* Washington Bureau Chief Al Hunt -- whose kids also attended Sidwell Friends. Journalists like *Newsweek*'s Joe Klein and *U.S. News* Editor-at-Large David Gergen attended the annual Renaissance Weekend with the Clintons at Hilton Head Island in South Carolina. Weisberg even said writer Taylor Branch was granted an inside-the-inauguration story for *Life* magazine only after he promised to help with Clinton's inauguration speech.[5] Appearances of objectivity would matter little in the Clinton years.

Strobe Talbott's appointment as ambassador to the former Soviet republics (later to be named Deputy Secretary of State) came at the very beginning. But other major reporters followed him into government service. ABC reporter Rick Inderfurth moved from covering foreign affairs to assisting United Nations Ambassador Madeleine Albright, who he also worked with in the Carter administration. National Public Radio President Douglas Bennet donated money to

Paul Tsongas, but joined the Clinton State Department. Long-time NBC legal reporter Carl Stern, who upbraided Supreme Court nominee David Souter's judicial philosophy on *NBC Nightly News* in 1990 as "narrow" and displaying "a certain insensitivity," became chief spokesman for the Clinton Justice Department.[6] CNN anchor David French joined the Central Intelligence Agency as a spokesman. ABC reporter Kathleen deLaski moved from covering Defense Secretary Les Aspin in the spring of 1993 to joining his staff during the summer as his chief public affairs officer.

Besides Talbott, the highest-profile revolver was *U.S. News* Editor-at-Large and *MacNeil-Lehrer NewsHour* pundit David Gergen, who'd been throwing verbal bouquets at the new President early on, even as he advised him through phone calls behind the scenes. In 1994, Gergen's *U.S. News* colleague, assistant managing editor Don Baer, who before joining the magazine in 1987 hosted a $75,000 fundraiser for Jim Hunt, Sen. Jesse Helms' Democratic opponent, became Clinton's chief speechwriter. Some revolvers even replaced other revolvers: the Pentagon replaced deLaski in late 1994 with *Wall Street Journal* reporter Kenneth Bacon.

The dramatic movement of media personnel into the administration amounted to more than twice as many reporters joining Clinton's executive branch in the first two years (33) as signed up for the Bush administration in its entire four years (15). These numbers became more impressive when the appointees' high media profiles came into the picture. While no on-air network TV reporter joined the Bush Administration, six took jobs with Clinton. Ten network producers, executives, and researchers made the leap to Clinton's staff, compared to three in the Bush years. Another 13 major newspaper and magazine reporters signed up for Clinton, compared to just eight with Bush.[7] Not only did these ex-reporters help the Clinton administration sell its policies, since they knew very well their former colleagues on major Washington beats, it demonstrated the liberal insider politics of reporters in the nation's capital.

23

The Victimized Stimulus

"The Senate Republicans are threatening to block the President's other big proposal, the $16 billion job creation program." -- CBS Evening News anchor Connie Chung, April 1.

"Let's start with the President's job stimulus package, if we could. It's hung up in the Senate, victimized by a Republican filibuster." -- Today co-host Bryant Gumbel to Clinton chief of staff Mack McLarty, April 7, 1993.

The first example of the media's determination to advocate White House economic policies came in Clinton's spring push for a $16 billion "stimulus" bill to jump-start the economy through government "investment." The bill died in the Senate in late April, much like George Bush's 1989 capital gains tax cut proposal, which was filibustered to death by a Democratic majority in the Senate.

In theory, the two failed proposals represented the liberal and conservative approaches to stimulating the economy. Conservatives argued that cutting capital gains taxes encouraged investment and reduced the cost of capital, helping the private sector to grow and create jobs. Liberals, on the other hand, traditionally created make-work jobs in the public sector, and the Clinton stimulus plan included a large amount of grants to big-city mayors for added local government jobs and summer jobs programs for teenagers.

But a Media Research Center study of network coverage on both morning and evening shows found that the Bush plan was never described in 1989 as a "jobs bill" or a "stimulus," but simply as a "capital gains tax cut" -- intended to help the wealthy only. But in 1993, the networks used the Democratic term "jobs bill" to describe the plan in 46 percent of the 180 news stories on the subject.[1]

In the April 19 *Newsweek,* Eleanor Clift noted the White House's pleasure with the trend: "Watching reports on CNN, a top aide noted that the network flashed 'Jobs Bill' on the screen each time the impasse was discussed. 'We'll take it,' he smiled, knowing a debate framed by jobs was one Clinton could win."[2]

CBS led the networks in cheerleading. While the others described the Clinton package as a "jobs bill" or "jobs creation bill" in 31 percent of news stories, CBS used the terms in 83 percent of its segments. CBS repeatedly portrayed the "stimulus" package's holdup as a tragedy. On April 2, anchor Connie Chung reported: "The government says the unemployment rate held at 7 percent last month. Held up in the Senate is President Clinton's $16 billion program to bring unemployment down. Opponents are blocking a final vote." Reporter Bob Schieffer portrayed the blockage as economically harmful: "For sure, the tie-up couldn't have come at a worse time: in New York, today's gloomy economic news contributed to the stock market tumbling 68 points." On April 6, reporter Bill Plante explicitly hit the GOP: "At an unemployment office in Fairfax, Virginia, they don't understand why politics is getting in the way of helping people find work." On April 21, Dan Rather intoned: "Clinton's big jobs bill is still being held prisoner in Congress tonight."[3]

By contrast, on September 28, 1989, the night the House passed the tax cut, anchor Dan Rather hypnotically repeated: "A vote to support President Bush's idea to cut the capital gains tax cut *for the wealthy.* Sixty-four Democrats bucked their own House leaders, abandoned them, and joined the Republicans to support the measure. Mr. Bush says that cutting the capital gains tax *for the wealthy* will boost the economy and create jobs. Opponents don't believe that and call it simply a tax giveaway *for the wealthy.*" (Italics mine). On October 5, 1989, Rather reported the House passed a spending bill to "cut capital gains taxes for the wealthy...and repeal the overall catastrophic illness insurance program which stood to benefit mostly the poor and middle-income people." When the Bush plan failed on October 25, 1989, Rather noted Democrats said no to Bush on the capital gains cut "which would benefit mostly the wealthy."[4]

In 180 morning and evening news stories in 1993, viewers were reminded of the 1989 capital gains filibuster only once -- by ABC's Brit Hume. On April 5, Hume recalled: "For the record, four years ago, Senate Democrats filibustered to block a measure George Bush said would stimulate the economy -- a cut in the capital gains tax. The White House claimed the bill would, that's right, create jobs. Senate Democratic leader [George] Mitchell, who now complains about this filibuster, led that one, which succeeded."[5]

Of the 33 network reports on the Bush plan, only two used statistics. Both CBS and NBC relied on Democratic estimates of who would benefit. On September 28, 1989, NBC reporter Andrea Mitchell, stacked the deck by using simplistic Democratic averages to charge that taxpayers making $200,000 a year would typically receive $25,000 in tax breaks, while those making $50,000 would get $300. *CBS This Morning* also attacked the proposal in an October 5 segment with its then-"political columnist," Christopher Matthews, a former top aide to Speaker of the House Tip O'Neill. Matthews' self-described "sermonette" claimed 80 percent of the cut would go to those making over $100,000.[6]

Neither CBS or NBC invited anyone for the Republican response: that the tax benefits would depend on the size of the gain, not the size of people's income, or that the majority of capital gains taxpapers make less than $100,000, but their gains aren't as large. Most importantly, no one mentioned the potential to create jobs.

In 1993, only 28 morning and evening stories (15 percent) related that the GOP claimed to oppose spending on "pork" or "wasteful" items. In 180 news stories, CBS reporter Bill Plante was the only network reporter to note the GOP counted 20 projects that would create no new jobs, and another 103 projects would create 10 or less jobs each. Plante and NBC's Lisa Myers were the only ones to list pork-barrel items in the Clinton bill. On the March 30 *Nightly News,* Myers read from "wish lists of mayors" including "swimming pools in eight states, tennis courts in four cities."[7] Although they outscored ABC (8 percent) and CNN (10 percent) in mentioning pork, CBS usually sounded Democratic notes. On *CBS This Morning* April 8, co-host Harry Smith asked Sen. Al D'Amato (R-N.Y.): "Isn't the pork a small part? Aren't we talking about money for jobs programs that could be used effectively in New York City?"[8]

The pro-Clinton bias extended from TV to radio. In the Washington *City Paper,* reporter Glenn Garvin described how National Public Radio covered the story in one week in mid-April when the stimulus fight boiled passionately. "During the first three days of the week, NPR ran 11 stories on Clinton's campaign for the package, all of them centered around speeches by the President or Al Gore...It wasn't until the afternoon of April 15, the fourth day I listened to the network, that I heard a Republican voice on the subject of the filibuster." Even then, Garvin reported, the Republican analyst was wrongly conceding defeat. In the meantime, NPR reporter Cokie Roberts found "more than a little racism" in anyone who opposed the package's aid to the cities.[9]

Print reporters also touted the proposal. *U.S. News & World Report* economics writer Susan Dentzer asserted: "Amid a broader economic plan that has its share of flaws, Clinton's well-crafted stimulus is a piece worth keeping...The reason to pass a stimulus package is to chart a smoother course for the economy, boosting it toward full employment that much faster." Just as she was beginning to sound Keynesian, Dentzer added: "It's no Depression-style program of hiring workers to paint murals at the post office....The sorts of spending the President has picked -- for example on education or on long-planned highway projects -- tend to create lots of jobs, many which carry high wages and benefits."[10] What was most surprising about this coverage was not its blatantly promotional bias, but its failure to carry the day for the President's proposal.

CBS may have been especially guilty of rooting for Clinton, but the difference between the network portrayal of the Bush plan (sop to the rich) and the Clinton plan (jobs bill) is the same distinction made by liberal politicians. If the networks claimed its skepticism of Reaganomics or the rare supply-side Bush initiative came from its duty to critique the White House, often with statistics from liberals in Congress, then the media failed to highlight the opposing arguments to the Clinton stimulus. The networks led the cheers for the White House instead of balancing them.

24

The Fabulous First Budget

"Forty-five minutes into budget director Leon Panetta's briefing on the economy, it was clear that something was missing. After 12 years of Ronald Reagan's voodoo economics and George Bush's decaffeinated, nondairy, sodium-free imitation voodoo economics, there was suddenly no ideology in the federal budget. Panetta talked like a cheerful, no-nonsense accountant trying to balance the books the hard way -- honestly." -- New York Daily News Washington Bureau Chief Lars-Erik Nelson, March 15, 1993 column.

"Doesn't Clinton deserve some credit here for beginning to tackle the problem of getting people to pay taxes? I mean, for 12 years in this country, it's become patriotic not to pay taxes, to avoid paying taxes. And Clinton is at least trying to turn that around. Why isn't he getting more credit for that?" -- Washington Post columnist and chief foreign correspondent Jim Hoagland on the PBS show Washington Week in Review, June 18, 1993.

Reporters continued the sales job just days after the stimulus plan's failure when Clinton proposed his budget plan, complete with a large tax increase. Candidate Bill Clinton harpooned GOP Presidents for adding $3 trillion to the national debt in the last 12 years. In 1993, President Clinton's initial budget, according to Clinton's Office of Management and Budget, would cause the deficit to climb to $431 billion by 2003.[1] But reporters praised him for unprecedented courage in reducing the deficit.

On *CBS This Morning* on April 30, co-host Harry Smith asked Sen. Bob Dole: "Yesterday you came out and said 'Let's give the President an E for effort.' Shouldn't he get a better grade for at least passing a budget that takes the deficit seriously for the first time?"

On May 28, *This Morning*'s Paula Zahn asked Ross Perot: "Do you acknowledge that this is at all better than anything the Republicans attempted over the last 12 years?"[2]

On NBC, reporter Lisa Myers agreed on the April 30 *Today:* "The President deserves great credit for having the courage to come up with a deficit reduction plan and we shouldn't lose sight of that." Two days later on *Meet the Press,* NBC White House reporter Andrea Mitchell complained that Clinton's image was all wrong: "This is the first President in a generation who had the guts to try to do something about deficit reduction and to take on health care, and he's somehow not selling that. He's still being perceived as an old-style Democrat." Declared Bob Schieffer on the May 23 CBS *Sunday Morning:* "It's a plan that calls for massive cuts in federal spending."[3]

The canard continued in the news magazines. *Time* Chief Political Correspondent Michael Kramer saluted Clinton on May 3: "Great salesman that he is, Clinton can be viewed as a victim of his own success. His insistence on deficit reduction -- and his cajoling of Congress to support a multi-year plan to accomplish it -- is the very definition of courage in modern American politics."[4] *U.S. News & World Report* Editor-in-Chief Mort Zuckerman crowed in a May 17 column: "The political climate has changed in large measure because of Clinton's determination to address the deficit seriously for the first time in 12 years."[5]

The staunchest Clinton defense came from *Newsweek* reporter Eleanor Clift on the May 15 *McLaughlin Group:* "Essentially, the plan maintains the balance which undoes the '80s: 70 percent of the taxes fall on wealthier people. He does have a dollar in spending cuts for every dollar in tax increases. It's true...It's the first serious attempt to cut the deficit in this country."[6] Earlier, *Newsweek*'s "Conventional Wisdom Watch" box praised Clinton twice on his budget. On February 22, it read: "Bubba's got guts. But watch out for Congress's days of whine and poses." On March 1, the President drew another up arrow: "Old CW: Not ready for prime time. New CW: Almost ready for Mount Rushmore."[7]

While Republicans charged that like past budget deals, the Democrats preferred tax hikes to spending cuts, reporters stuck to the White House line that the budget plan proposed an even mix of the two. *Newsweek* Senior Writer Joe Klein complained that "Republicans...have a curious way of calculating the spending-cuts-to-tax-increase ratio: they consider loophole closing -- like Clinton's proposal to reduce the deductibility of business meals from 80 to 50 percent -- a tax increase; thus, Bob Dole can say that the Clinton plan is 3-to-1 taxes to cuts."[8]

Gloria Borger of *U.S. News & World Report* also went to bat for the Clinton budget on *Washington Week in Review:* "The Republicans argue that it's three dollars in tax increases for one dollar in spending cuts, but I think it's really more 50-50. That's an important thing to get out to the American public." *U.S. News* agreed, in its July 5 issue, saying the Democrats "verge on a 50-50 mix of tax increases and spending cuts, according to *U.S. News* calculations."[9]

Reporters ignored the many Democratic gimmicks. Most of the proposed "cuts" were really projected debt service savings from projected low interest rates, a "rosy scenario" that crumbled as the Federal Reserve raised rates in 1994. Other "cuts" were reductions in projected increases. Many were completely unspecified and were scheduled to take place after 1996. Worst of all, the entire talk of a five-year budget plan did not take into account the billions or trillions of dollars a Clinton health plan would cost.

But reporters who used the term "smoke and mirrors" so freely during the Reagan years touted the honesty of Clinton's budget experts. In *U.S. News,* Gloria Borger stressed that Panetta "has been the affable and honest budget broker, serving as the Democrats' budgetary conscience, opposing all bills that exceeded spending targets."[10] *Washington Post* reporter Steven Mufson claimed: "For the past 12 years, the job of balancing the federal government's books has been rife with avoidance and obfuscation. Reagan budget director David A. Stockman began the process with his 'rosy scenarios' and 'magic asterisks,' accounting tricks that helped him submit what looked like balanced budgets even as he added billions to the deficit." Bush budget director Richard Darman had "hollow spending caps that helped him keep the budget ruse going," but Clinton budget director Leon Panetta's "talk of honest budgeting [is] part of a cultural change that seems to be underway at OMB."[11] Borger and Mufson ignored that Panetta and Darman's 1990 budget compromise aimed to reduce the deficit by $500 billion to the debt, but it actually increased the debt $500 billion.

Heritage Foundation analyst Daniel Mitchell argued the Clinton package which claimed to save $336.6 billion over five years consisted of $301 billion in tax increases to just $20 billion in actual cuts in projected spending increases, making the real ratio of tax hikes to spending "cuts" 15 to 1. Mitchell noticed one obvious irony reporters ignored: Clinton suggested in his first address to Congress that the Democrat-appointed Congressional Budget Office would be the official arbiter of the budget numbers, but the CBO calculated the tax-hike-to-spending-cut ratio at about 2.5 to 1.[12] The most political thing reporters could do -- helping sell Clinton's budget -- involved insisting that there were no politics or political gimmicks in the budget.

25

Hillary's Fan Club

"She is the duty-bound, disciplined Methodist, carrying her favorite Scriptures around in her briefcase and holding herself and others to a higher standard....Perhaps a First Lady who consults lawbooks rather than astrologers doesn't look so frightening after all. And perhaps Bill Clinton, rather than seeming weak by comparison with his wife, has proved that it takes a solid, secure man to marry a strong woman." -- Time's Margaret Carlson, January 4, 1993.

"Feminaut explores gender cosmos. The most fabulous woman in U.S. history?!?!" -- Newsweek's "Conventional Wisdom Watch," February 15, 1993.

While Bill Clinton drew some adversarial barbs from the White House press corps, the new First Lady received a much more positive press. In a remarkable study by the Center for Media and Public Affairs, President Clinton received only 34 percent positive coverage from the network evening news shows from January 20 to July 20, but in the same time period, the First Lady scored a startling 79 percent rate of positive coverage.[1]

That may have been partially due to Mrs. Clinton's reluctance to grant interviews. With the exception of a mid-summer NBC tour of the White House, the First Lady completely avoided a network interview until the President's health care address in late September. Even when her office parceled out print interviews, the reporting often seemed as soft as a month-old banana. Instead of presenting a full picture of the First Lady, reporters assisted the Clintons politically, as Clinton biographer Elizabeth Drew explained: "The essence of these articles was a portrait of a whole woman: a working mother who struggled to keep all her roles intact, a normal, warm person. An anecdote about Mrs. Clinton making scrambled eggs for an ill Chelsea was featured in three of the articles, which served only to suggest how rare this kind of thing must have been. The softening of her image from the sometimes chilly and remote person that much of the public had perceived was obviously, and not too subtly, designed to give her more of the benefit of the doubt when the health care plan was unveiled."[2]

Seeing in Mrs. Clinton their own aspirations and struggles as working women, female reporters remained her most enthusiastic cheerleaders. Before she had scored an interview, *Washington Post* reporter Martha Sherrill honored the First Lady in a three-part series from January 11 to 13. Or was it an honor? Sherrill devoted only one paragraph to Mrs. Clinton's career at the Rose Law Firm and two to her legal writings, but twelve paragraphs to changes in her hair and wardrobe. Sherrill did not touch on Mrs. Clinton's tenure as chairman of the federal Legal Services Corporation from 1978-81. But Sherrill still attacked Hillary's critics: "At one extreme, you had Pat Buchanan at the Houston Astrodome, spitting out the words 'lawyer spouse.' On the other side, she's provoked a certain amount of weeping. Old girlfriends...[think] the world has so grossly misunderstood their warm, funny, smart, tough, loyal Hillary."[3]

The journalistic tributes to Hillary said little about her important role heading the task force which would produce a dramatic new proposal of nationalized health care. When *Time* published a 20-question interview in White House reporter Margaret Carlson's May 10 cover story on Mrs. Clinton, three concerned health care reform. The other 17 dwelt on trivial questions, such as the President's crossword puzzle habit: "Does he ask you for a six-letter word for a river in Germany?" And: "Do you get a chance to exercise?" Carlson explained that *Time* wanted to include the questions that no one else had asked: "We have a lot on the record about health care, and three questions out of 20 about something we have her on the record for seemed enough when you can get in stuff that nobody'd ever seen." Asked at the time how the media treated Hillary, Carlson proclaimed on CNN: "I think we actually try to cover her as hard news."[4]

Carlson's cover story proclaimed: "As the icon of American womanhood, she is the medium through which the remaining anxieties over feminism are being played out. She is on a cultural seesaw held to a schizophrenic standard: everything she does that is soft is a calculated coverup of the careerist inside; everything that isn't is a put-down of women who stay home and bake cookies."[5] But Hillary benefited from a different double standard -- heading a task force doing the hard-news work of redesigning one-seventh of the economy while riding a wave of soft-news puff pieces.

Despite the media's disdain for poking into the Clintons' marriage, Carlson actually contended, both in *Time* and *Vanity Fair,* that the Clintons were much more affectionate than the Bushes. In *Vanity Fair,* she described the First Couple's Valentine's Day trip to the chic Washington restaurant Red Sage: "They have painted soup and the lamb baked in herbed bread. They exchange gifts and touch each other more in two hours than the Bushes did in four years."[6]

Washington Post reporter Martha Sherrill returned to polishing the First Lady's apple in a loving May 4 article on the inner Hillary's political and spiritual influences: "In the midst of redesigning America's health care system and replacing Madonna as our leading cult figure, the new First Lady has already begun working on her next project, far more metaphysical and uplifting." Hillary's mission was nothing less than "redefining who we are as human beings in this postmodern age." Sherrill also wrote: "She has goals, but they appear to be so huge and so far off -- grand and noble things twinkling in the distance -- that it is hard to see what she sees...She is both impersonal and poignant -- with much more depth, intellect, and spirituality than we are used to in a politician."[7]

Both reporters caricatured the conservative criticism of Mrs. Clinton as extreme and unthinking. Wrote Sherrill: "All this children business, children business -- keeps reminding the far right of communist youth camps, early indoctrination, Marxist brainwashing." Despite claiming she voted for Reagan twice, had an aunt in the John Birch Society, and is "the only Republican in the *Post* building," Sherrill told *Media Watch:* "This is something I got from a couple of people, and I'm not going to say who they were, conservatives. I think [conservative criticism] comes from a lot of emotion and not very much thinking." Carlson also caricatured the Right: "In a state where Gloria Steinem was considered by some a communist, Hillary started out being regarded as a stuck-up feminist from Wellesley and Yale who wouldn't change her name and ended up being a popular and admired First Lady." Asked who considered Steinem a communist, Carlson confessed to *MediaWatch:* "That was overly glib, and I regret it now. But 20 years ago, a woman came from Yale Law School and the House Judiciary Committee and kept her own name. This was a very conservative group of people, and she was deep in a hole. She had to prove herself."[8]

As Sherrill explained later on CNN: "I think there's an intensity of interest in her, and I think it's very hard for career women, working women, to not be rooting for her."[9] Carlson concurred: "As much as we try to think otherwise, when you're covering someone like yourself, and your position in life is insecure, she's your mascot. Something in you roots for her. You're rooting for your team. I try to get that bias out, but for many of us, it's there."[10] Carlson went further in an appearance on C-SPAN with host Brian Lamb and two male reporters: "Wouldn't all of you rather just keep the goodies to yourself and not share them in general?"[11]

Jokes about the new First Lady were psychoanalyzed as the traumatized last refuge of male chauvinist pigs. In the April 6 *Boston Globe,* reporter Nathan Cobb posited: "Not since the days of Dan Quayle -- has it really been two months already? -- has a national figure been such a triple star of joke, one-liner, and song as is Hillary Clinton...Not everyone thinks it's funny. Hillaryesque humor is seen by some people as a comment on how many Americans, from TV monologists to water cooler wiseguys, are made uncomfortable by a powerful and ambitious woman." Cobb quoted National Organization for Women leader Patricia Ireland: "They're trying to take a threat, and their fear of it, and make it a joke. Many men are threatened by strong women."[12] Hillary's boosters continued to tout her as a new kind of First Lady who could do anything a man could do, but that apparently did not include taking a joke.

26

The Health Campaign

"I say the Clintons are almost heroes in my mind for finally facing up to the terrible problems we have with our current health care system and bringing it to the attention of the public. Most people, I think, will be better off." -- ABC medical reporter Dr. Tim Johnson on 20/20, September 24, 1993.

"I saw a Hillary Clinton that I'd never seen before. She was funny, charming, sexy -- yes, gang, sexy. We are both Scorpios, which tells you a lot....Meanwhile, she's earned the respect of everyone (except the wackos) with her handling of the health care issue. Indeed she has gotten everyone (except the wackos) to agree that we need health care for everyone. This is a very formidable idea, ladies and gentlemen." -- CNN talk show host Larry King in his USA Today column, October 4, 1993.

In proposing a nationalized health care system, the Clinton administration must have known that its plan would get a very favorable journalistic reception. In a Media Research Center study of the 20 network stories aired from 1990 through July 1993 on more socialized health systems in other countries and two liberal states, 70 percent of them were decisively positive; talking heads favoring government-run systems outnumbered opponents by two to one; and 65 percent also described the socialized systems as "free" or less costly than the United States.[1]

Another MRC study, focusing on network morning show interview segments on health reform from Election Day 1992 through August 1993, found a significant tilt to the left (featuring 21 guests from the left, six from the right, and five from medical industry groups). Despite the left-wing tilt of the guests, interviewers did not play devil's advocate from the right, asking questions that were classified as evenly split (25 left, 25 right, 95 informational). Only in the study's last month, September 1993, as the Clinton health plan was unveiled, did coverage move right. Guests in September grew slightly more balanced (24 left, 13 right, 4 industry), and questions reflected more of a devil's-advocate approach (57 right, 17 left, 130 informational). The study classified as "right" any guest advocating less government than the Clinton plan, including many politicians who were endorsing government-mandated universal coverage at the time.[2]

As the Clintons prepared to unveil the details of their health proposal in the fall of 1993, ideologically confused reporters actually placed the Clinton plan, with its massive government takeover of health spending and decisionmaking, on the right end of the political spectrum. *The Washington Post* promoted Clinton the New Democrat on the front page September 6 with the headline "Post-Vacation Clinton Swims Toward Mainstream: Health Care, Trade Pact, Reinventing Government Give President Chance to Alter His Image." Reporter Ann Devroy wrote that Clinton's health plan and the other proposals were "intended to restore the image he had last November as the 'new Democrat' who would be a change, not only from Republican refusal to deal with domestic problems but also from the old Democratic ideology."[3]

On September 9, *Post* economics columnist and Democratic cheerleader Hobart Rowen described the many ways Clinton had been backsliding on full-scale nationalization, adding: "Clinton's more conservative initiative on health care anticipates a slower phasing in of his proposals...The drift clearly is toward a more centrist presidency."[4]

Some reporters actually equated the Clinton health plan with the "free market." On CNN's *Inside Politics* August 30, CNN health reporter Jeff Levine explained the health policy factions within the White House: "On the one hand, you have the regulators and there are many of those in government...And then there are the free marketeers, more of the Ira Magaziner people, who would like to see the marketplace somehow do its job and solve the health care crisis."

Wall Street Journal health reporter Hilary Stout seconded Levine's confusion on that show: "I think that everyone within the administration at this point is agreed on the general direction of their health care plan, the sort of free-market managed competition that Jeff just described plus some significant federal oversight. The federal government would set caps on private and public health care spending."[5]

Levine's coupling of "free market" and "Ira Magaziner" in the same sentence demonstrated the media's ideological incoherence. The Clinton health plan, heavily influenced by Magaziner, would have created a maze of new federal agencies and allowed state governments to throw all but two or three insurance companies out of business in each state. The plan even allowed states to employ a single-payer option and ban insurance companies. The label "free market" should have been left for plans to remove government interventions from the medical system, not add them.

In the September 20 issue of *Time*, Washington Bureau Chief Dan Goodgame found the struggle between Republicans on his right and supporters of a Canadian-style system banning insurance companies on his left "leaves Clinton where he wants to be: somewhere near the political center with a plan that incorporates some market mechanisms and a lot of government regulation, cuts in some spending programs, and new health benefits in other areas."[6]

The reality of "reform" -- a nationalized health care system forcing Americans into a government-run system of lessened services and higher taxes -- was lost. The President's ideological-chameleon tactics -- promising no new income taxes, claiming there wouldn't be price controls, slowing down the pace of the government takeover -- were presented as Clinton's allegiance to the right wing of the Democratic Party.[7]

The unveiling of the Clinton health plan drew rave reviews from reporters, especially Hillary Clinton's appearances without notes before congressional committees in late September. "There seemed no detail she did not know, no criticism she had not considered...It was a boffo performance. Republicans were impressed, Democrats just loved it," announced CBS reporter Bob Schieffer on September 28. The next day, CNN's Candy Crowley found "more rave reviews for Hillary Rodham Clinton, who put in yet another virtuoso performance...This is a lady who knows her stuff...Pro and con on the issue, lawmakers seem unanimously ga-ga." On September 24, ABC named her "Person of the Week," with Peter Jennings proclaiming: "This particular individual had come a long way in the last year or so. And then we thought -- no, maybe it's the country which has come a long way."[8]

In *Time*, three reporters penned their own tribute: "Perhaps the most striking thing about Hillary Clinton's performance last week on Capitol Hill was the silent but devastating rebuke she sent to her cartoonists. This was not the Hillary as overbearing wife, the Hillary as left-wing ideologue, or even the Hillary as mushy-headed spiritual adviser to the nation. This was Hillary the polite but passionate American citizen -- strangely mesmerizing because of how she matched the poise and politics of her delivery with the power of her position. No wonder some of Washington's most acid tongues and pens took the week off."[9]

But reporters had yet to delve into the classic question of all major political debates: how much would it cost and how would it be paid for? Throughout the campaign, reporters insisted that insuring 37 million uninsured Americans could be done with no tax increase, the mother of all rosy scenarios. Some of that delusion remained. *Time*'s Dan Goodgame attempted a salesmanlike pitch: "The Clinton plan is surprisingly persuasive in supporting the long-time claim of the Clintons, and their top health care strategist, Ira Magaziner, that reform can be almost entirely from savings, without broad-based new taxes and without enough left over to reduce the federal budget deficit."[10]

Just weeks before the health plan's unveiling, reporters repeatedly explained that Clinton would reduce the deficit by $500 billion over five years with a package containing half tax increases, half spending cuts. But nowhere in their calculations did media outlets factor in massive new health care spending, which would eventually be estimated by the Democrats' Congressional Budget Office at $784 billion over the seven years from 1996 to 2002.[11]

27

The Big Red "Wrong" Returns

"Before Clinton gets the maximum bang out of health care's buck, he'll have to address all the lingering myths and fears, but none more than this one: that reform will mean giving up what we've already got." -- NBC reporter Jim Maceda on Today, September 22, 1993.

"Independent experts say the GOP commercial is just wrong, that the Clinton plan will not cost anything close to three million jobs." -- CNN reporter Brooks Jackson voicing over a big red "WRONG" on the screen, October 22, 1993 Inside Politics.

After praising both Clintons for proposing ambitious health "reform," reporters moved on to defend Bill and Hillary against the substantive arguments of their opponents. Reporters resumed their role as a truth squad against conservative critiques. Despite the questionable validity of the Clintons' claims that their non-government-run health plan would somehow pay for itself, their foes were not allowed to predict the harm of "reform" without being declared dishonest or wrong.

On the morning of Clinton's September 22, 1993 address to Congress introducing his health plan, two networks marshaled attacks against Clinton critics. *CBS This Morning* consumer reporter Hattie Kauffman judged the accuracy of anti-Clinton ads, using as an expert the Clinton partisan Ron Pollack of Families USA. Pollack criticized an ad by the Coalition for Health Insurance Choices, accusing them of concealment: "It's the Health Insurance Association of America's money that's behind that so-called coalition. That, I think, is unethical to the worst degree." But the HIAA listed themselves as the Coalition's funders at the end of the commercial.

Kauffman did not tell viewers that what she called a "health care consumer group" was pushing the Clinton plan. The February 6, 1993 *Washington Post* reported that at Clinton's request, Families USA "hired eight field representatives to wage a health care reform campaign of its own in 60 'swing' congressional districts where support for Clinton's general themes....are not firm."[1] Kauffman's story begged the question: How fair is the debate when the judge is on one of the teams?

NBC's Jim Maceda did not focus on any commercials, but he did set out to address what *Today*'s Bryant Gumbel called "a few common misconceptions" about the Clinton plan with the aid of Arthur Caplan, a liberal medical ethicist. Caplan announced that doctor choice is a myth: "I think I can nominate as the mother of all myths the idea that choice exists. What you've got is consumers who get no information about their doctor, about their hospital, about their hospice, about their mental health facility. They don't know whether it works or doesn't work. They have no idea who is doing things to them, whether they're any good, what the costs are."[2] In other words, choice did not exist because Americans did not have the brains to choose.

The next myth was "Managed Care." Maceda explained: "Also looming, the specter of managed care, something good for those so-called socialist countries abroad, but surely not for us. But guess what? American health care is already largely managed... Managed care already works in ten U.S. states, and, the reformers insist, is saving money." NBC changed its mind once the Republicans proposed giving Medicare patients the option to choose managed care through health maintenance organizations (HMOs): on October 16, 1995, when NBC anchor Tom Brokaw introduced a story asking: "Under the reforms now before Congress, many more would be encouraged to do the same thing [join HMOs], but will they really save money?" Reporter Robert Bazell told Brokaw "experts" said using HMOs for Medicare patients would mean "increasing costs for the traditional Medicare program as it covers more of the sickest people."[3]

Maceda's 1993 story concluded: "Before Clinton gets the maximum bang out of health care's buck, he'll have to address all the lingering myths and fears, but none more than this one: that reform will mean giving up what we've already got." How could Maceda claim it's a "myth" that Americans would have had to give up what they have? Maceda told *Media Watch:* "I didn't say giving up something, I said giving up everything, if I recall, I said starting from scratch, losing all the good things." When he was reread the transcript, including "giving up what we've already got," Maceda replied: "Okay, in context, giving up everything we've already got is what that means, giving up and going plunging into the unknown, giving up the known, is what that means." Wouldn't people have to give up what they have for the new plan? "Sure, people will have to sacrifice. Of course."[4]

Maceda insisted the story "was done not as a news report, it was done as an essay. I had freedom to do what I wanted, it was a more subjective piece, and I tried to be thought-provoking, rather than simply informative...[Caplan] happens to be one of the best I know to raise those issues. Obviously, he is a reform advocate, and I say that throughout." But Caplan was never identified as a liberal or "reform advocate" in the story, and NBC never told viewers that they were seeing an essay or commentary.[5]

The Republican National Committee released an ad predicting three million jobs would be lost if the Clinton plan were implemented. On the October 22, 1993 *Inside Politics,* CNN reporter Brooks Jackson proclaimed: "Independent experts say the GOP commercial is just wrong, that the Clinton plan will not cost anything close to 3 million jobs." CNN aired the graphic "Fact Check" and put a big red "WRONG" on the screen. Jackson defended his story and CNN's graphic by arguing that "I didn't say that was wrong. I said 'independent experts say it is wrong.'...The Republicans aren't using an independent expert."[6] Jackson did not note that "independent experts" also predicted Reagan's tax cuts would be wildly inflationary and that the 1990 budget deal would solve the deficit problem. How could it be "wrong" that the Clinton plan would cost 3 million jobs when the plan had yet to be implemented?

Reporters like Jackson had every right to air "independent experts" saying the Republicans were wrong, but to declare it "WRONG" in big capital letters amounted to blatant editorialization on a matter of prediction, not fact.

Reporters carried their campaign for health reform into the new year. Even a few days before the Congressional Budget Office released its estimate that the Clinton health plan would add modestly to the deficit, many reporters were still leaving a potential tidal wave of new health spending out of their overall budget analysis. In January 1994, reporters passed on that the CBO "issued a new forecast saying the deficit crisis is effectively over." By February, anchors like CNN's Judy Woodruff introduced Clinton's new annual budget as "one of the tightest fiscal proposals in memory."[7]

The national media's reporting on budgetary matters simply could not be trusted. In 1993, reporters touted the fiscal solidity of a budget with a massive magic asterisk in the middle, with no estimate of the increased costs of adding 37 million Americans to a nationalized health program. Simply frustrated by a government which had grown too large and demanded too much, the public would reject the media's sales job in the year to come.

V. THE TRAVAILS
OF 1994

28

The Great Beast of Need

"I suspect that as long as the peccadilloes remain within reason, the American people will have great tolerance for a President who has not only seen the sunshine of Oxford, but also the dusky Dunkin' Donuts of the soul." -- Newsweek's Joe Klein, January 3, 1994.

"To watch this President connect with people emotionally is an awesome thing. It's a raw, needy, palpable, electrifying thing that happens. There was no smile. It's as if he's soaking up the people like he's soaking up the sun, with the warmth pouring deep and direct into his political soul and recharging him, refilling him somehow once again with his humanity and some sense of his role in the destiny of the country. Then the hunger slaked, the great beast of Need fed once again, it seemed you could almost see the gratitude pouring off his brow like sweat as he made his way." -- Washington Post reporter Phil McCombs with Clinton on his California vacation, March 30, 1994.

Since Bill and Hillary Clinton developed very early in their national fame a thinly disguised loathing for the "objective" national media, one can only imagine their feelings about the nascent alternative conservative media complex. Focusing anew on investigative journalism, the alternative media outlets labored to expose the mainstream media's lack of vigilance in covering the Clintons during the 1992 campaign.

Days before Christmas 1993, *The American Spectator* published the revelations of Arkansas state troopers that as Governor, Clinton had used them to solicit women for sexual favors, and then offered the troopers federal jobs in exchange for their silence when he became President. Charges in the *Spectator* article spurred an even richer display of media bias on sexual harassment a few months later.

While Anita Hill's charges against a Supreme Court nominee were an immediate national scandal, former Arkansas state employee Paula Jones' February charges of harassment against the President went ignored for three entire months. When Jones filed suit in May, reporters portrayed it as cheap hillbilly political theater.

By themselves, the sexual charges caused only a few weeks of embarrassment. On both the trooper story and the Jones story, the national media belatedly devoted a few stories to the charges and then moved on. But new findings about the Clintons' partnership in Whitewater Development, coupled with the uncovering of Hillary Clinton's nearly $100,000 profit off a $1,000 investment in commodities trades, unraveled the Clintons' claims to represent those who "worked hard and played by the rules." Instead, new reports showed the Governor freely used his power to procure sex, and his wife used his power to make money from his campaign contributors.

The new Whitewater troubles actually began on October 31, 1993, when *The Washington Post* found that the Resolution Trust Corporation had named the Clintons as potential beneficiaries of wrongdoing in the bankruptcy of Madison Guaranty Savings & Loan. Judge David Hale charged that Bill Clinton pressured him to make a $300,000 Small Business Administration loan to Clinton's Whitewater partner, Susan McDougal, even though she was not financially disadvantaged -- a requirement. The story also surfaced that Hillary's Rose Law Firm partners, Webster Hubbell and Vincent Foster, told federal bank officials that their firm had not represented S&Ls when they sought federal business, when Mrs. Clinton and other Rose partners had represented Madison Guaranty.

But with the exception of *The Washington Post* and *The Washington Times,* the major media yawned again: other than one brief question to CNN's Wolf Blitzer on the November 2 *Inside Politics* and a November 11 *NBC Nightly News* story by Andrea Mitchell, the network evening newscasts continued to ignore the story through November and the first three weeks of December.[1] The news magazines dismissed the story with one page or less each. *Time*'s story actually claimed that Clinton's financial entanglements with Whitewater partner James McDougal were "coincidental."[2]

Ironically, part of what broke the Whitewater story open was the Troopergate story. Look at public broadcasting. The Nexis data retrieval system includes NPR features, not news summaries, but the word "Whitewater" cannot be found until December 21, 1993, when Mara Liasson and Linda Wertheimer stumbled over Troopergate. The same is true of *The MacNeil-Lehrer NewsHour* on Nexis, on which "Whitewater" first appears on December 24.[3] Print editors and television producers finally arrived on the Whitewater story, since it promised to be a scandal with dry, serious substance, free of the salacious tales of a President's past indulgences.

Another reason for increased attention came in the same week *The American Spectator* released its story on Arkansas state troopers. *The Washington Times* issued a story by investigative reporter Jerry Seper revealing that White House staffers removed Whitewater documents from the office of Vincent Foster after the deputy White House counsel died five months earlier in an apparent suicide.[4]

The impact of these stories made an important point. In 1993 and 1994, the Democrats controlled both the executive and legislative branches, but the alternative conservative media drew on political adversity to rise to a new level of influence. Spurred by a new dedication to investigating the liberal opposition, *The American Spectator* saw its circulation skyrocket from 40,000 to more than 220,000. *The Washington Times* may not have seen a dramatic circulation increase, but its team of reporters, led by Seper, broke a series of investigative scoops that frustrated the Democrats. Often single-handedly, the *Times* reported stories the liberal media did not want to report. Before Clinton came to power, the *Times* drove coverage of the House Bank scandal, which caused an exodus of retiring House members, mostly Democrats, and the House Post Office scandal, which eventually claimed very powerful Ways and Means Committee baron Dan Rostenkowski.

The new print media was matched by nationally syndicated talk radio, an idea that had been given up for dead, but was rejuvenated and dominated by Rush Limbaugh. Limbaugh was so successful that the media soon declared talk radio was firmly, angrily anti-Clinton. "Poll Says Conservatives Dominate Talk Radio," reported *The New*

York Times. "Misleading Medium of U.S. Politics: Talk Radio Callers Often 'Caricature Discontent,'" wrote *The Washington Post.* But the survey by the Times Mirror Center for the People and the Press included the findings that radio hosts preferred Clinton in 1992, 39 percent to 23 percent for Bush and 18 percent for Perot. Among self-identified liberal listeners, 20 percent said talk radio hosts were "more liberal" than they are, and 43 percent said their views were "the same."[5] The prospect of Limbaugh entertaining 20 million Americans a week with his analysis and satire of the Clintons clearly worried the media establishment as much as the White House.

The growing agenda-setting power of the alternative conservative media often forced the liberal media into covering potentially damaging stories, at least for a few days. As a result, for the Clintons, 1994 was a losing year long before the congressional elections and the collapse of their utopian health care dreams. The trooper story reopened the question of Clinton's abuse of power as Governor; the Paula Jones story pressed Clinton to become the first President to create a legal defense fund; the Whitewater story forced the Clintons to accept an independent counsel.

Clinton didn't profess to like any of the media. In a testy part of an interview with *Rolling Stone* magazine, he complained he had "not gotten one damn bit of credit from the knee-jerk liberal press, and I am sick and tired of it, and you can put that in the damn article." His fit of pique drew *New York Times* reporter Maureen Dowd to note: "Yes, that's the same knee-jerk liberal press than helped him get elected."[6]

29

The Trooper Truth Squad

"One of my losers of the year is David Brock, who wrote that slimy magazine article that revived all those charges about Bill Clinton's personal behavior, and I regarded that as journalism that was truly out of bounds." -- *PBS Washington Week in Review host Paul Duke, December 31, 1993.*

"There's criticism being directed at these groups but it seems to me this is in the American spirit. This is the oldest American tradition of lobbying, where people organize for their causes and band together....so I think some of the critics are off base when they condemn this so strenuously, because these groups are representing significant segments of the population." -- Paul Duke responding to Sen. John Danforth's condemnation of the liberal groups that worked to solicit Anita Hill's unproven charges against Clarence Thomas, October 12, 1991 PBS hearings coverage.

While the testimony of four state troopers to *American Spectator* investigative reporter David Brock sizzled throughout the conservative media, the liberal media tried to repeat the quick-punt coverage of previous Clinton sex revelations. The troopers' story received nearly an identical amount of network evening news coverage as Clinton's last "bimbo eruption," the Flowers story, which drew only 14 stories in a six-day period. Likewise, from its beginning on December 21, 1993, the trooper story attracted only 22 stories in a 12-day period, nine of them on CNN.[1]

Like the Flowers and Charlette Perry stories, Clinton's misuse of his office became a clear and separate issue from the tawdry tabloid tales of extramarital sex. But one magazine reporter expressed the media's reluctance: "I don't really want to be the first to do one of these stories. I don't think [the magazine] wants to be the first to do one of these stories." After researching coverage of Clinton's personal life, Larry Sabato and Robert Lichter proclaimed: "In the case of Troopergate and the Paula Jones story, the mainstream media were locked in a race to be second."[2]

What makes the media squeamishness more interesting is their underlying belief that the troopers were telling the truth. *Los Angeles Times* reporter William Rempel, who did write extensive stories on the troopers, said: "We didn't have any doubt that the stories we heard were true in substance." NBC's Jim Miklaszewski agreed: "Anybody who has ever covered a president or governor knows that his security force becomes a second skin around him. If anyone has intimate knowledge of what a president or governor does in private, it would be these guys." ABC's Jim Wooten admitted: "Yeah, I think they were telling the truth."

But Wooten also said Ronald Reagan told confidants of his affairs before his marriage to Nancy, and added: "This fellow Clinton...I don't have any interest in who he was sleeping with then or who he's screwing now. It doesn't make any difference to me." CBS reporter Scott Pelley spent ten hours questioning the troopers: "It just seemed a little bit tenuous, and you want to rise to a higher standard when dealing with the office of the presidency of the United States...We just felt, not to sound pompous in any way, but it didn't rise to the level of something we wanted to put on the evening news."[3]

Media outlets claimed these stories were unsubstantiated despite the facts, as *Wall Street Journal* columnist Paul Gigot noted: "Douglas Frantz of the *Los Angeles Times* said on CNN's *Reliable Sources* that 'All four troopers with whom we spoke extensively corroborated Gennifer Flowers' allegations.' Ms. Flowers now has more corroboration than Anita Hill ever did."[4] But their reluctance did not suggest a high-minded, universal resistance to investigating the personal lives of public officials -- just the liberal ones. The national press did not recoil from unproven charges of personal behavior made against Sen. John Tower in his failed nomination for defense secretary; or Kitty Kelley's gossipy book about Nancy Reagan and her sex life, including allegations of an affair with Frank Sinatra; or Anita Hill's sexual harassment charges against Clarence Thomas.

CBS Evening News Executive Producer Erik Sorenson delayed the trooper story for two days, until Mrs. Clinton denounced it. Sorenson told *The Boston Globe* it was just "circumstantial evidence. No women have come forward. I don't want to put these guys on the air because everyone else is doing it....I don't want to act holier-than-thou, but the walls [between the media and tabloids] are definitely tumbling down." But on March 2, 1989, *CBS Evening News* aired allegations of John Tower fondling women and abusing alcohol based on one source, Bob Jackson, who was discharged from the military for "mixed personality disorder and anti-social and hysterical features." On the April 8, 1990, *CBS Evening News* reporter Mark Phillips did a story on Kitty Kelley's book, concluding: "Is the stuff in the book true or just vindictive tales? Who knows? Who cares?" In 1992, *CBS This Morning* interviewed Susan Trento, whose book contained a footnote about George Bush's alleged affair. But the networks never invited the troopers for a morning show interview.[5]

"*The New York Times* is not a supermarket tabloid," proclaimed Washington Bureau Chief R.W. Apple, as his paper began its coverage with tiny wire dispatches. But Apple's paper printed a front-page Maureen Dowd story the day before the release of Kitty Kelley's book -- without any attempt to prove any of Kelley's allegations, and without printing any of the objections of Kelley's critics. The *Times* also ran a story describing the "wild streak" of Patricia Bowman, who accused Ted Kennedy's nephew, William Kennedy Smith, of rape in 1991.[6] Was it coincidence that the *Times'* greatest embarrassments came in attacks on conservatives or defenses of liberals?

Newsweek ran the trooper story, but accompanied it with attacks by the magazine's "Conventional Wisdom Watch" (usually penned by Jonathan Alter) calling the troopers "slimy fibbers." On *The McLaughlin Group, Newsweek* reporter Eleanor Clift denounced the Brock article: "It is full of innuendo and bias. The troopers themselves...want money for their story. They're angry they didn't get jobs. You have to look at the credibility and the motives of the people making the charges instead of just the President's credibility." But Alter wrote a long cover story on Kitty Kelley's book on April 22, 1991, concluding: "If even a small fraction of the material amassed and borrowed here turns out to be true, Ronald Reagan and his wife had to be among the most hypocritical people ever to live in the White House." The week before, *Newsweek*'s Clift hailed the book: "If privacy ends where hypocrisy begins, Kitty Kelley's steamy expose of Nancy Reagan is a contribution to contemporary history."[7]

U.S. News & World Report only mentioned Troopergate in one January 10 article. Asked if the magazine wasn't trying to avoid the story, reporter Greg Ferguson admitted: "Yeah, they tried pretty hard to." Assistant managing editor Harrison Rainie proclaimed: "Our mission always is to give our readers something they can't get elsewhere...We talked to the troopers and it was clear they told their stories very fully to the *Spectator* and the *L.A. Times*...It's not like vast numbers of our readers didn't already know about [the charges]." But *U.S. News* not only ran with the Anita Hill story, it revisited it a year later with a long pro-Hill cover story, heralding new poll results that showed more people now believed her story.[8]

National Public Radio reporters Mara Liasson and Linda Wertheimer interviewed Clinton in the White House, but asked only two questions about the troopers. Clinton stammered evasively: "I just don't want to -- don't want to do anything to prolong this. I have answered those questions and I don't have anything else to say." Instead of pushing forward, the NPR duo quickly knuckled under and moved on to questions like this one from Wertheimer: "I was up late last night, you know, working on this interview, three o'clock in the morning. And I -- and the thought popped into my head -- I wonder if President Clinton wakes up at three o'clock in the morning sometimes and thinks 'I am the President'?"[9]

NPR's Nina Totenberg, the leaker of Hill's unproven stories, had the audacity to decry the trooper story. "You get allegations that are printed in a fringe magazine, or at least a magazine with a very definite political agenda, and then you see...how long it takes the rest of the press to come and bite." But during PBS coverage of the Hill-Thomas hearings, she compared her Hill scoop to the McCarthy hearings, the Pentagon Papers, and Watergate: "That would have just been a third-rate robbery if there hadn't been a lot of leaks."[10]

30

Paula Jones: No Anita Hill

"Yes, the case is being fomented by right-wing nuts, and yes, she is not a very credible witness, and it's really not a law case at all...some sleazy woman with big hair coming out of the trailer parks." -- Newsweek Washington Bureau Chief Evan Thomas on Inside Washington, May 7, 1994.

"We've got an awful lot to talk about this week, including the sexual harassment suit against the President. Of course, in that one, it's a little tough to figure out who's being harassed." -- NBC Today co-host Bryant Gumbel, May 10, 1994.

Paula Jones drew new attention to the national media's divergent approach to sexual politics when she announced in a February 11, 1994 press conference at the Conservative Political Action Conference that she had been sexually harassed by Bill Clinton. While working for an Arkansas state agency at a conference in 1991, troopers delivered her to a hotel room to meet Clinton. There, she charged, the Governor asked her to perform fellatio on him, and even exposed himself. Jones offered two affidavits by corroborating witnesses who were told of Clinton's behavior that day.

Considering that the media made the uncorroborated Anita Hill into a heroine and portrayed sexual harassment as one of the gravest political sins, would this story dominate the headlines? Hardly. Of the four networks, only ABC's *World News Tonight* even mentioned the charges (in a 16-second anchor brief). *The New York Times* published a few paragraphs, and *The Washington Post*'s Lloyd Grove wrote a snippy Style section article on the "primal hatred" for Clinton at the conservative conference where Jones met reporters: he called it "another ascension of Mount Bimbo."[1]

In the March 7, 1994 *New Republic,* former *Newsweek* reporter Mickey Kaus described the scene at the Jones press conference: "Afterward...reporters conferred with each other to try to figure out whether what they'd just seen was 'a story' and...whether anybody was going to report it. The consensus was that if CNN carried it, the networks would carry it, which meant *The New York Times* might carry it, in which case it would be a big story." Now this scene looks funny coming from a media that ridicules critics by suggesting they believe in some grand media conspiracy. Obviously, on that day, in that hotel, reporters who were usually competitive for scoops were asking each other if they had to run this story.

Kaus then explained why the story didn't happen: "Clinton is also the best President we've had in a long time. That is the unspoken reason the sex charges haven't received as much play as you might expect. Reporters are patriots, too; it's their dirty little secret...Few journalists want to see the President crippled now that he is making some progress in cracking large, intractable domestic problems."[2]

In a February 18 appearance on C-SPAN, *Newsweek*'s Eleanor Clift, perhaps the media's foremost Clinton booster, was asked about Jones and Sally Perdue, a former Miss Arkansas who claimed to have had an affair with Clinton: "This rather reeks of exploitation, if these women had, you know, serious concerns, why didn't they speak out then? Why didn't they come forward earlier? There is no way to check whether they're credible, and it seems to me that a responsible press doesn't automatically just put people on the front page because they've made a charge...It seems to me that the discussions about Bill Clinton's sexual life came up during the campaign."[3] Clift might not have known that Perdue went public with her charges in 1992, even appearing on Sally Jessy Raphael's TV talk show that summer.

On May 4, after getting the hint that Jones would actually file a sexual harassment lawsuit against the President, *The Washington Post* ran its long-delayed investigation of Jones by *Post* reporter Michael Isikoff. Isikoff was suspended for two weeks on March 25 for insubordination after protesting the *Post*'s delay of his story.[4] While the networks reported 67 evening news stories in the first five days of Anita Hill's charges against Clarence Thomas, before the hearings even began, in the first five days after the media acknowledged the Jones story (May 4-9), the networks reported 15 stories, or less than one-fourth the attention paid to Anita Hill's charges. Unlike the Hill coverage, there were no evening news features on sexual harassment, no story sampling Washington reaction, no biographies of Jones.[5]

When Bryant Gumbel broached the subject on May 10, he told the *Today* audience: "We've got an awful lot to talk about this week, including the sexual harassment suit against the President. Of course, in that one, it's a little tough to figure out who's being harassed." Minutes later, Gumbel insulted Jones in a question to Democratic consultant Bob Squier: "Charging 'intentional affliction of emotional distress,' something she clearly thought out on her own, to your mind, does the suit have any merit or are we just looking at politics of the worst kind here?" Although Hill was adoringly interviewed by *Today*'s Katie Couric (sometimes in two-day segments), and Gumbel interviewed Kitty Kelley for three mornings about her Nancy Reagan book, Jones made no morning show appearances.[6]

Appearing on the CNBC show *Tim Russert*, NBC's Tom Brokaw defended the media: "Why didn't we put it on earlier? It didn't seem, I think to most people, entirely relevant to what was going on at the time. These are the kinds of charges raised about the President before. They had been played out in the Gennifer Flowers episode. The American public had made a decision about his personal conduct and whether it had relevance in his personal life. And it seemed at that time it didn't have the news weight."[7] How could media stars insist adultery (with the consent of the woman) and sexual harassment (without the consent of the woman) were the same?

Like Eleanor Clift, *Time*'s Margaret Carlson had no feminist qualms about always believing the woman in a sexual harassment case: "I think at least the American people are more likely to believe the President than they are to believe, you know, someone without a job, from Arkansas, whose lawyer says she's not in it for money, but clearly she's in it for something."[8]

NPR's Nina Totenberg finally moved on the story on May 6, the day the suit was filed. In her NPR story, Totenberg again defended her reporting on Anita Hill: "Paula Jones, according to her lawyer and her sister, was interested in money. Her lawyer acknowledges that he approached the White House, or tried to approach the White House, seeking money in exchange for her silence, and one sister says she was interested in money. Anita Hill never asked for money. Paula Jones made her charges at a press conference that was arranged for by Bill Clinton's sworn political enemies. Anita Hill went directly to the Senate Judiciary Committee, and when the committee didn't pay serious attention to her charges, her story was leaked."[9] Totenberg failed to note Anita Hill's speaking fees or $1 million book deal.

A week later, in an NPR commentary, ABC reporter Judy Muller decried the arrival of the Jones suit: "'Oh no,' said the cab driver, 'Not again,' and I knew just how he felt. As the two of us listened to the sordid details of the lawsuit, I realized my compassion fatigue had been replaced by scandal fatigue." Muller cited polls suggesting the public didn't care about Clinton's personal life: "For many Americans, it is much more than they want to know. For many Americans, scandal fatigue set in long ago, beginning with Gennifer Flowers and escalating in the torrents of Whitewater, a story few seem to care about, and even fewer comprehend. The Paula Jones story is much easier to comprehend, of course, but the question remains: How much do we care? I have a feeling that in places like Chicago's Robert Taylor Homes, where just walking to school is a life-threatening proposition, the answer to that question is 'not very much.'"[10] Notice her fatigue began with Clinton scandals.

When Jones did appear in a June ABC *Prime Time Live* interview with Sam Donaldson, who found her credible, *Good Morning America* co-host Charles Gibson asked Donaldson: "Sam, 'not trying to hurt the President?' Did she say that with a straight face?" Gibson also asked "Why does anyone care what this woman has to say?" and "Bottom line, Sam: Is she not trying to capitalize on this, in effect to profit from impugning the President?"[11]

Time and *Newsweek* interviewed Jones in June, but both failed to publish them. "We're certainly under no obligation to print anything," declared *Time* Washington Bureau Chief Dan Goodgame to *The Washington Post*. His opposite number at *Newsweek*, Evan Thomas, concurred: "We didn't learn anything we didn't already know." Instead, *Time*'s June 27 issue included a Michael Kramer column on "Why Paula Jones Should Wait" touting Clinton's "impressive" case. *Newsweek* repeated its attacks on Jones in the July 11 issue: "Former Clinton aides from Arkansas are depicting Paula Jones as a groupie, who, far from acting like a victim of harassment, hung around Clinton's office 'giggling and carrying on' after her alleged hotel encounter."[12] Reporters rejected this groupie line of attack with Hill, but in David Brock's book *The Real Anita Hill,* one of Hill's co-workers said: "My clearest recollection is of her sitting on a couch outside [Thomas's] office, very nicely dressed, flipping through magazines." Former top Thomas aide Armstrong Williams said Hill complained to him Thomas "didn't even notice me."[13]

While Anita Hill drew hosannas from reporters as a "Rosa Parks" of sexual harassment,[14] Jones emerged as a sleazy bimbo puppet of Clinton-hating right-wingers. *U.S. News & World Report* described Jones as one of "The Right's Flame Throwers" (although she had never been involved in the conservative movement), and managed to ally her with Larry Nichols, who charged without proof that the Clintons may have had a role in 29 mysterious deaths. But in 1991, *U.S. News* crowed that to some, Anita Hill "was Everywoman, the proxy for all who had ever had a degrading or threatening encounter with a male co-worker." Her attempt to level anonymous charges were not partisan or vengeful, but "her own political naivete." Her supporters were "a team of academics and lawyers...who were totally unschooled in the ways of hardball campaigns."[15]

But the difference in political sophistication between Jones and Hill was enormous. If Jones, with no history of political involvement, were sophisticated, she would not have allowed her advisers to choose the Conservative Political Action Conference to publicize her charges. On the other hand, after working for years in Washington in the executive branch, Hill was an active feminist at the University of Oklahoma, and told interviewers she opposed the direction Reagan and Thomas were moving on affirmative action during her time at the EEOC. Her testimony was solicited by liberal politicians (Ted Kennedy, Howard Metzenbaum) and interest groups (Alliance for Justice, People for the American Way) and supervised by a team of liberal lawyers, including Georgetown's Susan Deller Ross and Harvard's Charles Ogletree. To suggest they were "totally unschooled in the ways of hardball campaigns" ignored Robert Bork's Supreme Court nomination, which most of these people worked to defeat.[16]

In 1991, *Newsweek* portrayed Hill as a "quiet and intensely private...straight arrow" and that law school colleagues "say it is inconceivable that the never-married professor would fabricate the allegations against Thomas." But *Newsweek* Washington Bureau Chief Evan Thomas characterized Paula Jones as "some sleazy woman with big hair coming out of the trailer parks"[17] (he later apologized), and the magazine's coverage echoed that theme.

Newsweek cited Clinton attorney Bob Bennett, who "says he has 'people coming out of the woodwork' to discredit her story," then quoted brother-in-law Mark Brown: "She went with one man and when she got there, she spotted another one. She goes right up to him, puts her leg between the legs of the other man and rubs herself up and down on him...Promiscuity? Good gosh. Her mother is fixing to get the shock of her life when Paula's life comes out...She went out and had herself a good time. I've seen her at the Red Lobster pinch men on the ass." Of course, when Sen. Alan Simpson said that *he* had Anita Hill stories coming out of the woodwork, *Newsweek* called it "the lowest of many low points" of the hearings, and compared Simpson to Sen. Joseph McCarthy -- and Joseph Stalin.[18]

Newsweek's Joe Klein turned schizophrenic on the issue. The same columnist who'd believed the public would tolerate the President's experience with the "dusky Dunkin' Donuts of the soul" now claimed that life is a journey, but character is not, and "it is both tragic and quite dangerous that we find ourselves still asking if Bill Clinton will ever get there."[19] But in the same week on CBS, Klein inanely compared the Jones suit to the Salem witch trials and worried that "we're going to end up with government by goody-goodies, government by people who have done nothing in their life except walk the straight and narrow, who have no creative thoughts. We're going to look back on this 100 years from now and say we drove some of our best people out of politics. In the 20th century, having an interesting sexual history is a leading indicator of success in the presidency."[20]

31

The Whitewater Wimp Factor

"Whitewater so far is a parody of a political scandal, full of sound and fury, signifying next to nothing. If it walks like a duck and talks like a duck, it must be a...turkey." -- Newsweek Senior Editor Jonathan Alter, August 8, 1994.

"The trouble with Whitewater may be that there is less there there: no crime, as far as is known, no broken promise to the voters either." -- CNN reporter Bruce Morton, March 28, 1994 Inside Politics.

As with Clinton's adultery, reporters like CNN's Bruce Morton suggested whatever the President had done with Whitewater, it was all in the past and best forgotten. Morton blamed the Whitewater story on media competition and "gossip. Poorly sourced stories start out in the supermarket tabloids or on tabloid TV on Monday and are in the mainstream press and the network newscasts by Tuesday. Gossip's a lot easier to write than tough, investigative pieces or stories about the health care debate."[1] Just as Tom Brokaw casually blurred Paula Jones with Gennifer Flowers, now Morton blurred Whitewater into the Flowers story. But the tabloids and daytime talk hosts like Ricki Lake and Jenny Jones cannot be plausibly accused of searching through the eye-glazing technical details of the Whitewater story, which surfaced only on the occasional leads found by national newspapers like *The New York Times* and *Washington Times*.

The late-night raid of Vincent Foster's White House office, not the 1970s land purchase in northern Arkansas, had turned Whitewater into a full-blown scandal, including the appointment of an independent counsel, Robert Fiske. The focus shifted from Little Rock sweetheart deals to White House obstruction of justice.

By March 1994, the biggest month of Whitewater coverage in the first three years of the Clinton presidency, the attention grew to where average Americans would now be familiar with the Whitewater story. But media critics quickly pronounced it was overdone. *Washington Post* media reporter Howard Kurtz wrote a March 12 front page story headlined "Media Awash in Whitewater, Some Critics Warn," noting the disapproval of old CBS hands Walter Cronkite ("definitely overheated") and Marvin Kalb ("There is a rushing to judgment that is unprofessional and distasteful").[2]

Kurtz should have first reread his recommendations from his 1993 book, *Media Circus:* "Tell us the things authorities don't want us to know...When the President tells an obvious fib, let's call him out on strikes." It also complained of missing the S&L story: "Had more reporters trusted their instincts and made the case that the industry was collapsing, many billions of dollars may have been saved."[3] Madison Guaranty was part of that story.

Kurtz was not alone. *Boston Globe* Washington Bureau Chief David Shribman called Whitewater "a cheap dime-store novel transformed into a Washington page-turner" by an inept White House staff and the death of Foster. On CNBC's *Talk Live,* NBC's Bryant Gumbel described Whitewater coverage as "too much, off-target." The April 4 *Time* explained the entire media's behavior in a chart showing 75 articles in one month in major outlets used both the words "feeding frenzy" and "Whitewater."[4] *U.S. News* Editor-in-Chief Mort Zuckerman sounded the most panicked alarm: "The press is on a rampage....We cannot afford a failed presidency, especially if it is falsely damaged by innuendo, speculation, and hyperinflated innuendo of events of a decade or more ago."[5]

But how overdone was it? The Center for Media and Public Affairs reported that from March 1 to 20, the Big Three networks aired 86 stories, or 4.3 stories a night between three networks. For comparative purposes, the CMPA study also found that the Big Three networks reported 12.9 stories per night at the beginning of Iran-Contra in 1986, and 13.4 nightly during the eruption of Watergate in 1973, meaning Whitewater stories drew only a third the attention of other major scandals. As the political turmoil increased, so too did the positive spin control. CMPA found that the percentage of pro-Clinton talking heads actually went up in White-water stories. The White House may have preferred no stories, but they certainly were given the opportunity to air their spin.[6]

For example, *Time* and *Newsweek* published interviews with the First Lady in their March 21, 1994 issues. *Time*'s Ann Blackman and Nina Burleigh were formal, if not tough: "How do you respond to questions of conflict of interest raised by your representation of Madison?" But they also asked: "How do you and your husband explain this to each other...and Chelsea?"[7] *Newsweek*'s Eleanor Clift didn't so much ask questions as make supportive assertions. "The only thing I see comparable [to Watergate] is that a lot of people want to launch careers based on finding something." Clift added: "The attacks against you are really about more than Whitewater. They really go to the whole role you're taking on and whether you can be spouse of a president and a policymaker." Clift concluded the interview: "Edward Bennett Williams used to say that Washington likes to burn a witch every three months."[8]

Reporters did not pile on the President with terms like "sleaze factor." In fact, a Media Research Center study of major newspapers and magazines showed that through May 1994, Clinton had never been identified with the term "sleaze factor." Since its coinage by Walter Mondale in the 1984 campaign, reporters used the term "sleaze factor" 114 times in news stories to refer specifically to the Reagan administration or Republicans, and only on eight occasions referred to Democrats.[9]

One obvious sign of the networks' low level of interest in the Whitewater story was the lack of specials on the controversy. When the Iran-Contra story broke on November 25, 1986, the networks dove into the story. ABC dedicated its entire *World News Tonight* that night to Iran-Contra and expanded *Nightline* to 60 minutes. CBS aired a half-hour special, and NBC did an hour-long special. On December 18, ABC's *20/20* devoted another hour to the story. NBC aired two one-hour specials on December 15 and January 6. After the Tower Commission's report on February 26, 1987, CBS aired a special called *Judgment on the White House*. That added up to at least seven hours of specials.[10]

When the Whitewater story first broke on March 8, 1992, the networks barely touched it, noting some details in five stories on the four networks that month. When the story gained steam in early 1994, the only special came from ABC, which investigated not the scandal itself, but the media coverage: a *Nightline* special entitled "Whitewater: Overplayed or Underplayed?" The only magazine show segments touching on the Clintons' finances were two ABC *Prime Time Live* segments (one after a presidential news conference, another on Garrison Keillor's attack on the media for overdoing it), and an explanatory *60 Minutes* piece on commodity trading.After a few fitful weeks of congressional hearings, the story died for the rest of 1994. "Feeding frenzy" did not describe the media's attention.[11]

Potential hot potatoes in the Whitewater story continued to go unreported by the networks. When the White House released the Clintons' previously hidden tax returns from 1979 and 1980 (which the media didn't find important during the 1992 campaign), the *Los Angeles Times* found that while the Clintons claimed they invested $46,000 in Whitewater Development, "the tax records and supporting documents show only about $13,000 in such payments by the Clintons." None of the networks mentioned it.

The Washington Post reported that the Clintons' company made $50,000 by repossessing lots from 16 Whitewater buyers without any return of the buyers' equity, even if the buyers paid tens of thousands of dollars before defaulting. None of the networks followed up on this story with the obvious hard-luck angle of people who lost thousands at the Clintons' hands.[12] One exception to this pattern came from CNN's Terry Keenan, who focused in January on Whitewater Development's investment in a property called Lorance Heights. Keenan examined how black homeowner Henderson Gaddy suffered from Whitewater's default on the property: "In the midst of all this confusion, many land buyers didn't know where to send their mortgage payments, or if the money would ever be credited to their property, and some like Gaddy lost their land."[13]

The media's bias against Whitewater allegations surfaced again in the summer of 1994 when independent counsel Robert Fiske released his first report on June 30, finding no basis for criminal charges in White House contacts with the Resolution Trust Corporation, the agency managing the S&L bailout. CBS anchor Dan Rather announced: "For now, at least, President Clinton and his aides are entitled to say 'We told you so.'" Interviewers were harsher. NBC's Tim Russert asked: "Are the Republicans on a witch hunt?" CNN's Bernard Shaw inquired: "Should the Republicans shut up?"[14]

When the three-judge panel that appointed Fiske replaced him with Kenneth Starr, Rather switched from defending Fiske to accusing Starr: "There is growing controversy tonight about whether the newly named independent counsel in the Whitewater case is independent, or a Republican partisan allied with a get-Clinton movement. Among the questions about Kenneth Starr are these: the involvement of anti-Clinton activists in pushing for Starr's appointment to replace Robert Fiske. Also, Starr's public stand actively supporting a woman's current lawsuit against the President. This is a potentially important and explosive story....Rita Braver has the latest."

Braver asserted: "Democrats are raising questions about Starr, a former federal judge, because of how he was picked. Under the new independent counsel law, Chief Justice William Rehnquist chose fellow conservative David Sentelle to head the three-judge panel that selects independent counsels. Sentelle himself was appointed by President Reagan with sponsorship from Senate conservative Jesse Helms, and Sentelle was lobbied to replace Robert Fiske by constant Clinton critic Floyd Brown and congressional conservatives."

Four days later, Rather returned to his "explosive" story: "Questions abound about how and why Republican Kenneth Starr is an ambitious Republican partisan backed by ideologically motivated anti-Clinton activists and judges from the Reagan, Bush, and Nixon years." Reporter Eric Engberg repeated the story, with a more conspiratorial tone: "Kenneth Starr's history of partisan Republican activity is not the only thing troubling Democrats. The way Starr got the job, which bears the footprints of every Republican President from Nixon to Bush, is also becoming a hot issue. Independent counsels are chosen by a panel of three federal appeals court judges.

By law, the panel is selected by Chief Justice Rehnquist, a Nixon appointee to the Supreme Court named Chief Justice by President Reagan. Rehnquist chose Judge David Sentelle of the D.C. Court of Appeals, a Reagan appointee, to head the three-judge panel. Sentelle is from North Carolina where he was an active worker in the Republican organization run by Senator Jesse Helms, who is among Mr. Clinton's fiercest critics. Sentelle owes his job on the federal bench to Helms, who urged the Reagan White House to appoint him. Sentelle's two most famous rulings overturned the Iran-Contra convictions of Oliver North and John Poindexter."[15]

Engberg aired only three talking heads, all Democrats attacking Starr's integrity. Neither Braver nor Engberg noted that for this Republican plot to work, the Independent Counsel Act had to be reauthorized by a Democratic Congress. The bill setting up Rehnquist and Sentelle was supported 246-2 by House Democrats. Seven of the ten Republicans who signed a letter to the three-judge panel opposing Fiske voted against the bill making Starr's appointment possible. Neither Braver nor Engberg described GOP complaints about the inconsistencies in Fiske's report, his professional relationship with White House counsel Bernard Nussbaum, or his law firm's representation of firms with Whitewater connections.[16]

As for Sentelle, former Ed Meese lawyer Mark Levin wrote in *The Washington Times* that Sentelle upheld Iran-Contra prosecutor Lawrence Walsh's right to deny Meese access to parts of Walsh's final report: "If Judge Sentelle and the panel deserve criticism, it is for supporting Walsh's extra-constitutional conduct...To believe Judge Sentelle is not impartial in administering his legal duties is to believe a contemptible lie."[17] In the months after Starr's appointment, Rather often referred to him as "Republican prosecutor Kenneth Starr," which didn't make him sound very independent.

32

Hillary's Cattle Killing

"It was fun to learn about Yuppie Hillary, but the story belonged in the business pages, or perhaps the food section, where the Times usually runs its diagrams of cows." -- Newsweek Senior Editor Jonathan Alter, March 28, 1994.

"The public might be tickled to discover that the prim and preachy First Lady has a gambler's streak. Hillary's brief fling in commodities was possibly reckless, but it shows a glimmering of a more credible, if more flawed, human being." -- Newsweek reporters Eleanor Clift and Mark Miller, April 11, 1994.

The discovery that Hillary Clinton parlayed a $1,000 investment in cattle futures into $100,000 in 1979 threw a curve into the media's portrayal of the First Lady as a Scripture-toting Methodist moralist. What was this trail-blazing governor's wife with a hunger for policy wonkery doing selling 42,000 pounds of cows at a time? How did she achieve such an astounding capital gain in nine months? Mrs. Clinton first claimed she just read the financial pages. Later, it was discovered her trades were arranged through James Blair, a friend who was also a lawyer for Tyson Foods, one of the largest businesses in Arkansas. Could Blair have been helping Tyson gain favor with the Clintons by providing some quick cash through "allocated trades," where brokers might have rewarded Mrs. Clinton with gains, while Tyson accepted losses?

Two years after his seminal Whitewater scoop, *New York Times* reporter Jeff Gerth had unearthed another difficult scandal out of the Clinton finances on March 18. Despite the First Lady's changing stories, the four networks reported only 18 stories between them on

Mrs. Clinton's curious trading. None of the Big Three evening newscasts devoted a full story to the mysterious trades until 11 days later. Twelve of the 18 stories appeared on the three days the White House released documents or met the press: March 29, April 11, and April 22, the day of Mrs. Clinton's press conference.[1]

By holding a press conference which shed no light on the strange affair, the First Lady hoped to put an end to the story -- and the networks granted her wish, dropping the story after a set of excessively positive reviews. "Hillary Rodham Clinton today summoned the White House press to, as you can see, that meeting in the Lincoln Room at the White House. And she was cool, articulate, and for the most part very responsive to all questions," NBC's Tom Brokaw pronounced immediately afterward. ABC's Peter Jennings repeated Mrs. Clinton's charge that attacks on her show "the country is having some difficulty adjusting to a working woman in the role of First Lady," and added: "I think most people will regard this as certainly an enormous effort by Mrs. Clinton to set the record as straight as she can." CNN White House reporter Jill Dougherty proclaimed: "It was an extraordinary performance."[2]

In a sentence not reminiscent of the Reagan years, *Time*'s Michael Duffy emphasized Hillary may have been light on substance, but her style was all that mattered: "What happened was a riveting hour and 12 minutes in which the First Lady appeared to be open, candid, and above all unflappable. While she provided little new information on the tangled Arkansas land deal or her controversial commodity trades, the real message was her attitude and her poise."[3]

Among television reporters, only ABC's Brit Hume suggested on the 22nd that "Mrs. Clinton may not have answered all the questions about the Clintons' financial dealings." Another exception to the encomiums came on April 10, when CBS *60 Minutes* reporter Lesley Stahl presented an informative segment on how commodities markets work, which suggested the First Lady's gains were not ordinary. Newspaper reports were tougher on the substance. *The Washington Post* ran an article inside the paper titled "First Lady's Explanations Yield Little Information," and *The New York Times*' Maureen Dowd, who called it "an exceptionally polished and calibrated performance," conceded later in her story that "she never fully resolved the central questions of Whitewater and the commodities trades."[4]

Conservative columnist Tony Snow ignored the media's politesse: "She promised to 'be as forthcoming and accessible as you need me to be' but answered precise questions with lawyerly evasions: 'There's no evidence of that...I don't think there's any evidence of that...I know of nothing to support that.' She evoked the amnesia defense more often than Ronald Reagan did in the days of Iran-Contra." She said "I don't remember" at least six times.[5] The obvious question became: why would the same media that celebrated Hillary's ironclad memory without notes in testifying on health care reform give her a free pass on this performance?

On the April 22 *Washington Week in Review* on PBS, *New York Times* legal reporter Linda Greenhouse exemplified journalistic wishful thinking: "About halfway into the hour, somebody asked a non-Whitewater question. Somebody asked a question about health care. And one of my colleagues said 'That's it. She's exhausted them. Whitewater's over.' And I'd really like to know what you think -- is this basically the end of Whitewater?"[6]

Time reporter Elaine Shannon bought the First Lady's story of her lucky reading of the financial pages: "I believe her story that it was smarts and luck and some good advice. Who of us at the age of 30 hasn't taken a few risks, and I wish my risks had been that successful....Of course, maybe she took some advice of some people who later ran into legal problems in terms of lawsuits, but I think all of us may have done that at one time or another. You can't be responsible for the lives of every broker and banker you ever run across."[7]

When the White House released documents a month after the press conference proving that the First Lady received preferential treatment by not being required to post margin (pay cash when her shares' value dropped), the networks were nowhere to be found. Yet when *Roll Call,* a small-circulation Capitol Hill newspaper, revealed in June that Sen. Al D'Amato made $35,000 on stock in an initial public offering closed to most investors, ABC reported the story the very next day, despite taking 11 days to devote a full story to Mrs.

Clinton.[8]

Perhaps most ironically, both Bob Woodward and Carl Bernstein, the reporters who broke Watergate for *The Washington Post,* pooh-poohed the Clinton scandals. On NBC's *Meet the Press,* Woodward presented a lawyer's defense of the First Lady's high-profit commodities trading: "Would it be possible that there's a crime involved in the $100,000 in the futures market? This was what, 15 years ago, so the statute of limitations automatically means it's not a crime." How would Woodward have greeted that claim during Watergate? Woodward then attacked journalists for suggesting Hillary was greedy: "Look at journalism today. There are people, there are journalists who go out and give five, six speeches at universities, make $100,000 doing this. They take that money out of the university system, and there are minority and poor students working in the cafeteria scraping garbage. And if you were to lay all that out before the public and say 'Who's greedy? Who has the moral high road?', there might be a different answer."

On National Public Radio, Bernstein bashed his former colleagues for overplaying the Whitewater story: "Journalism is part of popular culture, and popular culture right now is consumed by controversy, manufactured controversy, by Rush Limbaugh, by *The McLaughlin Group* yelling at each other, by *Donahue,* by freak shows. You can't separate the coverage of Whitewater from that atmosphere."[9]

Reporters not only ignored the real victims of Whitewater Development, but also those who lost when Hillary Clinton made her $100,000. *Money* magazine told the story of "midwestern ranchers who allege that the manipulation of the futures market undermined the prices they got for their cattle...to this day the ranchers remain convinced that [Thomas] Dittmer [the sole owner of Mrs. Clinton's brokerage firm, Refco] led to some of the financial hardships they suffered."[10] The ranchers sued in federal court, but the networks never bothered to look into it. *Dateline NBC* went looking for victims of Neil Bush's loans from the Small Business Administration, but the Clintons apparently never caused anyone hardship.

33

The Policy Wars Continue

"So at least from the physicians represented here, you get a 100 percent vote, including mine, for universal coverage." -- ABC reporter Dr. Tim Johnson to Hillary Clinton, July 19, 1994 Good Morning America.

"Without health care reform, there is nothing to stop insurance discrimination. And anyone can get sick. Anyone with a job can lose it -- lose benefits, lose protection....Without reform, only the richest will be protected from a debilitating new kind of disease -- a virulent strain of worry about their health care, their security. Worry that is becoming epidemic." -- ABC reporter Beth Nissen in an "American Agenda" story, July 29, 1994 World News Tonight.

Despite their political significance, scandal stories remained a small part of the general news flow. The Center for Media and Public Affairs found that ethics stories only accounted for five percent of the administration's news coverage in its first 17 months in office.[1] Meanwhile, the 1,300-page Clinton health plan and the crime bill continued to receive positive coverage.

A crime bill passed Congress in August. The bill professed to implement President Clinton's campaign promise to put 100,000 police on American streets, but Republicans objected the bill had become a vehicle for all of the big-city pork projects that didn't pass in the ill-fated "stimulus" package of 1993. During the month of August, crime bill supporters outnumbered opponents by nearly 2-to-1. Stories referring to the bill's "crime prevention" provisions surpassed stories on "pork-barrel" spending by 19 to 5, almost a 4-to-1 ratio. Another ten stories carried both sides. After it passed, ABC's Tom Foreman noted "no comprehensive nationwide data" showed how often 19 assault weapons banned by the crime bill were used illegally, "although it's believed to be less than one percent."[2]

In health care coverage, a Free Enterprise and Media Institute study of evening news stories from June 15 to July 15 demonstrated the health care story focused mostly on the horse race: 56 of 68 stories concerned the legislative battle, while only nine looked at the possible economic effects of various plans. Politicians dominated the soundbites (141 of 208), and Democrats outnumbered Republicans by more than 2.5 to 1 (102 to 39). By contrast, the networks aired only two soundbites of economists, and only 16 of businessmen -- six of those soundbites came from two businessmen brought to Washington by the Clintons to support hefty employer mandates.[3]

The largest block of network time devoted to health care came from NBC (which did no special on Whitewater). The Robert Wood Johnson Foundation, "a nonprofit group with close ties to the Clinton reform effort," as the August 1 *Time* described it[4], paid $3.5 million for a two-hour prime-time NBC News special on health care. The Johnson Foundation had at least five of its fellows on Hillary Clinton's health care task force, which met to redesign the American health care system in sessions closed to the public. When that secrecy became an issue, the foundation doled out $500,000 for four town meetings. The *Los Angeles Times* reported: "Like a campaign event, the first of four hearings sponsored by the Robert Wood Johnson Foundation...was carefully controlled to bolster the Clinton Administration's fundamental premise in health care policy." The foundation funded polls for the Clintons and studies for liberal groups like Families USA doubling estimates of the uninsured.[5]

When Republicans complained of the conflict of interest, NBC News President Andrew Lack denied political motives: "Newt Gingrich would say that the Central Park Zoo has a political agenda."[6] On CNBC's *Tim Russert*, Tom Brokaw declared: "I can assure you that I wouldn't be involved with that program in any fashion if it were being directed or if it were being engineered by a special interest group." The special, taped at Washington's Warner Theater, tilted left in its selection of speakers. NBC's main attraction was Hillary Clinton: the program opened and closed with tributes to her for bringing this important issue to public attention. On-stage panelists leaned two to one in favor of the Clinton plan or a single-payer plan. Speakers from the audience also leaned to the liberal side by two to one. The program's pre-packaged news segments were mostly horror stories: uninsured parents of kids with dramatic medical problems, or a woman who couldn't find home care for her elderly mother. The audience clapped loudly in favor of socialized medicine.[7]

ABC also did its best to promote the Clinton plan. In February, *Good Morning America* ran a week-long series called "Closeup on Health Care." All five reports touted the desirability of the Clinton plan, and 12 of 18 soundbites favored dramatic health reform, with only two opposed. On Monday, George Strait found an employer who feared a minimum wage increase, but said "the sky didn't fall in then, and predicts it won't when health care reform is passed either." On Tuesday, Ann Compton found nothing but support for the Clinton plan among doctors, quoting one member of the Clinton task force and two doctors who thought the Clintons wouldn't go far enough. Compton declared: "Last year President Clinton complained that paperwork wastes a dime of every health care dollar. His plan's architects would fix that."

Bettina Gregory addressed the elderly's drug costs that Thursday, noting: "The American Association of Retired Persons says at least ten percent of seniors have to choose between buying food and buying drugs. Horror stories abound." Gregory listed the drug coverage offered by Clinton's plan, then added: "Because of these benefits, many seniors' groups heartily endorse health care reform proposals. Some believe the Clinton plan is the best blueprint for health care." But the AARP had not yet endorsed the Clinton plan, and AARP polls showed that about half its members doubted whether they'd be better off under the Clinton plan.

In the week's final report, Karen Burnes quoted three supporters of Clinton and no critics, and concluded: "Under the plan, everyone will be covered: employed, unemployed, and suddenly laid off." But *Investor's Business Daily* reporter John Merline noted that month that "Hawaii [where universal coverage is guaranteed] has an uninsured rate equal to or greater than 16 other states according to the Urban Institute, and not too far below that of the U.S. as a whole."[8]

ABC's *World News Tonight* aired a similar series in late July which resumed the networks' attack on ads opposing the Clinton plan from the right. Reporter Tom Foreman based his entire story on a study by the University of Pennsylvania's Annenberg Public Policy Center that said "the reason for the confusion is simple: many of the ads focus on a narrow portion of reform that tell only half the story." While the study often supported Clinton's statistical claims for health reform, the report singled out some liberal ads and said "questionable claims are not the unique property" of either side, but ABC focused on the right. Foreman mentioned seven claims, and all but one criticized the Clinton plan. ABC chose the Annenberg Center's Kathleen Hall Jamieson as their referee, but never told viewers their study was funded by the Robert Wood Johnson Foundation, whose funding aided the Clintons and liberal groups.

Foreman explained: "Consider this commercial by Empower America, a conservative political group. It says the Clinton reform plan will mean patients losing the right to choose their own doctor." ABC aired part of the ad: "The bureaucracy will decide when and even if you see a specialist. Under this plan, you will lose choice and control." Foreman "corrected" it: "In reality all the plans being considered would offer consumers a relatively wide choice of doctors within a selected coverage pool. If patients want to go outside of the pool, they can, but it will cost more." Jamieson added: "The notion that the Clinton plan will remove choice is fundamentally false." That was not a question of fact, but a matter of prediction.

Foreman also attacked conservative direct mail: "Some of the worst scare tactics have come from highly conservative groups through thousands of direct-mail flyers aimed primarily at older people. The Heritage Foundation warns the first people to be rationed out of health care are the elderly. The Seniors Coalition says doctors will have less time to treat patients. And the American Council for Health Care Reform says the government would use health records to end privacy for all Americans and determine who shall live and who shall die. Although there is little evidence to support any of these claims, each group asks for substantial contributions to help fight for seniors' rights."

Foreman concluded: "Scare tactics and misinformation could strangle fair debate and special interest groups will effectively rob Americans of the right to choose for themselves." But Foreman's story strangled fair debate by not allowing the purveyors of "misinformation" to defend themselves: ABC asked none of them to provide evidence or respond to charges of inaccuracy.[9]

In the year after Clinton's health care address on September 22, 1993, Media Research Center analysts identified 19 examples of print and TV reporting on ad accuracy. Of the sample, 11 stories attacked anti-Clinton ads exclusively, six stories critiqued both sides, and only two focused solely on a liberal ad, despite a profusion of ads by pro-Clinton groups like the AARP and HealthRIGHT.[10]

Print stories also attacked conservative ads. On July 17, the *New York Times'* Catherine Manegold evaluated ads produced by the liberal American Association of Retired Persons and the conservative Citizens for a Sound Economy. Both cited fear of the future. In the AARP ad, "because the actors are convincing and the concerns they articulate are common, the advertisement hits home." But Manegold panned the CSE ad: "While the ad plays effectively on many peoples' fears, its Darth Vader tone works against it. It has an overblown quality that slips dangerously close to the tone of a spoof."[11]

A *Wall Street Journal* story was headlined "Truth Lands in Intensive Care Unit As New Ads Seek to Demonize Clintons' Health-Reform Plan." Reporter Rick Wartzman charged: "Many of the groups twisting the facts are hard-line conservatives, bent on stopping any government presence in health care." *The New York Times* carried a story headlined "'Liars' Try to Frighten Elderly On Health Care, Groups Say." Reporter Robert Pear began: "Two large consumer groups charged today that conservative direct mail organizations were scaring elderly people with inaccurate attacks on President Clinton's health care plan." The "consumer groups" were the AARP and the National Council of Senior Citizens (NCSC), a liberal group funded largely by unions and grants from the federal government. Pear didn't declare the claims inaccurate, but the story dwelled on liberal attacks on "liars for hire." He did not evaluate the ads of AARP or HealthRIGHT, which was partially funded by the NCSC.[12]

When the Democratic National Committee quoted Gov. Carroll Campbell (R-S.C.) out of context in an ad ("you can't say there's no health care crisis" was shortened to "there's no health care crisis"), only a few outlets covered it. *The Washington Post* did the story on February 16; but the story didn't make CBS, *U.S. News & World Report* and major newspapers like the *Los Angeles Times, USA Today* (which promoted the ad in a February 10 story), and *The New York Times* (which two weeks before had quoted one of the Campbell ad's creators, Clinton consultant Mandy Grunwald, saying "I think there will be a barrage of cynical advertising like we have never seen"). CNN's Brooks Jackson covered the Campbell hubbub on February 15, but CNN reviewed none of the other liberal ads.[13]

Liberal ads were even presented as nonpartisan. On January 28, *USA Today* reporter Judi Hasson's ad review ended: "Not all ads are partisan. Monday, the Henry J. Kaiser Family Foundation philanthropy and the League of Women Voters launch a $4 million ad campaign and 60 town meetings to urge reform, without taking a position on Clinton's plan or competing proposals." But Hasson did not mention both groups helped create or advocate the Clinton plan: the "nonpartisan" Kaiser Foundation had fellows on the Clinton task force, or that the League of Women Voters was a paying member of the Health Care Reform Project, a group that openly coordinated strategy with the White House.[14]

While CBS and CNN critiqued the HIAA's ads in 1993 for inadequately underlining their funding, with Families USA chief Ron Pollack leading the attack, the Health Care Reform Project's commercials never drew a critique, even though its ads did not explain they were funded (in part) by Families USA, which refused to release its donor information. The HCRP's ads also did not disclose they were also funded by self-interested big businesses like American Airlines, Ford, and Chrysler, which supported socialized medicine as a way to pawn their health costs off on the taxpayer.[15] Clinton's opponents were held to a higher standard.

34

Probing the Conservative Mind

"Clinton is giving the best evidence yet of his approach to leadership. It's about understanding, not threats; accommodation, not confrontation; about getting people (or at least Democrats) to sing the same song. The style is reminiscent of another patient, nonjudgmental figure given to hugging in public: Barney the Dinosaur." -- Newsweek reporters Howard Fineman and Eleanor Clift, August 9, 1993.

Host Tina Gulland: "Are we agreed generally that it was a plus week for Clinton in the sense that he was viewed as presidential and in charge of foreign policy?"
Nina Totenberg, NPR: "He was there in the middle of the desert. I mean, it was biblical!" -- Exchange on Inside Washington about a Clinton trip to the Middle East, October 29, 1994.

Their obvious enthusiasm for a President who finally shared their baby-boomer liberal outlook left journalists puzzled by conservative charges of the Clintons' ethical abuses and tax-and-spend liberalism. A small boomlet of reporters took that puzzlement to publication in 1994, psychoanalyzing the unfamiliar territory of the conservative mind. Politics inspires passions, passions that inflame the whole range of our emotions -- joy, sadness, anger, inspiration, disillusionment. Bill Clinton, like Ronald Reagan, fueled all of these. But some liberal analysts believed that conservatives hated Clinton with such intensity it deserved a spate of news stories to expose it.

The trend began on December 28, 1993, with *Washington Post* columnist E.J. Dionne, a respected, savvy former political reporter for *The New York Times* and the *Post* who became a surprisingly leaden liberal columnist. Dionne charged in the wake of Troopergate: "Why do conservatives hate Bill Clinton so? If you listen to conservatives a lot, you routinely hear ugly and salacious jokes about the President and First Lady and talk suggesting that this President is the most evil, dishonest, scheming character ever to live in the White House."[1]

In the April 11, 1994 *Time,* reporter Nina Burleigh wrote a story titled "Clintonophobia! Just who are these Clinton haters, and why do they loathe Bill and Hillary with such passion?" Burleigh found the same suspects: "Two men who have benefited as professional Clinton haters are behind-the-scenes activist Floyd Brown and conservative celebrity Rush Limbaugh." After tagging them as haters, Burleigh explained "Both profess not to hate Clinton." But Burleigh ignored them and proceeded to label again: "The Arkansas branch of Clinton haters is led by two attorneys, Sheffield Nelson, who is a Republican candidate for governor, and the quixotic Cliff Jackson," the former Clinton friend who helped bring out the stories of Arkansas state troopers and Paula Jones.

Burleigh's oddest passage came at the story's end, when she quoted (unlabeled) liberal historian Alan Brinkley: "Brinkley says Clinton is also a victim of a political fact of life: he's on the wrong side of the tolerance fence. 'Liberals tend to value tolerance highly, so there's a greater reluctance to destroy enemies than among the right. Democrats are historically more likely to cooperate with Republican administrations than Republicans with Democratic administrations.'"[2]

Like Alan Brinkley, the liberal media saw the conservative Other through their ideological prism as naturally mean-spirited. For four years, the victory of George Bush was portrayed as a victory based on exploiting hatred and racial divisiveness. David Duke was the party poster boy, Willie Horton its victim. In every year, they portrayed Republican aims to streamline government as an intentional agenda to pollute the planet and dump the poor out on the streets. But how much did the Democratic Congresses of the 1980s cooperate with the Reagan administration in cutting government? Did they seek to aid the Reagan presidency -- or destroy it? Liberal media arrogance began with the notion that liberals are never guilty of attack politics.

The Washington Post topped their front page on Sunday, May 22, with the story "Clinton Foes Voice Their Disdain, Loud and Clear: On Talk Shows and in Angry Mail, 'Visceral Reaction' to President Seems Unusually Intense." White House reporter Ann Devroy wrote: "Bill Clinton's enemies are making their hatred clear, with a burning intensity and in some cases with an organized passion."

Who "hates" with "organized passion"? Devroy named names: "At least three conservative talk show hosts -- Rush Limbaugh, G. Gordon Liddy, and Ron Reagan, the son of the former president -- have made Clinton-bashing the basis of their shows, [talk show magazine editor Michael] Harrison said, with no comparable liberal or moderate figure on the other side." (Devroy erred: the talk show host son is Michael Reagan, not liberal young Ron.) Devroy later added conservatives Floyd Brown, Reed Irvine, and Jerry Falwell.[3] None were allowed to defend themselves. Their "hate" was simply to be accepted as fact.

On October 17, *Wall Street Journal* reporters Jeffrey Birnbaum and James M. Perry asserted: "The tone of these attacks is like nothing Americans have seen in years. Opponents sometimes said George Bush, a World War II hero, was a wimp, or an aristocrat who went to grade school in a limousine. People laughed at Ronald Reagan's sleeping habits and his reluctance to grapple very often with legislative or political substance. But this is raw hate being directed at Mr. Clinton."[4]

But the *Washington Post* headline's use of the phrase "unusually intense" to describe hatred of Clinton underlines the journalistic difficulty of this trend: how do reporters quantify a "passionate hatred"? In these cases, they didn't. These stories demonstrated the ideological distance between the media and conservatives. Reporters and commentators implied opposing the Clintons in the defense of conservatism wasn't the product of intellectual reasoning, but an unusually intense, perhaps irrational, wave of emotion.

The growing wave of opposition to the Clinton administration wasn't so much explained as impugned by a befuddled media elite. They failed to see in the public's revulsion the seeds of their own actions: that at least in part, reaction to Clinton was based on voters feeling betrayed by the pretty picture that journalists painted for them in 1992. Reporters knew conservatives opposed Clinton; their coverage suggested they were more concerned about everyone else changing their mind. The media's response to this growing wave became a more determined attempt to defend the President and his achievements as the fall campaign approached.

VI. THE COLLAPSE
OF THE OLD ORDER

35

Retooling the Clinton Record

"Stocks had their best performance in months this week, on news of sustained growth with negligible inflation, and the job picture is good as well. But does the President get credit? No." -- ABC's Jack Smith on This Week with David Brinkley, August 28, 1994.

"In less than two years, Bill Clinton has already achieved more domestically than John F. Kennedy, Gerald Ford, Jimmy Carter, and George Bush combined. Although Richard Nixon and Ronald Reagan often had their way with Congress, Congressional Quarterly says it's Clinton who has had the most legislative success of any President since Lyndon Johnson. Inhale that one...The standard for measuring results domestically should not be the coherence of the process but how actual lives are touched and changed. By that standard, he's doing well." -- Newsweek Senior Editor Jonathan Alter, October 3, 1994.

As President Clinton's approval rating dropped and the 1994 midterm congressional elections approached, national reporters began buffing up the President's image. It's as if months later, the media collectively decided Clinton had been right when he complained to *Rolling Stone* that he had "not gotten one damn bit of credit from the knee-jerk liberal press." A common argument developed among the media that he was not getting much-deserved credit for his accomplishments. On the other hand, Republican proposals in the "Contract with America" were criticized as both economically foolish (the return of Reaganomics) and politically foolish (a recipe for Republican losses).

On CNN's *Larry King Live* August 3, *Los Angeles Times* Washington Bureau Chief Jack Nelson argued: "I think we make too much of polls...The economy's doing well, he's accomplished a lot." NBC White House reporter Andrea Mitchell appeared on King's show August 18: "He doesn't get credit for a lot of the good positive things he's done. Somehow he's the opposite of Ronald Reagan. The message is not getting through...The economy is in better shape...He should be getting some credit for the economy."[1] NBC *Today* co-host Katie Couric asked ex-Congressman Tony Coelho, who had taken on an advisory role at the Democratic National Committee: "Why do you think that he doesn't get credit for the good news that's going on? And if Reagan was the Teflon President, it seems like Bill Clinton is the Velcro President. Every bad piece of news just sticks to him."[2]

One of the boldest pleas for Clinton came from Ted Koppel on the August 16 *Nightline:* "He is receiving little or no credit for his accomplishments. He has, after all, cut the deficit, slashed about a quarter of a million jobs out of the federal bureaucracy, presided over a strong economy with low inflation, and deserves, one would think, some points at least for boldness of vision on welfare and health care reform."[3] That wasn't even accurate: Vice President Gore's "reinventing government" plan estimated an *eventual* reduction of 250,000 jobs. In *The American Spectator,* Byron York noted that Clinton and Gore claimed credit in September 1995 for a reduction of 160,000 jobs. But York showed that of the 156,900 jobs the Office of Personnel Management reported were cut, more than 90 percent were either civilian employees of the Department of Defense or workers at the phased-out Resolution Trust Corporation.[4]

But what credit have past presidents gotten for a recovery or deficit reduction? Pro-Clinton reporters' attempts to correct a negative impression of Clinton's leadership ignored the benefit Clinton derived from coverage of George Bush in 1992. Whether he deserved credit or not, a recovery was well under way in the last year and a half of Bush's presidency. But when economic growth rose 2.7 percent right before the election (and was later revised upward to 3.9 percent), reporters made sure he didn't get any credit. Reporters might have remembered ABC's Peter Jennings dismissing Bush: "All over the country, millions of people hardly need any statistics to tell them what is happening."[5]

Reporters also ignored the history of national economic reporting on Ronald Reagan. As professor Ted J. Smith documented in his book *The Vanishing Economy,* as the economy improved from 1982 to 1987, the number of TV economic stories dropped by two-thirds, and the negative tone of stories intensified, from 4.9 negative stories for each positive story in 1982-83 to 7 to 1 in 1986-87. This bizarre trend came despite the numbers: inflation went down from 13.5 to 4.1 percent; unemployment, from 9.5 to 5.2 percent; the federal discount rate, from 14 to 6.5 percent; the number of jobs up almost 20 million; median family income up every year from 1982 to 1989.[6]

But it wasn't only on economic issues that the media felt Clinton deserved more credit. Former *Newsweek* reporter Jacob Weisberg wrote in the September 6, 1994 *New York* magazine: "Far from being pathologically dishonest, Bill Clinton has been more faithful to his word than any other chief executive in recent memory...On policy issues, he has done almost exactly what he said he was going to do, despite setbacks and enormous obstacles. And by so doing, he has made himself an excellent President."[7]

ABC's Jack Smith also touted a Democratic era of accomplishment, and awarded some of the credit to the Congress on the October 2 *This Week with David Brinkley:* "It was sworn in two years ago as the Reform 103rd, but this week collapsed in partisan backbiting over the failure of health reform....Indeed, look at what the 103rd did pass: North American free trade, substantial deficit reduction as well, a popular family medical leave bill, and gun control. But all this was drowned out in partisan bickering, especially on the crime bill."[8]

On *Face the Nation* October 23, host Bob Schieffer asked: "Why is it that so many things don't seem to help this President? I mean, you know, I can remember in days past when Ronald Reagan would get credit if the sun came up in the morning, and yet Bill Clinton, I mean, we're in a situation here where the economy is in fairly good shape. There's no real threat from any overseas power right now. And yet, the President just sort of humps along and just kind of people say, 'Well, if it was good, it wasn't his fault.' Why do you think that is?"[9] On CNN's *Late Edition* October 23, Bruce Morton noted: "On the other hand there's no doubt Mr. Clinton doesn't get credit for some of the things he's done. Republicans have signed a contract promising, among other things, to cut taxes and the deficit. President Reagan promised to do that: cut taxes, boost defense spending, and balance the budget. He got two out of three, the tax cut and defense boost, but the deficit, of course, went through the roof. Mr. Clinton has not balanced the budget, but he has reduced the deficit. Really. He is routinely denounced for the biggest tax increase in American history, but that's wrong, too. In constant dollars, Ronald Reagan's was the biggest."[10]

Reporters expected their colleagues to have renewed sympathy for Bill Clinton as the midterm elections approached. *Newsweek's* Howard Fineman noted on *Washington Week in Review* that while the Republicans appeared to have the edge in public opinion polls, the Democrats had time, and "guilt: media guilt. I think there's a certain amount of revisionism going on among pundits, not reporters, but pundits. 'Gee, we've been too hard on Bill Clinton. He's actually gotten some things done. Let's look at it.' I detect a slow shift on the C.W. [conventional wisdom] on that, and that'll probably help him, especially since some of the people who will be writing that are the ones who raised Bill Clinton up to begin with."[11]

Some reporters complimented Clinton by doing ideological pirouettes around his record. Since Clinton suffered rejection on the liberal legislation he wanted, especially the nationalization of health care, he actually appeared to be a business-loving moderate. *Wall Street Journal* reporter Jeffrey Birnbaum touted this theory in an October 7 news story: "Based on the measures that Mr. Clinton succeeded in getting through Congress in his first two years, he looks like Mainstream Bill...The Clinton record is surprisingly pro-business and centrist."[12] By that same theory, since social spending never decreased in the 1980s, Ronald Reagan was actually a Rockefeller Republican. That would never fly with the media, who saw Reagan as conservatives saw Clinton: fundamentally opposed to their worldview.

36

Newt's Welcome Wagon

"Newton Leroy Gingrich, former history professor, came to Congress in 1979. From the start, modesty was not his style. Rejecting the House's gentlemanly ways, he waged such constant guerrilla war against the Democrats he was attacked for McCarthyism...Gingrich himself -- bombastic and ruthless -- would be the most dramatic change imaginable, a change the Administration can only dread." -- CBS reporter Eric Engberg, November 2, 1994 Evening News.

"A lot of people are afraid of you. They think you're a bomb-thrower. Worse, you're an intolerant bigot. Speak to them." -- ABC's Sam Donaldson to Gingrich, November 13, 1994 This Week with David Brinkley.

Bill Clinton complained of being introduced to the public through Gennifer Flowers and the draft. But reporters also presented Clinton as a talented, solution-oriented politician, and never openly suggested that the election of Clinton was a threat to the country. In sharp contrast, national reporters presented rising Republican star Newt Gingrich as a bomb-throwing, destructive radical. The Center for Media and Public Affairs found that in political stories on the networks between Labor Day and October 20, Gingrich drew 100 percent negative evaluations from reporters and talking heads. By the end of the campaign, a few appearances by Gingrich himself helped narrow the negative percentage to 81 percent.[1]

CBS reporter Eric Engberg blasted away with a personally produced negative ad on November 2: "If he is reelected and the Republicans win the House, the Speaker's chair will belong to Gingrich, who treats Democrats like a disease....From the start, modesty was not his style. Rejecting the House's gentlemanly ways, he waged such constant guerrilla war against the Democrats he was attacked for McCarthyism."

Engberg saw a hypocrite: "It's a record filled with contradictions: the family values candidate who divorced his ailing first wife, the avowed enemy of dirty politics who bounced 22 checks at the House Bank, and runs a big-dollar political action committee that won't disclose its contributors." Engberg concluded: "Gingrich himself, bombastic and ruthless, would be the most dramatic change imaginable, a change the administration can only dread."[2]

Days before the election, *Time*'s November 7 "Mad As Hell" cover story on Gingrich by Richard Lacayo displayed a mastery of liberal cliches: "Gingrich has been preaching and practicing a strategy of confrontation intended to break the Democratic hold on Congress by fracturing the place itself....Gingrich has been perfecting his ability to disrupt the majority and move the opposition into an increasingly radical position on the right." Lacayo found Gingrich less intellectual than obnoxious: "In the end, his ideas, which don't often come to grips with the particulars of policymaking, may be less important than his signature mood of righteous belligerence."[3]

Newsweek took the negativity to a new level the same week with an article on Gingrich's personal life titled "How 'Normal' Is Newt?" Reporter Mark Hosenball explained: "The answer is just as normal as many Americans -- at least the ones who see their marriages fail, change their views and don't always practice their professed beliefs." Hosenball discovered some real bombshells, like his student protests at Tulane in favor of an "obscene" picture, that Gingrich didn't serve in Vietnam, and that he worked for Nelson Rockefeller, then omitted any reference to it in his 1974 campaign literature. A *Newsweek* caption of his college picture actually read "RADICAL GEEK," a caption *Newsweek* would not have used under a picture of the bearded Oxonian Bill Clinton.

An old faculty colleague of Gingrich was found to tell *Newsweek* readers: "There's the Newt Gingrich who is the intellectual, appealing and fun to be with. Then there's the Newt who is the bloodthirsty partisan who'd just as soon cut out your guts as look at you. And who, very candidly, is mean, mean as hell."[4] This rhetorical excess sounds a little like NPR's Sunni Khalid, who compared Gingrich's situation to radical-left Haitian President Jean-Bertrand Aristide on C-SPAN: "I think there's a big difference when people told Father Aristide to sort of moderate his views. They were concerned about people being dragged through the streets, killed and necklaced. I don't think that's what Newt Gingrich has in mind. I think he's looking at a more scientific, more civil way of lynching people."[5]

Despite all the media hype, NBC's Tom Brokaw and CNN's Bernard Shaw asked if Gingrich would moderate *his* tone. The morning after the Republican sweep to control of both houses, between 5:30 and 10, CNN employed the words "partisan bomb-thrower" three times, "combative" three times, and "fierce partisan" once.[6] *CBS This Morning* co-host Paula Zahn asked Sen. Bob Dole: "Clearly, Mr. Gingrich is no wallflower. The day after the elections, he called the President and the First Lady countercultural McGov-erniks. Do you think he's going to have to tone the rhetoric down?"[7] On November 13, Sam Donaldson asked Gingrich on *This Week with David Brinkley:* "A lot of people are afraid of you. They think you're a bomb-thrower. Worse, you're an intolerant bigot. Speak to them."[8]

A week after the election, Tom Brokaw profiled Gingrich on *Dateline NBC:* "You can call him an archconservative or an archen-emy of President Clinton's policies, but in less than two months, you'll have to call Newt Gingrich Mr. Speaker -- the new Speaker of the House." Brokaw honed in on Gingrich's rhetorical flourishes -- his calling Democratic efforts to prevent reform "Stalinist" and the Democrats, according to one quote from an off-the-record meeting, "the enemy of normal Americans." Brokaw recounted that Gingrich "referred to Bill and Hillary Clinton as counterculture elitists, McGovernites." Brokaw said: "You have a long string of those things, Congressman.....I get the impression, you're so pugnacious that what you say is hard for you to reel it back in right away."

In his interview with the ascendant Speaker, Brokaw sought to force Gingrich on the defensive, including "Newt Incorporated," the network of political organizations and financial supporters around Gingrich, including GOPAC, a political action committee and recruitment agency for House candidates. Brokaw explained: "GOPAC, with a two million dollar annual budget is the center-piece...GOPAC helps pay for and arrange a lot of Gingrich's travel. Over the past year he visited 41 states to stump for conservative candidates. Gingrich's frequent mode of travel? Well, the man who so stridently complains about the Washington elite flew thousands of miles on jets provided by corporate friends. This one [plane featured on-screen] came from a tobacco company." Brokaw asked Gingrich: "If this is all so appropriate and ethical, why not disclose the names of the contributors to GOPAC?"[9]

Brokaw also mentioned Gingrich's "Renewing American Civiliza-tion" college course, supported by the Progress & Freedom Founda-tion, another favorite charity of Gingrich supporters. Brokaw kept at Gingrich: "People who are running the Progress & Freedom Foundation are some of your oldest and closest friends and intellec-tual advisers. Forty percent of the people who gave to that founda-tion also gave to GOPAC. Obviously, there is a political, partisan agenda here because you're not a nonpartisan man....But can't you see how voters who are looking at this for the first time would say, 'Hey, these guys must be trying to buy his heart if not his vote, at the least'?" Brokaw added: "In a letter obtained by *Dateline* two weeks ago, the House ethics committee asked Gingrich to answer charges that his tax-exempt foundation is purely political and not purely educational."[10] NBC, which put off Gingrich's ethical charges against Speaker Jim Wright for more than a year, publicized charges against Gingrich before he even became Speaker.

37

Reaganomics Redux?

"Their agenda: tax cuts for just about everyone. Seniors, business, families with children, even new 'American Dream' savings accounts for the middle class. Also promised: more money for defense and a balanced budget amendment. An independent budget expert called it standard political bunk." -- NBC reporter Lisa Myers, September 27, 1994 Nightly News.

"The Republicans have no shame at all. Bob Dole, for example, bailed out the Reagan administration in 1982 by restoring a lot of the tax money that had been lopped off. We'd probably have a five-times-higher deficit otherwise, and this Contract with America is nothing but gimmicks and silly stuff, and nobody can govern with it." -- National Public Radio reporter Nina Totenberg on Inside Washington, October 1, 1994.

Republican candidates from across the country gathered on the Capitol steps on September 27, 1994 to announce their unity behind a historic agenda for change in the House of Representatives. The Contract with America promised the voters action on ten legislative items, from tax cuts to term limits. During the last month of the election campaign, pro-Clinton reporters greeted the Contract as a boon for Democrats who could now run against Reaganomics.

On the night of the Republicans' Contract-signing ceremony, NBC's Tom Brokaw began his *Nightly News:* "Here in Washington, fear, loathing, and anticipation, and among Republicans, unrestrained glee about the November elections...Today GOP congressional candidates were summoned to Washington and given a battle plan. However, as NBC's Lisa Myers tells us tonight, it is long on promises but short on sound premises." *U.S. News* writer Gloria

Borger called it "a collection of GOP golden oldies that pander to the public's desire to get something for nothing."[1]

Media figures could not admit Republicans could have a positive agenda, a positive vision of limited government. *Newsweek's* Joe Klein complained: "The Republicans have resorted to demagoguery and transparent bribes (like lower taxes). The legislature they promise seems a blustery, selfish, self-righteous desert."[2]

Washington Post reporter Clay Chandler asked: "Why are the Republicans, who generated so many new ideas a decade ago, suddenly reaching backward on economic issues? One possible answer, analysts say, is that the GOP is, in effect, hoping to bribe the electorate -- by appealing so directly to the public's interest in lower taxes that other issues, such as the nation's fiscal solvency, fall away....GOP critics say another possibility is that the chief architects of the House compact...are betting that voters have short memories. They may assume that few may recall -- let alone care -- that the Reagan experiment with supply-side economics quadrupled the federal deficit and left average Americans saddled with higher taxes."[3] These same reporters did not use words like "bribery" or "something for nothing" to describe the Clinton health plan, which promised extending insurance to 37 million Americans without raising taxes.

At *USA Today,* financial reporter Mark Memmott took to writing commentaries beating on the Republicans: "The temptation to be really snide and sarcastic about the Contract with America that House Republicans unveiled last week is almost unbearable. Here's what they want us to believe: They can cut taxes, 'restore' defense spending, and balance the federal budget in eight years...Seems to me that's what the public was told by candidate Ronald Reagan and his advisers in 1980 -- back when the federal debt was $900 billion. Look what's happened since. The federal debt's now $4.5 trillion and heading higher." A week later, Memmott saluted Clinton's plan to put his economic record up against Reagan's: "Have the President and his advisers gone mad? No. They've got solid political and economic arguments to back their argument."[4]

Tax cuts drew the most fire from reporters, who tried in the aftermath of Clinton's election to suggest that tax increases were no longer politically damaging. On June 14, 1993, *Time*'s Margaret Carlson proclaimed: "I think we're going to find out that taxes are okay. I think the Congress should look at the race in New Jersey and see that [New Jersey Gov. Jim] Florio has come back from the dead and vote for Clinton's plan." *Newsweek*'s Eleanor Clift echoed Carlson months later: "Florio will win substantially. [Christie] Whitman's offer of a 30 percent tax cut -- she lost all credibility. Last year's hustle doesn't work. Supply-side economics is dead."[5]

Even "objective" news reports trumpeted the new line. On October 7, 1993, ABC's Jim Hickey reported: "Many voters across the country no longer believe it when told their taxes will go down. Furthermore, taxpayers, say some analysts, have come to accept they have to pay for government that works."[6] Florio lost.

Reporters really haven't liked tax cuts, no matter who proposed them. Even in 1992, when Bill Clinton wanted one, reporters were indignant. After one of the fall debates, NBC's Andrea Mitchell complained: "[Clinton] said he would never tax the middle class, and if things didn't turn out right, he would still not tax the middle class...He really took a pledge last night not to talk about things that would hurt the middle class, and I think it's intellectually one of the worst things I've seen Bill Clinton do." After the election, Margaret Warner, soon to join *The MacNeil-Lehrer NewsHour* as an anchor, said: "I think it would be entirely to the good if [growth] made him abandon this ridiculous middle-class tax cut."[7]

In 1992, *CBS This Morning* touted Clinton's plans to "help just about everybody." On September 30, 1994, *CBS This Morning* co-host Harry Smith asked Gingrich: "There were 300 of you on the Capitol steps a couple of days ago, got together to sign this pledge which kind of harkened up a lot of memories of Ronald Reagan. The papers over the last couple of days have been filled with praise and criticism for this pledge. Among the things you talk about wanting to do, raise defense spending, cut taxes, balance the budget, but did y'all neglect to figure out how you're going to pay for all of that?...If we're talking about Reaganomics, which this seems to be harkening back to, tax cuts for the rich and everything else...You're talking back to the days when deficits ran out of control."[8]

On October 2, Gingrich met a dramatic challenge from Tim Russert on NBC's *Meet the Press*. Armed with a chart of a future federal budget, Russert demanded eight times that Gingrich list specific cuts: "Looking at this chart, this is the year 2002 where you said you'd have a balanced budget. Could you explain to our viewers what areas of the budget you would seek cuts in?" Russert also asked: "There's a new book out called *Dead Right* by David Frum -- you're quoted regularly in the book -- which says that Ronald Reagan never cut or eliminated a major social program. You don't dispute that?"[9] Russert, in effect, was suggesting Republicans were cynical to offer tax cuts without offering specific spending cuts in tandem.

After the networks created and sustained for years the fiction that Republican administrations warred on the poor, of "spending cuts" that were at best reductions in planned increases, how could Russert have the audacity to turn around and suggest that Republican politicians shouldn't be trusted with the purse strings because they couldn't cut spending? Russert's "how will they pay for it" line did not extend to the Democrats. After he pummeled Gingrich, Russert asked Tom Foley three questions about spending cuts in the same show, none of which challenged the legitimacy of Democratic policy.

On *Washington Week in Review, U.S. News* writer Gloria Borger talked about Democratic savvy: "I think it's the Democrats who want to nationalize this, but not to Clinton, but to Reaganomics...that's how the Democrats are using Newt Gingrich's Contract with America, and I think with some success."[10]

Newsweek's Jonathan Alter summed up the conventional wisdom in an October 10 story: "The problem is the contract's main idea has been tried and discredited. House Republicans are now pledged to tax cuts, increased defense spending, and a constitutional amendment to balance the budget. Sound familiar? 'This was a dopey political move,' [then-Rep. Fred] Grandy says. 'We were holding the high ground on welfare, foreign policy, so why would be go back and shoosh down the Laffer Curve? This is like giving the Democrats a nuclear weapon.'"[11]

38

Psychologists Call It Denial

"Some thoughts on those angry voters. Ask parents of any two-year-old and they can tell you about those temper tantrums: the stomping feet, the rolling eyes, the screaming. It's clear that the anger controls the child and not the other way around. It's the job of the parent to teach the child to control the anger and channel it in a positive way. Imagine a nation full of uncontrolled two-year-old rage. The voters had a temper tantrum last week." -- Peter Jennings' ABC Radio commentary, November 14, 1994.

"My memory after that '92 convention the Republicans held in Texas, is that a lot of people, even Republicans, said 'Good Lord, what have we done?' Because the party seemed to have skewed so to the right. Well, the whole country gets to see that now. It's at least conceivable they set up their own defeat in '96, isn't it?" -- CNN anchor Mary Tillotson on election night.

U naware of the rejection their beliefs would take at the polls, reporters and editors quickly warned of the political damage the Contract would cause. But when the Republicans took their issues to a dramatic victory, gaining 52 seats in the House of Representatives after 40 years in the political wilderness, reporters did not apologize for promoting the Clinton presidency and its legislative agenda. But they did balk at the thought that the decisive sea change signaled that voters wanted conservatism or limitations on government.

On election night, CNN political analyst Bill Schneider pro-nounced: "The cynics would say this was a vote for gridlock. But I think it's easier to say, and the data points to the conclusion, that it was a vote for bipartisanship, for centrism." *U.S. News* Senior Writer

Steven Roberts told CNBC *Equal Time* host Mary Matalin: "They are not voting Republican tonight, Mary. They are voting against a lot of unhappiness in their own lives...This is not an anti-government vote tonight." The next morning on *Today,* NBC reporter Gwen Ifill explained: "They're dissatisfied with the idea that nothing happened. In fact, Bill Clinton did a lot of things, he kept a lot of promises. But there's a real surliness afloat out there of people who feel as if things they were entitled to didn't come to them."[1]

When post-election polls showed the public wanted Clinton to adjust to the initiatives of the new Republican Congress, rather than Congress adjusting to the President, all three analysts changed their mind, without admitting their switch. Within three days, Roberts suggested to his colleagues on the November 11 *Washington Week in Review:* "I was very struck when looking at the exit polls. Fifty-one percent of the people said they disapproved of Clinton, and of those, four out of five voted Republican....Doesn't this all add up to a picture of a referendum on the Clinton presidency?" Ifill agreed: "Certainly...It wasn't just a series of bad luck, and it wasn't just bad spin."[2] On December 1, Schneider conceded that "1994 was one of the most ideological elections in the country's history. The election was a referendum on government. The voters said firmly and unmistakably: 'We want less of it.'"[3]

Some media figures turned downright ugly. *Newsweek* Senior Writer Joe Klein blamed the public, and the media: "The public seemed more intolerant than involved, uninterested in what the candidates have had to say, blindly voting against...The President might argue, with some justification, that it's the media's fault: we're allergic to good news."[4]

After a stunned President Clinton held a post-election news conference, Tom Brokaw asked NBC Washington Bureau Chief Tim Russert if the media deserved blame for the Democrats' losses: "During the course of the last two years, they have passed the crime bill. They have made progress on the deficit. They have done things like the national volunteer service. Do you think the press has been too fascinated with other ancillary issues like the feud between the President and some more conservative members of Congress, like

Whitewater and Paula Jones?" Russert agreed: "Yes, I do."[5]

But the strongest reaction came from a disgusted Peter Jennings in his November 14 ABC Radio commentary: "Some thoughts on those angry voters. Ask parents of any two-year-old and they can tell you about those temper tantrums: the stomping feet, the rolling eyes, the screaming. It's clear that the anger controls the child and not the other way around. It's the job of the parent to teach the child to control the anger and channel it in a positive way. Imagine a nation full of uncontrolled two-year-old rage. The voters had a temper tantrum last week." Jennings ended: "Parenting and governing don't have to be dirty words. The nation can't be run by an angry two-year-old." After thousands of angry reactions, Jennings apologized, sort of: "The change in Washington is surely exhilarating. But it's a lot more difficult to build and to govern."[6]

Voters told pollsters it was the President's traditional liberal ideology that sealed their decision. An NBC News/*Wall Street Journal* poll found: "By 67 percent to 28 percent, voters want Clinton to revise his agenda rather than hewing to promises."[7] The public had definitely noticed that the Heritage Foundation-quoting "New Democrat" the media presented to them in 1992 governed more like a big-government Old Democrat.

Reporters had trouble admitting the obvious ideological shift in the President's policies from his campaign speeches. The Media Research Center conducted a study of news stories using the words "Clinton" and "liberal" within 25 words of each other (in *Time*, *Newsweek*, *U.S. News & World Report*, and *USA Today*) from 1991 through 1994. The study found that in 1991, no story identified Clinton as liberal, while 26 claimed he was not liberal.

In 1992 stories featuring the words "Clinton" and "liberal," reporters vastly preferred the not-liberal claim to the liberal label 84 to 11. In the February 10, 1992 *Newsweek*, Eleanor Clift explained that Clinton's invulnerability to charges of liberalism led him to popularity among reporters: "Truth is, the press is willing to cut Clinton some slack because they like him -- and what he has to say. He is a policy wonk in tune with a younger generation of Democrats eager to take the party beyond the liberal stereotype." *USA Today*'s

Adam Nagourney and Bill Nichols wrote on March 18: "This moderate Southerner benefited from the fact that the Democrats seemed to have finally kicked their addiction to nominating liberals doomed to failure against Republicans."

In the first year of Clinton's presidency, the number of labels in the sample dropped dramatically (19 not-liberal, 20 liberal). In the February 8, 1993 *U.S. News,* Editor-at-Large David Gergen described his future boss: "He has come down decisively in favor of a new age of liberal rule, picking up where Franklin Roosevelt and Lyndon Johnson left off." By 1994, reporters used only three not-liberal protestations in the sample, compared to 19 liberal labels. In total, not-liberal tags still outnumbered liberal descriptions, 132 to 50. Instead of labeling Clinton a liberal frequently, reporters mostly stopped using labels.[8]

By the autumn of 1994, a few reporters were admitting that Clinton had promoted an unpopular liberal agenda. In October, *USA Today* reporter Bill Nichols wrote: "Not only did the Clinton health plan fail, but it was almost universally perceived as a bureaucracy-laden liberal expansion of government." Eight days later, Nichols explained: "Voters really believed Clinton was much more conservative than his Democratic predecessors and feel his agenda has been a liberal ruse."[9] Nichols, like his colleagues, did not take any responsibility for forwarding this ruse of Clinton's conservatism before the 1992 election.

VII. CLINTON vs. GINGRICH

39

The Benefits of Irrelevance

"As a milepost, then, we offer 'How the Gingrich Stole Christmas'....
For pianos and parsleys, peanuts and pajamas
Why he'd even take kiddies away from their mamas
The Gingrich said things that Whos thought were shocking
He'd take back each present and empty each stocking." -- CBS anchor
Charles Osgood, December 11, 1994 Sunday Morning.

"Uncle Scrooge: 'Tis the season to bash the poor. But is Newt Gingrich's
America really that heartless?" -- Time cover, December 19, 1994 issue.

"How the Gingrich Stole Christmas!" -- Newsweek cover, December 26,
1994/January 2, 1995 issue.

Bill Clinton joked in the campaign that electing him would give
voters "two for the price of one" -- President Bill and President
Hillary. But the astonishing and sudden ascent of the Republicans
marked the beginning of an entirely different co-presidency in 1995:
of Clinton and Newt Gingrich.

Overnight, Gingrich became Washington's number one story.
The shock at the House turnover after 40 years brought him two
battling identities: strategic genius of the new majority and primary
lightning rod for political attacks. The media treated Gingrich more
like a President than Speaker of the House: polls tracked his approval
ratings along with Clinton's, something the media never considered
for Gingrich's Democratic predecessors, Jim Wright or Tom Foley.
The long-ignored approval rating of Congress was now watched on
a weekly basis to gauge any possible waning of support for the
Republicans.

After decades of placing the center of Washington news at the White House, the center of media scrutiny shifted to Capitol Hill. Republican strategists joked of Clinton's "irrelevance," but the shifting spotlight conveniently spared Clinton, along with his Cabinet officers and Democratic allies, of the kind of ethical and personal scrutiny the media would apply to the new Republican majority.

Clinton's designated irrelevance was no excuse for the media's failure to pick up other reporters' scoops on continuing scandals coming from the White House. On December 16, 1994, *The Washington Post* reported in a front-page story that the Clinton presidential campaign had paid $37,500 (including $9,675 in federal matching funds) to settle a sexual harassment claim against longtime Clinton friend David Watkins. Watkins had served as head of the White House Office of Administration until he was fired for taking a presidential helicopter to a nearby golf course. Other than one mention on ABC's *Good Morning America,* the networks and news magazines totally ignored the Watkins story.

Five days later, U.S. District Judge Royce Lamberth asked the U.S. Attorney for the District of Columbia to investigate Clinton health care aide Ira Magaziner for perjury. Lamberth declared Magaziner must have known his declaration that the Clinton health care task force had only federal bureaucrats on it was false, since employees of his private consulting firm worked on the task force. Again, while some newspapers reported the story, the networks and news magazines were silent.[1]

Ethical troubles also shadowed Clinton's cabinet. On January 14, 1995, *The Washington Post* reported that Clinton's Commerce Secretary, Ron Brown, had taken $400,000 since he joined the Cabinet from Nolanda Hill, who defaulted on more than $20 million in debt guaranteed by the Federal Deposit Insurance Corporation. The three networks aired only one story each -- 13 days later. Clinton's HUD Secretary, Henry Cisneros, accused of misleading the FBI about the size of payments he made to an ex-mistress, gained an extension on the deadline for an independent counsel appointment. But the networks reported nothing. In time, both Brown and Cisneros were assigned independent counsels. With the exception of a lone *60*

Minutes story, no network touched the story of the new Senate Minority Leader, Tom Daschle, who was accused (and later cleared) of intervening with federal aviation officials on behalf of a friend's company who owned a plane that was destroyed in a deadly crash.[2]

The clearest example of the media's transformation from ethical watchdog to Democratic lapdog had to be *Frontline,* the PBS documentary series. Produced out of public station WGBH in Boston, the program spent the late 1980s and early 1990s concocting grand theories of Republican conspiracy, such as the "Secret Team" selling drugs to fund the Contras in Nicaragua, and the "October Surprise" theory that the 1980 Reagan campaign conspired to delay the release of American hostages in Iran. But in the Clinton era, *Frontline*'s investigative nose for the high and mighty went cold.

Despite the wealth of scandal stories to investigate -- Whitewater, the Travel Office, the sex scandals, the Foster suicide, the commodity trading, the Waco fiasco, the ethical quandaries around Cabinet members Cisneros, Brown, and former Agriculture Secretary Mike Espy's improper acceptance of gifts from big business -- *Frontline* aired nothing. Its October 25, 1994 installment "Is This Any Way to Run A Government" investigated the Agriculture Department, but presented Espy, whose ethical troubles also drew the appointment of an independent counsel, as a force for reinventing government who "sees himself as a victim of his reforms." Weeks later, *Frontline* eschewed its hard-boiled style in "Hillary's Class," a look at the First Lady's Wellesley classmates since their countercultural heyday in the '60s. When *Frontline* finally devoted an hour to the Waco fiasco on November 1, 1995, Attorney General Janet Reno was barely mentioned, and Bill Clinton's name never came up.[3]

Frontline's only focus on the Clinton presidency came in January 1995 with the documentary "What Happened to Bill Clinton?" Sherry Jones, a *Frontline* veteran and former Democratic Party activist, answered the program's title question: "In 1992, the American people elected a man who had campaigned as an outsider. They expected change. What has happened to Bill Clinton is not about draft-dodging or Whitewater, but the political choices he made at the beginning. He had promised to change the money politics of

Washington, to reform how the Congress does business. But within days of his election, the Democratic barons would travel from Washington to Little Rock to argue their view of what was possible."[4] Jones did not resolve her contempt for the "money politics of Washington" with her one-sentence dismissal of Whitewater, a classic demonstration of money politics: James McDougal brought the money, and both Clintons attended to his needs.

President Clinton continued to draw sympathetic coverage after the Republican takeover. On the December 12, 1994 *Today*, Bryant Gumbel asked Harry Truman biographer David McCullough: "Like Truman, Clinton has a long list of achievements he can point to -- including a robust economy, a crime bill, NAFTA, GATT. How did Truman ultimately win credit for what he was doing?"[5]

In a January 5 interview with the President, ABC anchor Peter Jennings also trumpeted Clinton's achievements: "I'd like to start, if I may, with what I think you may think is a puzzlement. You've reduced the deficit. You've created jobs. Haiti hasn't been an enormous problem. You've got a crime bill with your assault weapon ban in it. You got NAFTA, you got GATT, and 50 percent of the people don't want you to run again. What's the disconnect there?" Jennings then asked: "Here's another one. In our poll today, the absolute critical items for Congress to address. Number one, cutting the deficit. Number two, health care reform. The two issues which were absolute priorities for two years, and you don't get any credit for them?"[6] Despite his apology for comparing the electorate to "angry two-year-olds," Jennings retained a tone of puzzled condescension over the choices voters made in 1994.

40

A Bounty of Scrutiny

"You called Gingrich and his ilk, your words, 'trickle-down terrorists who base their agenda on division, exclusion, and fear.' Do you think middle-class Americans are in need of protection from that group?" -- Today co-host Bryant Gumbel to House Minority Leader Richard Gephardt, January 4, 1995.

"According to a friend at the time, Newt said he was divorcing [first wife] Jackie because she wasn't young enough or pretty enough to be the wife of a President, and, besides, she has cancer." -- One of CBS anchor Connie Chung's questions to Gingrich's mother, January 4, 1995 Eye to Eye with Connie Chung.

Since he obviously lacked the love-hate relationship with liberalism that occupied President Clinton, Newt Gingrich's personal life and ethical behavior suffered from an abundance of politically inspired media curiosity. Gingrich's decision to accept a $4.5 million advance from Rupert Murdoch's HarperCollins publishing firm for a political book became the first dominant political story of the new Congress. Gingrich quickly decided to forego the advance, but in the five weeks after the story broke on December 22, the networks questioned Gingrich's integrity in 27 evening news stories -- more than the networks devoted to individual Contract with America items such as regulatory reform, legal reform, or term limits in the first 100 days of the 104th Congress.[1] In February, another five network stories investigated "Newt Incorporated," the Speaker's network of financial supporters.

A dramatic disparity remained in coverage of Gingrich scandals and Democratic scandals. All four networks filed reports on February 16 when the Department of Justice opened a preliminary investigation into Commerce Secretary Ron Brown's personal finances. Dan Rather sounded almost regretful: "New legal trouble tonight for a widely respected member of President Clinton's cabinet, Commerce Secretary Ron Brown." Unlike the Gingrich book deal story, however, the networks' curiosity quickly ebbed. In all, the networks devoted eight stories to the Ron Brown scandal during February. Even reporter Jerry Knight's revelation in the February 25 *Washington Post* that NBC had forgiven a loan made to a partnership Brown was a member of failed to pique their curiosity. The networks weren't nearly so hesitant to question Newt Gingrich's ties to Rupert Murdoch's Fox broadcasting empire.[2]

Only CBS, which barely mentioned Troopergate at the end of 1993, reported on the February arrival of the new Clinton biography by *Washington Post* reporter David Maraniss, which confirmed what *The American Spectator* revealed about Clinton's use of troopers to secure women.[3] But without obvious hesitation, reporters jumped on rumors about of Gingrich's divorce from his first wife, Jackie.

In his November 15, 1994 profile on *Dateline NBC,* Tom Brokaw also pointed out that Gingrich smoked marijuana and sought a marriage deferment from the Vietnam War. Brokaw, who worried that "we've made it almost unbearable [for candidates] to enter the public arena" when the issue was Gennifer Flowers, took a moralistic tone about the divorce: "For many of his friends, that divorce, from Jackie Gingrich, was a breaking point...The day after her cancer surgery, Gingrich went to his wife's hospital room to discuss the terms of the divorce. She threw him out....Gingrich, who makes so much of family values, is touchy on this issue, blaming personal grudges of former friends. He can be quick to blame. It has served him well in politics. In his 16 years in Washington, Gingrich has distinguished himself, not for his legislative record, but for carrying the conservative torch and burning Democratic initiatives."[4]

In *Newsweek,* reporter Howard Fineman also aimed for the jugular: "Gingrich's opportunism, often a virtue in politics, can be devastating in private life. Gingrich has a deep feel for human history, but not always for human beings." He added: "The story of his first marriage is familiar: a wife seven years his senior who helped him through school, bore him two daughters, and whom he divorced once he hit the big time in Washington."[5]

The networks also devoted ten stories to Gingrich's mother whispering to Connie Chung on the show *Eye to Eye with Connie Chung* that Gingrich had called Hillary a "bitch." Chung gained this revelation by whispering to the Speaker's mother: "Why don't you just whisper it to me, just between you and me?" CBS saved this spitball of a story for two weeks, until the day before Gingrich was to be sworn in. Then, CBS trumpeted its B-word exclusive in press releases and on its own news programs.

By contrast, on the first episode of her show in 1993, Chung aired a profile of Roger Clinton that included a very soft interview with Virginia Kelley, Clinton's mother. She asked questions that sounded like Barbara Walters: "It seems that both of your boys have this desire to be famous, to be loved, and to be stars." But when Chung interviewed Mrs. Gingrich, the questions were often hostile: "According to a friend at the time, Newt said he was divorcing Jackie because she wasn't young enough or pretty enough to be the wife of a President, and, besides, she has cancer." She also ran down a list for Mrs. Gingrich: "These are some of the things said about your son: a very dangerous man....visionary....bomb-throwing guerrilla warrior....abrasive."[6] These attacks again underlined the media's partisan-flavored hypocrisy: those who pleaded that Clinton's private failings weren't relevant to his job performance had now returned with a vengeance to the sixties maxim that the personal was political.

On March 7, *NBC Nightly News* commentator Bill Moyers discussed the Speaker's sister: "A polite and soft-spoken woman, Candace Gingrich works two jobs and plays softball on the weekends. She is also a lesbian. Her brother is the fire-breathing leader of the conservative coalition that includes an intolerant religious right. It took courage for Candace Gingrich to come out, to lobby Congress for protection against discrimination. Her brother received her gracefully and for a moment family values triumphed over the culture war. But what she herself called his loaded language values winning over caring. Newt Gingrich uses words as if they were napalm bombs. He told Young Republicans their mistake was in not being nasty enough. He sent conservative candidates a long list of words to smear their opponents -- words like 'sick,' 'pathetic,' 'traitors,' 'corrupt,' 'anti-family,' 'disgrace.' With talk radio quoting it all back to us, our political landscape is a toxic dump." All this from the same Bill Moyers who helped create the 1964 "Daisy" ad using an imperiled little girl to imply Barry Goldwater would start a nuclear war, perhaps the nastiest TV ad in political history, and the same Bill Moyers who called Gingrich "Joe McCarthy with a Southern accent." NBC actually promoted Moyers in its advertising with the slogan "Bold, clear, balanced, and fair."[7]

After two years of relative calm, the media's gaffe patrol returned to deconstruct the utterances of Clinton's opponents. Reporters knew gaffes can strengthen media caricatures in the public mind, creating character sketches in 25 words or less: the flighty Third Wave volubility of Newt Gingrich, the stop-lying-about-my-record nastiness of Bob Dole, the spelling talents of Dan Quayle, or the clumsy ethnic satire of Al D'Amato. Gaffes were not something the media thought the Democrats made. Outrageous Democratic rhetoric went mostly uncovered.

Sen. Jesse Helms roiled the media in late November when he suggested on CNN's *Evans and Novak* that Clinton wasn't up to the job of commander-in-chief and later joked to a reporter that Clinton would need a bodyguard to visit military bases. *Today*'s Bryant Gumbel scolded: "His two most recent outbursts against the President are just the latest in a long line of outrageous remarks that have earned Helms the disrespect and disgust of people from coast to coast." NBC's Jim Miklaszewski added: "Critics call him a bigot, a sexist, a homophobe, and he seems to wear it like a badge of honor." *Time* insisted Helms "was widely regarded, even by some of his ideological brethren, as very nearly unpatriotic."[8] But in November 1988, Sen. John Kerry joked that "the Secret Service is under orders that if George Bush is shot, to shoot Quayle." While the Big Three networks did nine stories on Helms, only *NBC Nightly News* mentioned the Kerry joke in 1988.[9]

In late January, the networks struck a similar pose of outrage when House Majority Leader Dick Armey misspoke by calling openly gay Congressman Barney Frank "Barney Fag." *CBS Evening News* made the gaffe its number one story January 27. That same night, ABC's *World News Tonight* flagged the story in its opening seconds. A couple of minutes later, anchor Catherine Crier asked: "Was it a slip of the tongue or a sign of deep prejudice?....Mr. Armey wields enormous power over all kinds of legislation, including laws that deal with discrimination and civil rights. What Mr. Armey says matters."[10]

When Senator Al D'Amato mocked O.J. Simpson trial Judge Lance Ito on the Don Imus radio show, sporting a bad Japanese accent Ito did not have, the network news pounced. NBC's *Today* followed up a feature story on the mini-scandal with an interview with Rep. Norman Mineta (D-Calif.). For effect, co-host Katie Couric solemnly underlined: "Democratic Congressman Norman Mineta and his family were among the 120,000 Japanese Americans placed in detention camps in the United States during World War II."[11]

Even simple ideological labeling became an impolite slur -- if the label was liberal. In a CNN interview after his speech to the nation April 6, Newt Gingrich called the Democratic leadership "a small, left-wing clique." That offended reporter Bob Franken, who asked: "Why would somebody want to sit down with you -- and this gets to basic Newt Gingrich -- why would someone want to sit down with you who you call names, you call left-wing, for instance."[12]

Much like the contrast in "tone" coverage of the 1992 conventions, reporters ignored rhetorical excess on the left. On the campaign trail for Sen. Charles Robb (D-Va.) in his tooth-and-nail battle with Republican Oliver North, Vice President Gore claimed on October 28 that North's support came from "the extreme right wing, the extra-chromosome right wing." Advocates for those with Down's syndrome, which is caused by an extra chromosome, reacted with outrage, reported *The Washington Times*. But Gore's remark never made the network news.[13]

Reporters didn't just exempt Clinton and Gore, but Democrats in general. In December, Jesse Jackson declared: "The Christian Coalition was a strong force in Germany. It laid down a suitable, scientific, theological rationale for the tragedy in Germany. The Christian Coalition was very much in evidence there." No coverage followed on ABC, CBS, or CNN; NBC aired a brief mention.[14]

The Jackson outrage was not a one-time occurrence, but a recurring theme of liberal Democrats. In early March, Rep. Charles Rangel used the words "just like under Hitler" to complain about Ways and Means Committee tactics to its new GOP chairman, Rep. Bill Archer -- but attracted no network coverage. On March 21, Rep. John Lewis took to the House floor and compared the Republicans to the Nazis, paraphrasing an anti-Nazi saying from World War II: "They're coming for our children, they're coming for the poor, they're coming for the sick, the elderly, and the disabled." No network considered it news that night. When NBC's Jim Miklaszewski aired Lewis's remarks on the *Today* show the next day, he followed with Republican Clay Shaw calling them "an outrage." Miklaszewski abstained from judgment on the remark, as if it were subject to debate: "Outrage or not, Democratic attempts to paint Republicans as heartless budget cutters are beginning to hit home." The closest thing to criticism of Lewis came from Miklaszewski and Bob Schieffer calling the debate -- the debate, not Lewis -- "nasty." ABC's Bob Zelnick termed the debate "emotional."[15]

But then, the media, too, had compared Republicans to Nazis. In a 1992 ABC Radio commentary, avuncular *20/20* host Hugh Downs attacked the religious right, saying in times of stress, people often "regress into the family....In the 1920s, the Ku Klux Klan urged the nation to adopt family values and to return to old-time religion. Similarly, Adolf Hitler launched a family-values regimen...fanatics censor the thoughts of others and love to burn books. In the modern United States, new proponents of family values continue this tradition of fear and intolerance."[16] The media's approach to rhetoric appeared schizophrenic: caught between wanting to denounce uncivil language from above the fray while thriving on the expressive joys of partisan hyperbole.

41

A Contract Hit

"Perhaps emboldened by November's results and maybe even covered by the public's fascination with the O.J. Simpson trial, Republicans have succeeded in attacking a variety of social programs without much of a public outcry. Are you disappointed that the public seems to -- I don't know if 'care so little' is the appropriate term -- but not seem to care as much as they have in the past?" -- Today co-host Bryant Gumbel to Sen. Ted Kennedy, March 15, 1995.

"House Republicans denied any impropriety when they approved federal budget reductions of $17 billion and outlined $190 billion more, slashing programs that largely benefit women, children, and the poor, to pay for that 'pouting sex kitten' of their dreams -- tax cuts." -- U.S. News & World Report Senior Writer Gerald Parshall, March 27.

Bill Clinton became a hallowed "New Democrat" when he promised in his 1992 campaign a middle-class tax cut, a dramatic end to "welfare as we know it," and a notable hostility to rigid affirmative action programs. But when some of these promises became planks of the Contract with America and passed the House, the networks shifted to a decidedly negative approach. In a Media Research Center study of 229 policy stories on Contract items from January 1 to April 8, 1995. Talking heads opposing the Contract outnumbered supporters by 442-330, or 58 percent to 42 percent. Stories with a decidedly anti-Contract spin (with a disparity greater than 1.5 to 1 in arguments or talking heads) outnumbered pro-Contract stories by 127 to 21.[1]

For example, 34 stories asserted that a balanced budget would harm the poor or valuable government programs, while each network aired just one story that focused on the benefits of a more limited government. Lavishing their attention on victims of spending "cuts" in the face of the fall election results, only two stories focused primarily on taxpayer demands for smaller government. CBS's Dan Rather demonstrated the heated tone of network rhetoric in a March 16 report on $17 billion in budget rescissions: "The new Republican majority in Congress took a big step today on its legislative agenda to demolish or damage government aid programs, many of them designed to help children and the poor."[2] Weeks earlier, Rather had tried out his colorful language of destruction: "There was no doubt Republicans had enough votes to pass tonight another key item in their agenda to rip up or rewrite government programs going back to the Franklin Roosevelt era. It is a bill making it harder, much harder, to protect health, safety, and the environment."[3]

Despite Clinton's putative attachment to tough welfare reform, the networks' welfare coverage tilted heavily to the left and against welfare reform, with 45 of 68 stories (66 percent) dominated by liberal arguments and spokesmen. Only one of those 68 covered welfare fraud. ABC's Peter Jennings lectured viewers on January 12: "Widespread sympathy for those in need has given way to resentment....The welfare debate has been getting more intense, ever since President Reagan regularly vilified what he referred to as the 'welfare queens.'"[4]

Of 17 reports on the school lunch program, reporters in 15 stories claimed Republicans would "cut" school lunches, when the program was slated to grow 4.5 percent a year. On February 23, NBC *Today* news anchor Matt Lauer announced: "A House committee is working on legislation that would dismantle childhood nutrition programs." Lauer repeated himself the next day: "A Republican plan to wipe out the federal school lunch program is a step closer today to passage in the House."[5] On the March 21 *CBS Evening News,* reporter Bob Schieffer claimed: "Republicans want to wipe out some heretofore untouchable federal programs -- such things as aid to poor single mothers with children, school lunch programs, foster care, and aid to disabled children."

On the networks, only NBC reporter Joe Johns mentioned Republicans were slowing the program's rate of growth from 5.3 percent to 4.5 percent. CNN's Eugenia Halsey was the only reporter to note that any student is eligible for the program, not just the poor. Even so, she concluded on the February 23 *World News:* "The GOP must battle the perception that the Contract with America is a contract against children."[6]

As decisions moved from the House to the Senate, reporters expressed hope the Senate would reject the conservative extremism of the House. NBC weekend *Today* co-host Giselle Fernandez expressed her personal frustration with Labor Secretary Robert Reich on May 20: "This time around, why are *we* leaving such critical decisions, then, up to the Republicans? Why didn't *we* come up with another, more perhaps realistic deficit reduction budget plan?" (Italics mine). Others were even more obvious. *Newsweek* Washington Bureau Chief Evan Thomas declared the resignation of Sen. Bob Packwood was "too bad...he would be an important force, for instance, in stopping the Senate from passing this stupid tax cut."[7]

When Clinton decided to introduce his own plan to balance the budget in ten years rather than the Republicans' seven, Dan Rather acted like a White House spokesman in introducing Clinton's June 13 budget address to the nation: "President Clinton will outline his version of a plan he says will balance the federal budget without what Mr. Clinton sees as a radical and extremist Republican plan to gut programs that help the old, the young, and the poor in order to bankroll tax giveaways to the rich. Republicans, of course, see it a different way."[8]

This raises an intriguing question: what was the difference in tone or ideological intensity between Gingrich's rhetoric and that of the media covering him? Go beyond the list of words used about Gingrich personally -- "McCarthyite," "bombastic and ruthless," "bomb-thrower," "radical geek" -- to the words used for the Republican agenda. To reporters, the Contract with America was best described with words like "slash and burn," "destroy," "gut," "attack," "assault," "wipe out," and "making war on kids." Their coverage exemplified a negative political campaign.

In the February 27 *Time* magazine, Gingrich was caricatured again, not as Uncle Scrooge, but as George Washington taking a chain saw to the cherry tree. The headline read: "Congressional Chain-Saw Massacre: If Speaker Newt Gingrich gets his way, the laws protecting air, water and wildlife may be endangered." Reporter Dick Thompson warned the new Republicans "signal a radical shift in Congress's attitude toward environmental issues -- a shift that may bode ill for the health of snail darters, spotted owls, and even the human species."[9] A week later, a *Time* headline read: "To Be Leaner of Meaner? A congressional proposal to eliminate nutrition programs raises an outcry." Despite the slated spending hike, Senior Writer Elizabeth Gleick brought in hunger "expert" Larry Brown of Tufts University to charge that "We're going to see levels of damage that we have not seen in 40 or 50 years." Rep. David Obey (D-Wis.) argued: "The American public expects us to cut spending...but I don't think they expect us to make war on kids." For emphasis, *Time* put the Obey quote in large letters beneath a photo of two schoolgirls eating.[10]

On race relations, ABC's Carole Simpson announced on February 26 that "Affirmative action is under attack not just in Congress but in the courts." Days earlier, Dan Rather said the same on CBS: "It's one of the hottest and most divisive issues in the country, the future of the civil rights policy called affirmative action....under serious attack in the Republican-controlled Congress."[11]

In a nutshell, Republicans never "ameliorate" the burden of government, "liberate" the taxpayer, or "protect" the small businessman from intervention. Democrats never "assault" employers with regulation or "attack" property owners with wetland seizures. The Republicans were routinely described as "radical," but when the White House proposed adding a socialistic health plan to the federal budget, the President was a "centrist." The language of reporters signaled the audience that they should join them in being appalled by the new Congress and its ideology. Newt Gingrich's greatest struggle may not have been with the Democrats, but with a media which never saw government growth outside the Pentagon as anything but an unalloyed social good.

42

Timothy McVeigh: Newt's Protégé?

"If the perpetrators of the Oklahoma City bombing really view government as the people's enemy, the burden of fostering their delusion is borne out not just by the nut cases that preach conspiracy but also to some extent by those who erode faith in our governance in the pursuit of their own ambitions." -- Time Senior Political Correspondent Michael Kramer, May 1, 1995.

"The Oklahoma City attack on federal workers and their children also alters the once-easy dynamic between charismatic talk show host and adoring audience. Hosts who routinely espouse the same anti-government themes as the militia movement now must walk a fine line between inspiring their audience -- and inciting the most radical among them." -- Los Angeles Times staff writer Nina J. Easton, April 26, 1995.

The attempt to discredit the cause of relimiting government continued only four days after the dramatic April 19 bombing of a federal building in Oklahoma City. By Sunday, April 23, reporters were suggesting that anti-government rhetoric had encouraged terrorism. On *This Week with David Brinkley,* ABC's Sam Donaldson asked a left-wing expert on "right-wing extremists," Morris Dees: "To what extent, if any, do you think the political rhetoric to which you just referred has helped cause a climate in which people could go in that [violent] direction?" On *Face the Nation,* CBS host Bob Schieffer asked Clinton's chief of staff, Leon Panetta: "There's been a lot of anti-government rhetoric, it comes over talk radio, it comes from various quarters. Do you think that somehow has led these people to commit this act?"[1]

That evening, Clinton began blaming the Oklahoma City bombing on "purveyors of hate and division," clearly interpreted by the national media as conservative talk radio and anti-government ideology. Though Clinton hadn't, the press quickly took to naming names. *Today*'s Bryant Gumbel argued on April 25: "The bombing in Oklahoma City has focused renewed attention on the rhetoric that's been coming from the right and those who cater to angry white men....Right-wing talk show hosts like Rush Limbaugh, Bob Grant, Oliver North, G. Gordon Liddy, Michael Reagan, and others take to the air everyday with basically the same format: detail a problem, blame the government or a group, and invite invective from like-minded people. Never do most of the radio hosts encourage outright violence but the extent to which their attitudes may embolden and encourage some extremists has clearly become an issue."[2] Pundits wondered whether Clinton's attacks helped or hurt him politically, but the intellectual authors of the salvo against anti-government talk radio were members of the fourth estate.

Clearly, the media's interpretation of Clinton's remarks was plausible. The President had condemned "hate radio" in the past and named Rush Limbaugh personally. The media took Clinton's new attack and ran with it. Acting once again as the national nanny of public discourse, *Washington Post* reporter David Broder declared on in an April 25 column: "The bombing shows how dangerous it really is to inflame twisted minds with statements that suggest political opponents are enemies. For two years, Rush Limbaugh described this nation as 'America held hostage' to the policies of the liberal Democrats, as if the duly elected President and Congress were equivalent to the regime in Tehran. I think there will be less tolerance and fewer cheers for that kind of rhetoric."[3] In *Time,* Richard Lacayo argued: "In a nation that has entertained and appalled itself for years with hot talk on the radio and on the campaign trail, the inflamed rhetoric of the '90s is suddenly an unindicted co-conspirator in the blast."[4]

The networks' animus against talk radio, touted as the sounding board of the Republican revolution, lasted all year long. A Media Research Center study of the four evening news shows found that of 22 stories on talk radio, primarily negative stories aired three times as often as positive ones: 14 were negative, five were positive, and three were neutral. CBS led the charge with six negative stories to one positive. The only positive story focused on conservative Boston talk show host David Brudnoy, whose audience rallied around him when he announced he had AIDS. But Rather's introduction wasn't exactly positive: "The hottest thing on the radio these days is the call-in talk show. Most of the hosts are self-described conservatives, what their opponents call reactionaries, and their topics are about what you might expect. Well, something unexpected happened on one of these programs, and perhaps the only thing more surprising than the host's revelation was the audience reaction."[5]

The most inaccurate smear of talk radio came on April 27, when Rather began: "Even after Oklahoma City, you can turn up your radio in any city and still dial up hate talk: extremist, racist, and violent rhetoric from the hosts and those who call in. President Clinton, among others, suggests that all this violent talk risks encouraging violent action. But is there any law to stop them from pumping out that venom?" The day before, CBS promoted the story with the question: "Has free speech gone too far? Hate radio under fire, and firing back -- the story tomorrow on the *CBS Evening News*."[6]

Media figures also blamed Republican politicians for Oklahoma City, as if suspected bomber Timothy McVeigh was a Newt Gingrich "bomb-thrower" protégé. Columnist Carl Rowan suggested Gingrich and Senate leader Bob Dole created a "climate of violence" with their rhetoric. *Washington Post* reporter Juan Williams told CNN's *Capital Gang* the bombing showed the "angry white men here, sort of in their natural state...it's the same kind of idea that has fueled so much of the right wing triumph over the agenda here in Washington."[7] These remarks were not seen as part of an unfair attack on innocent politicians who had not urged the bombing of federal buildings, or the product of an "unusually intense hatred" of conservatives.

Boston Globe Washington Bureau Chief David Shribman saw doom for conservatism on April 25: "Public antagonism toward government has been voiced and amplified by the new Republican House, which just this month completed its 100 days of action, much of it aimed at paring back the growth of the federal government. But now that an attack on a government building has left scores dead, the allure is coming off the anti-government rhetoric."[8]

This blame-the-conservatives game wasn't new. When a disturbed man crashed his plane into the White House in September 1994, *Today*'s Katie Couric asked: "Some people are saying this incident is eerily reminiscent of a novel by Tom Clancy called *Debt of Honor.* Do you see any similarities and do you think this book might have played a role in the whole affair?"[9] When Francisco Duran shot at the White House in October 1994, Bob Schieffer asked on *Face the Nation:* "Did the Secret Service ask him as to whether there might have been connection with, was he mad about the President signing the crime bill?" Bryant Gumbel asked: "There's so much talk of voter anger out there, Mr. Panetta. Do you think in any way that contributes to a climate where the President is not safe?"[10]

These critiques lacked any sense that rhetorical excess could be a two-way street, and the media were often lobbing bombs from the other side. On January 4, Bryant Gumbel had blithely asked House Minority Leader Richard Gephardt: "You called Gingrich and his ilk, your words, 'trickle-down terrorists who base their agenda on division, exclusion, and fear.' Do you think middle-class Americans are in need of protection from that group?"[11] CBS *Sunday Morning* television critic John Leonard compared the Republicans to mass-murderous Cambodian communists: "From the *pronunciamentos* out of Washington, you'd think the new Congress were a slash-and-burn Khmer Rouge."[12]

The double standard continued from April 25 to June 1, when the evening news shows devoted 30 stories to the National Rifle Association, 25 of which featured a fund-raising letter in which the NRA called the Bureau of Alcohol, Tobacco, and Firearms "jack-booted government thugs." But when the Democratic Congressional Campaign Committee (DCCC) sent a fundraising letter accusing Newt Gingrich of "promoting the policies of a terrorist" by favoring Drug Enforcement Agency spending cuts, the media yawned. ABC and NBC gave it brief mentions, while the CBS and CNN evening shows did not. *Time, Newsweek,* and *U.S. News & World Report* also ignored the DCCC.[13] Bias by omission again left a false impression.

43

A New Obstacle Course

"While others are running as Mr. Right, or Mr. Far Right, Senator Lugar is stressing his foreign policy expertise." -- Dan Rather on the CBS Evening News, March 3, 1995.

"Even your sister concedes, although some supporters might like what you have to say about the economy and these very specific issues you just mentioned, they're very turned off by some of your social policies. And you know you've got political enemies out there calling you an isolationist, a bigot, you're anti-gay, and some even go as far as saying that your social stands are reminiscent of Nazi Germany. How are you to win them over?" -- CBS This Morning co-host Paula Zahn to presidential candidate Pat Buchanan, July 5, 1995.

The first outlines of 1996 presidential campaign coverage emerged with the announcements of a large Republican field of candidates. Just in the stories announcing the challengers, the networks signaled Republicans would be attacked on all of Bill Clinton's presumed weak points -- an out-of-the-mainstream ideology, personal troubles, real-estate deals, abuse of staff, the lack of military service or private-sector employment -- all to show that Republicans had as little integrity as the President they wanted to replace.

The Media Research Center looked at the first evening news announcement and profile stories of the Republican presidential candidates in 1995 and compared them to the introductory stories on Democratic candidates in 1991. The 29 stories in 1991 on six major candidates (Clinton, Sen. Bob Kerrey, Sen. Tom Harkin, Paul Tsongas, Gov. Doug Wilder, and Jerry Brown) differed dramatically from the 40 stories for the eight major announced Republican candidates who had thrown their hats into the ring by May 1995 (Sen. Phil Gramm, Lamar Alexander, Sen. Bob Dole, Pat Buchanan, Alan Keyes, Sen. Richard Lugar, Sen. Arlen Specter and Rep. Bob Dornan). Of 54 labels found in the 1995 GOP stories, 49 depicted the candidates and the party as either conservative, or in terms further to the right. Terms such as "right," "far right," "hard right," "hard line," "extremist," "right-wing," "Republican fringe," and "ultra-conservative fringe," accounted for 19 tags, or 35 percent of all labels. On the February 24 *CBS Evening News,* reporter Linda Douglass alleged: "For years, critics have called Gramm an extremist. But he argues these days his ideas are in the mainstream." On the April 13 *Inside Politics,* CNN's Gene Randall proclaimed Bob Dornan came "from political stage far right."[1]

In 1991, only 15 of 27 labels (56 percent) characterized the Democrats or their party as liberal. And while none of the networks referred to Democratic candidates or the party as "far left," 12 labels referred to candidates moving away from the left and toward the center. CNN's Randall described Sen. Bob Kerrey in these fuzzy terms: "a populist, liberal enough to challenge Senator Tom Harkin of Iowa, Kerrey would also compete with Arkansas Governor Bill Clinton for his party's moderate center."[2]

Suggesting that a pro-life position hurts the GOP, the 1995 sample identified Republicans' position on abortion more often than the uniformly pro-abortion Democrats in 1991 by a margin of 20 to 1. CNN's Jeanne Meserve explained the advantage of a pro-choice position on *Inside Politics* March 30: "The latest CNN/*USA Today* Gallup Poll should encourage Specter. In a survey of 361 Republican voters this week, better than 6 of 10 said they would support a candidate who favors current abortion laws...Specter vowed to fight to remove the tough anti-abortion plank from the GOP platform."[3]

Overall, network stories mentioning the military record of 1996 GOP candidates outnumbered those of Democrats in 1991 by a margin of 16 to 6. Seven Republican profiles disclosed a lack of service; no reporters mentioned that any Democrats lacked military service, including Clinton. Five of the six mentions in 1991 high-lighted Kerrey's and Wilder's decorated war records.[4]

Reporters were especially focused on Phil Gramm's record. On the February 23 *Inside Politics*, CNN's Bruce Morton declared: "Like the man whose job he now wants, Gramm never served in the military -- had legal deferments during the Vietnam War." ABC's Jim Wooten, who delayed the Clinton draft story for days at a crucial juncture in 1992, proclaimed on the February 24 *World News Tonight*: "But Gramm has not been a paragon of consistency...He urged Texans to reject a Democratic candidate because he hadn't been in the military. Neither was Gramm." The media repeated their imbalance of the Clinton and Quayle draft stories: since Republicans favored the Vietnam War, their draft avoidance merited a bigger story.[5]

Questions about the public and private behavior of Republicans in the first stories on a campaign surpassed those of Democrats by a ratio of greater than 3 to 1. CNN again led the way with four references to the past conduct of GOP candidates, two of them full-length exposés, something that no one did on the day Clinton announced his run for President.

CNN's Brooks Jackson introduced Phil Gramm with a lengthy piece on his Maryland vacation home and the S&L owner who helped him build it, but had to admit: "Gramm may now be the first Senator cleared by the Senate Ethics Committee twice on the same question." Jackson quickly added that "in a couple of ways this looks, looks, I stress looks, worse for Gramm than the original Whitewater allegations did for the President." Four days later on *Inside Politics*, Jackson concluded an investigative report on how Lamar Alexander became a millionaire: "Nothing illegal here...But the sheer size of his deals makes Hillary Clinton's commodities profits look like a widow's and orphan's fund."[6]

In a profile of Bob Dornan (a candidate given no chance of being nominated) on the April 12 *Inside Politics*, CNN's Gene Randall disclosed that "His announcement coincides with his 40th wedding anniversary. The irony: Sallie Dornan filed and then dropped four separate divorce actions against her husband between 1960 and 1976. She told the *Los Angeles Times* she lied about charges of physical abuse and that the real problem was her own addiction to alcohol and prescription drugs." But on the day Clinton announced his candidacy in 1991, Randall noted that "There has been an attempt to bolster Governor Clinton's image as a family man." He went on to point out that Clinton himself, in his announcement speech, acknowledged that his marriage "has not been perfect or free of difficulties," yet Randall still wondered: "Why did Clinton even say that much?"[7]

Reporters singled Phil Gramm out for early coverage very unlike the kind of comparatively easy treatment Bill Clinton received in 1991. In *U.S. News & World Report,* Steven Roberts announced that he'd put Gramm through a "*U.S. News* investigation of his real-estate transactions, draft record, fund-raising, 1969 divorce and personal finances." These were areas where *U.S. News* failed to investigate Clinton throughout 1992. Among the questions Roberts raised: "Though he crusades against government, Gramm has received government help all his life, from his father's death benefits to a federal scholarship. For the past 17 years, both Gramm and his wife, Wendy, have worked almost exclusively for the federal government."[8]

Gramm also suffered an attack on a very old personal charge. *The New Republic* reported that Gramm invested in 1974 in a R-rated bimbo film called *Beauty Queens* that was never made. The magazine advertised the story on its cover with the question: "Phil Gramm, Porn Entrepreneur?" John Judis's story was headlined "The Porn Broker." A number of media outlets described the film as a "soft-porn" project, including CNN, PBS, Reuters, Knight-Ridder, the *Chicago Tribune,* the *Los Angeles Times,* the *Houston Chronicle,* the *Boston Herald,* the *Sacramento Bee,* and the *San Francisco Examiner.*[9]

Major media outlets that scorned stories on Clinton's personal life jumped on the anti-Gramm bandwagon. ABC's Peter Jennings led off the May 17 *World News Tonight:* "The private lives of three important politicians are making news. One is the presidential candidate Phil Gramm. There are questions about a film in which he invested." So in his introduction, Jennings put Gramm before both Commerce Secretary Ron Brown's new independent counsel and Sen. Bob Packwood's sexual harassment troubles. When Jim Wooten did his report on the controversy, ABC put *The New Republic*'s "Porn Broker" headline on screen for a full 18 seconds.[10]

On May 29, *Newsweek* ran a story headlined "Senatorial Skin Flicks" that dominated page 44, despite writer Jerry Adler admitting the story "barely reaches the ankles of Chappaquiddick." In a two-inch-high box at the bottom of the page, *Newsweek* devoted three paragraphs to Commerce Secretary Ron Brown, who pocketed $400,000 since taking office from Nolanda Hill, who defaulted on $20 million in debt guaranteed by the FDIC.[11] This was an interesting demonstration of the magazine's left-leaning news judgment.

Within weeks, Judis and the magazine suffered the embarrassment of its main source, former Gramm brother-in-law George Caton, telling the *Houston Chronicle:* "Where this story has gone haywire is there was no pornography at all." Mark Lester, the director of the follow-up film project, an anti-Nixon spoof called *White House Madness,* told CNN: "I have to laugh. There's no pornography at all in it...I never made a soft-core movie or a pornographic film."[12] Unlike David Brock's Clinton exposés, no mass of media stars rushed forth to denounce the Judis story as a politically motivated and journalistically shoddy work, which left the impression that the major media's journalism judges didn't care *what* was reported on, but *who* was reported on.

On August 31, PBS *Washington Week in Review* host Ken Bode appeared on CNN's *Inside Politics* and complained that in 1996, Republicans may decide on a nominee too quickly for the people to have adequate information: "It's always better to know everything you can about a candidate before you elect him President, rather than find out afterward, and Whitewater is an example of something like that. There's just not time, unless you begin now, to do really intensive work reporting on every one of these candidates." But Bode worked at CNN in the "investigative unit" in 1992 and did nothing on Whitewater. He had reported an eight-minute biography of Clinton with no mention of Whitewater or his draft record.[13]

Not every potential Republican candidate would be put through the journalistic wringer. In September, Colin Powell, the retired Chairman of the Joint Chiefs of Staff, began teasing the media with the idea of running for President. That he was also promoting his book, for which he received a $6 million advance, did not trouble the boomlet of reporters his candidacy soon attracted. Some latched onto Powell to denounce the Republicans as extreme. On NBC's *Today* September 18, Bryant Gumbel wondered: "But could a moderate Republican survive in a system that favors those who flirt with the far right?" NBC Washington Bureau Chief Tim Russert replied: "Good question." Two days later on NPR's *Morning Edition,* reporter Mara Liasson worried that "dealing with the far right is just one obstacle Powell will have to overcome."[14]

Critics of the notion of liberal media bias may have cited the Powell boomlet as a pro-Republican fawning frenzy. But the hosannas began long before Powell declared himself a Republican in announcing he would not run on November 8. Instead, the excitement signaled not just the forward-looking hope of electing a black President, but the backward-looking dream of resurrecting a Republican Party that joined the Democrats in aggrandizing federal power in the 1960s and 1970s, a party of Nelson Rockefellers. ABC *World News Tonight* reporter John Martin mourned the absence of Powell's liberal views on welfare and abortion in the presidential race: "It was the glimpse of these views from someone speaking from within the Republican Party that might have made for change in American politics. For the last generation, the Republicans have moved even further to the right. Here with candor and some skill, it was a political figure willing to move it back toward the center. That is what made today's announcement so bittersweet."[15]

Newsweek's Howard Fineman sounded a similar note on the talk show *Equal Time* November 8: "Most of them [reporters] are centrists. They're not liberals, they're sane centrists, and Powell appealed to the image of why they think they got into politics -- journalism, to begin with...A lot of my colleagues are trying to accept the fact that the Republican Party has the upper hand, and Powell is a guy they could live with."[16]

44

Mangling the Medicare Math

"Democrats and Republicans in Congress late today came close to actual physical blows over proposed cuts in Medicare. That's the separate U.S. government health care coverage for 37 million older Americans of all income levels. There's no doubt that Medicare spending will be cut. The question is how much and for how many." -- CBS Evening News anchor Dan Rather, September 20, 1995.

"Just after midnight the [Senate Finance] committee voted 11 to 9 along party lines to approve an anti-deficit plan mandating massive cuts and changes in Medicare, Medicaid, and virtually every federal welfare program." -- Washington Post reporters Eric Pianin and Judith Havemann, September 30, 1995.

The media play an important role in what political scientist James Payne calls "the culture of spending." Like many other Washington players, from those in government, corporate lobbyists who used to be in government, and nonprofit advocates of more government, reporters have a bias in favor of more federal "activism," with an emphasis on more spending.

Perhaps because of that, reporting on Medicare and Medicaid reform did not resemble the media's coverage of Clinton-style health reform. The media sometimes reflected the Republican number of reducing Medicare *growth* by $270 billion over seven years, and sometimes used the word "cut." But in 1993 and 1994, they never used a precise dollar figure for the Clinton plan over a similar time period, since Clinton had no seven-year balanced-budget deadline. They certainly never acknowledged that they praised Clinton's 1993 budget plan as "the first serious effort to reduce the deficit" when it

completely excluded calculations for the health plan. Would reporters have allowed the Republicans to present a balanced budget plan
with no number for Medicare savings?

In 1993, reporters simply relayed the Clinton claim that his plan
would cost almost nothing in new taxes, although the Congressional
Budget Office eventually estimated the first seven years of the
Clinton health plan would require $784 billion in new spending. On
the September 15, 1993 *CBS This Morning,* Linda Douglass explained: "Well, they have a very elaborate plan to pay for this
revolution in health care. It doesn't provide for much new in the way
of taxes, just a sin tax, cigarette tax. They claim the money's going
to come from savings in spending."[1]

By contrast, Republican budget proposals were greeted with
hostile word-pictures of "slashing" and "bloodletting," even as spending was projected to grow well beyond the rate of inflation. Republicans proposed to reduce the growth of federal spending on
Medicare from over 10 percent a year to about 7 percent. Republicans projected increased spending per recipient -- from $4,800 per
recipient to $6,700. For Medicaid, the Republicans planned to send
the program's administration back to the states, but with a 39
percent increase over seven years, from $89.2 billion to $124.3
billion.

Republican plans were regularly described as "cuts" instead as
reductions in the rate of growth, sometimes in lurid terms. "The
House Republican budget bloodletting will infuriate lots of people,"
CNN's Bob Franken announced in heralding "cuts" in Medicare and
Medicaid. It might have reminded the viewer of Judy Woodruff's
earlier declaration: "March Madness has begun on Capitol Hill, and
almost as predictable as a B horror film, the slashing has begun."[2]

USA Today wrote of "huge cuts in Medicare and Medicaid."
Newsweek said Republicans would "slash funding for...medical care
for the poor and elderly." The *Los Angeles Times* also warned of "deep
Medicare cuts." Reporters often did not tell the public that Medicare
and Medicaid have grown more than ten percent a year. In the Bush
years, Medicare grew a whopping 72 percent, Medicaid an astro-
nomical 132 percent.[3]

Studies by the Free Enterprise and Media Institute found that network evening news stories used "cut" as an explanation of the GOP proposals over reductions in growth by a margin of two to one in the first two weeks of May. Medicare reports from July 15 to August 15 employed the terms "cut" and "slow the growth" about half and half. But only one reporter (CBS's Rita Braver) pointed out spending per recipient was planned to increase over that time span.[4]

In September, the formal introduction of a Medicare reform plan drew more heralding of "cuts." Bryant Gumbel charged on September 15: "Republicans in Congress are beginning to detail how they intend to cut $270 billion from the Medicare budget." Five days later, Dan Rather declared: "There's no doubt that Medicare spending will be cut. The question is how much and for how many." The next day, Rather added: "Republicans in Congress today unveiled their long-awaited and potentially most explosive proposal of all: to cut Medicare spending increases by more than a quarter trillion dollars."[5]

CBS This Morning co-host Paula Zahn warned on September 29: "The Republican plan to slash $270 billion from Medicare cleared its first hurdle in a Senate committee last night." On PBS, anchor Robert MacNeil reported October 2 that Senate Minority Leader Tom Daschle proposed to "cut $89 billion over seven years, a third of what the Republicans have proposed to slash."[6]

Once a Republican Congress had taken the policy-making reins, reporters suddenly discovered hypocrisy -- but only on the Republican side. CBS reporter Linda Douglass tried a cute comparison on September 14: "The basic components of the Republican plan have a strangely familiar ring: they were the main features of the Clinton health care plan, which Republicans defeated soundly last year."[7] Douglass may have been thinking of the Republican plan's reliance on some Medicare recipients opting for managed care, or the possibility that it would lead to greater price controls on Medicare providers, which the Republicans did decry in 1994. But the differences were larger than the similarities: the Republicans planned to move Medicare from a single-payer socialist system to a more private-sector system. Despite its skyrocketing growth and impending bankruptcy, the Clinton plan's proponents proclaimed Medicare a great American success story and said everyone should have an unlimited right to government-subsidized health care.

In mid-November, disagreements between President Clinton and Congress led to a brief shutdown. The networks often relayed Clinton's complaints that Republicans were extremists out to destroy programs like Medicare. A Media Research Center study of 104 evening news stories from November 13-20 found that none of the stories on Medicare pointed out that the Republican plan expected seven percent annual growth, or that spending per recipient would grow. Only one story mentioned the difference between the President and Congress on Medicare premiums -- the reason Clinton gave for his veto -- was only $11 per month. Instead, reporters talked again of "cuts." On *NBC Nightly News,* Tom Brokaw announced: "The House today did pass a bill to balance the budget in seven years with major cutbacks in big government programs and a tax cut of 245 billion dollars." In the same show, reporter Lisa Myers added "the President has promised to veto the bill because of what he calls extreme cutbacks in Medicare, Medicaid, education, and the environment."[8] Myers had been one of NBC's reporters on the "truth squad" in 1992. Why didn't she point out the President's claims of "extreme cutbacks" didn't match Republican projections?

The *Wall Street Journal* editorial page showed the uninformed state of public opinion on Medicare by publicizing a November poll of 1,000 Americans by the GOP polling firm Public Opinion Strategies. When asked what they thought the Republican Medicare plan would do, 27 percent said they thought the GOP would cut Medicare spending per recipient below $4,000; 24 percent replied it would keep spending the same; 25 percent did not know; and only 22 percent accurately answered the GOP's planned increase to $6,700. When the pollsters told the Americans "under the plan that recently passed Congress, spending on Medicare will increase 45 percent over the next seven years, which is twice the projected rate of inflation." When asked if that increase was too high, too low, or about right, 60 percent said too high, and 29 percent said about right. Only two percent said too low.[9] The media again belonged to a tiny minority.

45

Whitewater Bubbles and Boils

"You just heard Mr. Panetta and his comments on the proposed Senate Whitewater hearings. Polls in the past, Mr. Gingrich, have suggested that a) the American people don't really understand Whitewater and b) they really don't care about it. Is there a reason for hearings now, other than to inflict political damage on the President prior to the elections?" -- Today substitute host Matt Lauer to Newt Gingrich, May 18, 1995.

"The Whitewater scandal occupied key committees in both the House and the Senate last week -- a two-ring circus whose single goal seemed to be causing maximum political embarrassment to Bill and Hillary Clinton and their friends." -- Opening sentence of an August 21, 1995 Newsweek Whitewater story headlined "An End in Sight (Maybe)."

The hoariest of national news cliches is that Rodney King chorus chanting: "Why can't we all get along?" A regular nightly news watcher could quickly begin to believe that partisanship is an indelible stain on our democracy, a pox on both houses of the two-party system. But the national media, especially television, thrive on partisanship, overheated rhetoric, paper-waving pols in their angriest tones. After airing the juiciest combat soundbites, reporters often retreat to their studios and disdain the tone their coverage encourages.

Of course, liberal reporters' dislike of partisanship often appears when Republicans attempt to take advantage of Democratic scandal, just as the first Whitewater hearings under Republican control of Congress were scheduled. Take CBS correspondent Bob Schieffer, who told *Sunday Morning* host Charles Osgood: "It's a very mean summer....I think somehow there's a new mean-spiritedness in our politics and I think Washington was a lot better place when people were a little more amicable in how they conducted their business." Schieffer went on to cite the Watergate and Iran-Contra hearings as examples.[1]

The Republicans' Whitewater hearings began in the Senate on July 18, 1995. An August 14 *Washington Post* news analysis concluded the hearings drew "a more comprehensible picture of the controversy than has ever been presented before in a public arena" as "they made a strong case that the first family has not told the complete story of its relationship with former business partner James McDougal."[2]

But that's not the impression network coverage presented. The less productive 1994 hearings, held by the Democrats, and mangled on the House side by the constant restrictions of Banking Committee Chairman Henry Gonzalez, drew 40 evening news stories that featured on-site correspondents. But the 1995 hearings drew only 24 stories of that kind. How curious that as each new hearing added new details to the scandal, new proof of White House dishonesty and corner-cutting, the amount of network coverage lessened. A review of the network morning shows also found limited coverage of the hearings: on three networks in 18 days of mostly two-hour programs, the networks between them mustered only seven reporter-based stories, six anchor briefs, and seven interview segments with some mention of Whitewater.[3]

Ironically, CBS aired the most evening news coverage of the hearings (including ten reporter-based stories), but also seemed the most hostile in tone. On July 17, Dan Rather introduced a story: "From another offensive wave on Whitewater to a sweeping rollback of federal regulations on health, safety, and the environment, it's a political carpet-bombing attack, wall to wall, House to Senate." He added nine days later: "In Washington the Republicans' all-out offensive on Whitewater today featured contradictory testimony." Two days after that, Rather referred to concurrent hearings on the tragedy in Waco as "the Republican offensive against law officers' handling of the Branch Davidian siege." When the House joined the Senate in hearings, Rather began describing the committees as "the

Whitewater tag team."[4]

On the other hand, CNN and NBC barely noted the hearings, each airing just three evening reporter-based stories compared to ten and seven respectively in 1994. Not until the House opened hearings on August 7 did CNN's *World News* air its first reporter-based story.[5]

Significant discoveries and contradictions would have been missed by anyone relying on network news. On July 19, 1995, Patsy Thomasson, a White House aide who had worked for Clinton friend and convicted cocaine dealer Dan Lasater, who did not have a security clearance, but sat at Vince Foster's desk hours after his death while the FBI and Park Police were denied access to his office. ABC and NBC aired no story. CBS did a story on bungling the night of the death, but failed to note this news. When Dan Rather asked "What in terms of substance have they come up with?," Bob Schieffer responded: "Well, not a lot, really." CNN dedicated two and a half minutes to a photo exhibit of movie kissing scenes, but just 18 seconds to Whitewater without mentioning Thomasson.[6]

On August 2, former Deputy Attorney General Philip Heymann charged that White House Counsel Bernard Nussbaum betrayed a promise to allow a joint review of documents in Vince Foster's office. CNN ignored the story, but found time for a piece on the health benefits of tofu. After two weeks without a reporter-based piece, *NBC Nightly News* reporter Jim Miklaszewski narrated an "In Depth" segment on the history and political impact of Whitewater, but NBC relayed nothing about Heymann's testimony. When a second Justice Department lawyer, David Margolis, backed up Heymann's testimony eight days later, CNN and NBC had no story, but CNN did find time to report on Joe Namath donating the pantyhose he wore in a TV ad to the Planet Hollywood restaurant chain.[7]

NBC won the prize for ignoring the story on August 8. The other three networks did full stories on RTC investigator Jean Lewis, who told the House that after Clinton became President, officials tried to obstruct her investigation of Madison Guaranty. Lewis found McDougal involved in "rampant" fraud and check kiting to siphon money to the Whitewater project and Clinton campaign. But NBC led with the O.J. Simpson trial and devoted three minutes to a convention of Elvis "scholars," devoting only 13 seconds to Lewis.[8]

The news magazines weren't much better. As the hearings began, *Newsweek* ran a small feature on Clinton pal Susan Thomases, but nothing on the hearings, although it did publish seven pages on the merger of Disney and Capital Cities/ABC. Perhaps *Newsweek* didn't have room because of its earth-shattering cover story: "At 34, JFK Jr. Is Trying to Make His Mark."

That week's *Time* included this lead sentence in its news summary: "The Administration took its biggest lumps yet at the Senate Whitewater hearings." What followed was exactly one paragraph in its news summary, period. Instead, it put a homely orange fish on its cover and devoted seven pages to the Disney-ABC merger. *U.S. News & World Report* put Mickey Mouse on its cover and gave over nine pages to the ABC-Disney and CBS-Westinghouse mergers.[9] Whitewater could have been presented as a John Grisham potboiler of lawyerly intrigue and coverup at the service of a politician's greed. But the media seemed only obsessed with themselves.

More interesting details spilled out in the fall. When a federal judge tossed out Whitewater independent counsel Ken Starr's tax fraud indictment of Clinton's successor in Arkansas, Democratic Gov. Jim Guy Tucker, on September 5, CBS failed to note the judge's name, Henry Woods, or his partisan activities. After suggesting in 1994 that Starr could be "an ambitious Republican partisan backed by ideologically motivated anti-Clinton activists and judges from the Reagan, Bush, and Nixon years," where had CBS gone? CBS ignored Judge Woods' friendship with Hillary Clinton, who "once wanted Hillary to run for Governor when Bill was undecided," according to a September 7 *Wall Street Journal* editorial. Woods had been "active in Democratic politics in Arkansas for more than 40 years, and developed particularly close relations with Mrs.Clinton when he appointed her to a citizen's committee in his long-running school desegregation case." *The Washington Times* noted Woods was an overnight guest at the White House who monitored election results from the residence in 1994. But media that used to look for the minutest "appearance of a conflict of interest" never called for Woods to recuse himself.[10]

However, CBS did devote an October 8 *60 Minutes* story to an attack on investigative reporter Christopher Ruddy, who almost single-handedly kept the story alive of the inconsistencies in the investigation of Vincent Foster's death.[11] But reporters were used to blaming the conservative media for bad taste in the Foster matter. When Foster died in 1993, his suicide note became a central symbol of what was wrong with Washington. The media beat its collective breast over its own hard-boiled cynicism.

Newsweek's Jonathan Alter wrote in the August 23, 1993 issue: "Foster's note -- especially the line 'Here ruining people is considered sport' -- captured what so many people despise about the Washington media culture." Alter added his own lecture on journalistic history: "The [*Wall Street*] *Journal* editorial page, for instance, resembles nothing so much as the rabidly partisan 19th-century newspapers that routinely -- often brilliantly -- slandered anyone on the other side of their barricades. In the modern era *The New York Times* and other papers reacted against this by developing a cult of objectivity and respectable editorializing that is only now beginning to break apart."[12]

The Washington Post's David Von Drehle, who later became editor of the paper's Style section, mourned the indignities Foster had to face in a long August 15, 1993 front-page article, like the "personal agony" of quitting his all-white country club. Von Drehle also wrote of the "fiercely incandescent" *Journal* editorial page's inquiries into "Who Is Vincent Foster?," suggesting: "To Foster, whose whole career was spent in the courtroom, the lack of evidence supporting the *Journal*'s attacks was scandalous." Von Drehle quoted from the suicide note: "The *WSJ* editors lie without consequence."[13]

On October 25, a panel of three handwriting experts asserted that the Foster note was a forgery, and a bad forgery at that. Only *USA Today* mentioned it. The networks were silent.[14] If some reporters had not elevated the note into a morality play about overzealous conservative editorial writers, perhaps the oversight would seem less ridiculous. The question is obvious: if a Republican counsel like Boyden Gray had turned up dead, and liberals believed his suicide note had been forged in a Republican White House coverup, where would the media have placed that story?

On NBC's Sunday *Today*, co-host Jack Ford asked the network's Washington Bureau Chief, Tim Russert: "We've also seen some new questions raised about the death of Vincent Foster, the death back in 1993, and curiously didn't get much coverage at all, the idea now that some experts are questioning the legitimacy of that suicide note. How has that played down in Washington?" Russert said: "I think most people are determined to wait for the report of the special counsel and if this special counsel agrees with the first special counsel that in fact Vincent Foster's death was a suicide, it should put it to rest for most of official Washington. I do think, however, Jack, that for many people this will long remain a mystery and will become a cult issue, if you will, for a long time to come."[15]

The media's instinct to cover up information damaging to the Clinton cause appeared more amazing as each new disclosure was smothered. Justice Department officials were shocked to learn Vince Foster had kept a meticulous diary which included notes on Whitewater and the Travel Office controversy, the kind of documentary evidence that had been under subpoena for months. Again, the Foster suicide note, genuine or faked, was important; but the diary somehow was not. Michael Shaheen, the career civil servant who heads the Justice Department's Office of Professional Responsibility, was the essence of nonpartisan justice when Independent Counsel James McKay could find nothing to indict then-Attorney General Ed Meese. He told House investigators the Clinton White House's refusal to release documents was "unprecedented."[16] The media yawned.

In a November 2 hearing Senators questioned the First Lady's top aide Maggie Williams and friend Susan Thomases about early morning phone calls placed two days after Foster died. Phone records show Williams called the First Lady in Arkansas and then a call was made from the Arkansas number to Thomases who then called then-White House Counsel Bernard Nussbaum. That day Nussbaum reneged on an agreement to allow Justice Department officials to examine files in Foster's office. Network coverage? The *CBS Evening News* aired a full story from Bob Schieffer, CNN *World News* ran a brief anchor-read item, but no story appeared on ABC or NBC.[17]

These were not the only ignored revelations of that week. The House Government Reform and Oversight Committee released a May 14, 1993 memo from Clinton aide David Watkins suggesting the First Lady's wishes about the White House Travel Office: "We need those people out -- we need our people in." Career Travel Office employees were to be bounced in favor of Clinton buddy Harry Thomason's travel firm. This only contradicted two years of White House claims she had little involvement in the fiasco, but the networks and news magazines ignored it.[18]

It took the Senate Whitewater Committee's decision to issue subpoenas for information from an uncooperative White House and its cronies to draw some of the networks' attention. Even then, a 20-second anchor brief would be enough. On ABC's *World News Tonight* October 26, the curious order of news in descending importance: A school bus crash in Illinois, questions about the safety of Dodge minivans, sex abuse by Catholic clergy, child abuse allegations against a Disney film's director, new anti-smoking commercials from the American Cancer Society, the election of new AFL-CIO head John Sweeney, and an update on the budget battle.[19] After all that, the subpoenas came eighth in a lineup that clearly signaled a slow news day.

In his 1993 *Newsweek* essay, Jonathan Alter wrote: "When the White House delayed turning [the suicide note] over to the U.S. Park Police for a day so that his widow could see it first, the press reacted as if it were Oliver North's shredding party."[20] Late in 1995, reporters still couldn't imagine a conspiracy in the Clinton White House.

But each new revelation underlined the story of a desperate coverup. The First Lady who reporters had scorned investigating in 1992, suggesting a troublesome invasion of privacy, turned out to be very much worth investigating. In late December, notes from Hillary pal Susan Thomases suggested that the First Lady did plenty of legal work for the corrupt Madison Guaranty Savings and Loan, and did the billing, contrary to Hillary's 1992 claims. Those Rose Law Firm billing records had not yet been found. After a brief struggle of claiming attorney-client privilege, the White House relented on former White House lawyer William Kennedy's notes from a November 1993 Whitewater damage control meeting that included the notation "Vacuum Rose Law files."[21]

Until her notes surfaced, Thomases had not spilled the beans on the First Lady despite hours of testimony as a very forgetful witness in the Senate Whitewater hearings, and for good reason. In her Clinton biography *On the Edge*, Elizabeth Drew provided an explanation when she quoted a friend of both Mrs. Clinton and Thomases: "Susan gets into everything, protecting Hillary Clinton. She's her campaign manager for President of the United States, and I'm not kidding. Susan believes that somewhere down the road Hillary will be the first woman candidate for President of the United States. She's positioning her. Not that anybody thinks it's a bad idea. It's just a little early."[22]

With scandals like these, it became easier to understand the Clintons' loathing of the media: it must have come not only from the drubbings they felt they took in 1992, but from fear of what the media could do with the information they tried to withhold throughout the Clinton presidency. The dawning of 1996 may have presented them with a chance at re-election, after which they could claim again that the people did not care about these ethical squabbles. But they had to fear losing control of their political destiny, watching it pass into the hands of the media. Could they count again on the press to sell the public on their inherent goodness and the value of their service to the nation? Trust was not something the First Lady placed in the Fourth Estate.

EPILOGUE

The Media Merry-Go-Round

"There's a hollowness to the U.S. economy and -- as the President explained aboard Air Force One -- to the American spirit in this post-cold war era. Doubt and fear leave people vulnerable to the seductive voice of extremists, he said, drawing votes from centrists like himself." -- Boston Globe reporter John Aloysius Farrell, September 22, 1995.

"It's nice, of course, if we have a President we like. But there's more to governing than likability. We learned that from the likable Ronald Reagan, who charmed us with stories as he amassed huge deficits and spent billions on goofy defense plans. No, the record is more important. And Bill Clinton's record is nothing short of terrific." -- Former NBC News President Michael Gartner in his USA Today column, October 17, 1995.

CNN may have fired the first shot of politicized 1996 campaign coverage when on December 17, 1995, the network devoted an hour to *Time*'s selection of Newt Gingrich as their Man of the Year, a selection they signaled their distaste for with a gaudy, unflattering cover photo. CNN's Judy Woodruff created the same disturbed tone on television. She began by painting Gingrich as viciously ambitious, calling his hope to be Speaker of the House "an obsession that shaped almost every decision, every alliance, what some saw as every betrayal on his path to power." Woodruff included among the betrayed Gingrich's first wife, Jackie: "It has become part of the Gingrich legend that he would later go to her hospital room where she was being treated for cancer to discuss a divorce." In discussing his House career, Woodruff mentioned his "late-night tirades on C-SPAN" which made him "a clown prince of an out-of-favor group."

Gingrich critics outnumbered supporters by almost two to one in the show's documentary segments. Woodruff concluded the program with a decidedly negative spin: "He couldn't have envisioned the blizzard of ethics charges or the stir his fits of pique would cause.

Now that they've gotten to know him, more than half of all Americans say they don't like him. More than half say they don't trust him. The irony is that *Time*'s Man of the Year may wind up the biggest liability to the revolution he launched."[1]

The program was a 180-degree change from the show CNN aired on December 26, 1992, when Bill Clinton was named *Time*'s Man of the Year. The 30-minute show featured at least 18 positive talking heads, including Clinton allies such as future Cabinet officers Robert Reich and Ron Brown, staffers Dee Dee Myers and Betsey Wright, Democratic Reps. Tom Foley and Lee Hamilton, Democratic consultant Bob Squier, and black scholar Henry Louis Gates. Only one soundbite from conservative Arkansas editorialist Paul Greenberg offered any sign of balance.

The syrupy narration by CNN's Lou Waters and Natalie Allen said nothing about Clinton's private life, his ethics, his ambition, his fits of pique. Allen began the show with a quotation: "He was not born a king, but a child of the common people who made himself a Great Persuader, therefore, a leader by dint of firm resolve, patient effort, and dogged perseverance." Waters chimed in: "The words were written by Horace Greeley a century ago to describe Abraham Lincoln. They apply as well to this persevering young man from Arkansas, now leader of the Free World." Allen continued: "The election of 1992 was a leap of faith in a sour and unpredictable year. American voters were angry and disgusted and often afraid of the future. They took an enormous risk and made a fascinating choice."[2]

Some reporters were still sculpting a positive public image for Clinton as 1996 approached. On August 20, 1995, Knight-Ridder reporter Robert Rankin detailed Clinton's popular achievements: "Ordered sweeping regulations over sale and marketing of cigarettes to children," "restricted lobbyists' access to executive branch officials," and appointed two proponents of "clean government" to "spearhead campaign-finance reform." Rankin added that Clinton "ordered his Education Department to notify every school in America about the religious rights of students, and his Justice Department to defend students whose religious rights are infringed upon." Phrases such as "flexing his executive muscles" and "the public seems to like the newly assertive Clinton" were sprinkled into the story.[3]

USA Today reporter Richard Benedetto launched into campaign mode in a September 5, 1995 "news analysis" on Clinton's perform-ance during V-J Day festivities. Clinton's speeches "hardly seemed the words of a leader who has little respect for the military, wants to gut its budget and is unwilling to commit troops to battle, as many Clinton critics charge." In an effort to keep the draft issue off the table, Benedetto claimed Clinton had repaired his image with veter-ans: "Maybe the 50th anniversary of the end of World War II was a time when he came to the realization that his reluctance to answer his country's call to arms may have been a mistake, and those who answered without a second thought forgave him. How else to we explain aging World War II veterans, as giddy as children, jockeying to get their pictures taken with the President, and camouflaged young soldiers with shaven heads shouting out 'Four more years!'"[4]

But that may not have as much impact as the sales job did when the product was new. The surreal feeling of reporters applying a glossy new coat of paint on the Clinton legend would not return his appeal. It seemed like a media merry-go-round that stuck to the same circular pattern of self-defense without reporters considering that many people had jumped off.

Certainly, with the dawning of 1996, those who marked their ballot for Bill Clinton in 1992 had trouble recognizing the blur of images that their candidate had become. The Clinton presidency had spun 180 degrees from the Cuomo-bashing Clinton campaign began in 1991 to the ardent liberalism of his first two years. After the 1994 vote, the White House spun back and forth, never landing on any side for very long -- unless the polls were right. The Bill Clinton reporters presented at the dawn of Clinton's national career looked nothing like the Bill Clinton struggling to regain his footing in 1995.

As the Clinton-Gore '96 effort gathers its millions and prepares to spend the year fanatically selling itself in every medium that will take them, will the media reflect on how it covered Clinton's first election and try to correct its mistakes? Will they submit the Clinton record to the same damning skepticism that they applied to the sputtering Bush presidency? Will they realize that their fervent protests against Bush commercials claiming that Clinton would not raise taxes were unfair and inaccurate? Judging from the record of past presidential election years, it might be wise to suggest that this baby-boomer President will be able to count on his fellow boomers returning to some lyrics from their youth: "Love the one you're with."

But the man-from-Hope facade cracked like Humpty Dumpty, and all the President's men and women in the press cannot put the myth back together again. The man the media presented as offering America a clear moral vision that revered the social centrality of the American family had lost his moral authority, both in revelations of sexual recklessness and the political manipulation used to cover it up. The candidate who offered himself and his new administration as an ethical paragon in contrast to the "sleaze factor" dogging Republican Presidents saw his closest friends and old business partners suffer criminal indictments. The Governor who pledged to reinvent government and create a new Democratic Party of federal restraint pursued a radical course of new trillion-dollar entitlement programs. The alternative to a President derided as a "wimp" for his indecision drew near-universal worry that his positions would change from day to day, from conversation to conversation.

Bill Clinton had not changed. The image had. That shining vision of a new Democratic President to bring a triumphant end to the Reagan and Bush eras crumbled under the weight of his presidency. Much like Clinton, the national media had engaged in a pattern of deception. They painted a pretty picture during the campaign, and labored mightily to avoid any story that could damage that picture. Much as they might have liked to restore an "old media" that acted as gatekeepers restricting damaging information, a new media stepped forward and investigated the real story behind the Clintons' mysterious past. Mysteries remain, but the pretty picture stands exposed -- as a yellowing fairy tale of campaign public relations, a tale the national media not only bought, but sold.

NOTES

INTRODUCTION: THE MOST TALENTED CANDIDATE

1. Sabato, Larry J., and Lichter, S. Robert, *When Should the Watchdogs Bark? Media Coverage of the Clinton Scandals* (Washington: Center for Media and Public Affairs, 1994), p. 34.

2. Starobin, Paul, "Unplugged," *National Journal* (November 4, 1995), pp. 2733-36.

3. Weaver, David H., and Wilhoit, G. Cleveland, "Journalists -- Who Are They, Really?," *Media Studies Journal* (Fall 1992), pp. 63-79.

4. Broder's statement on the June 13, 1994 edition of CNBC's *Tim Russert* quoted in "Very Reassuring," *Notable Quotables* (July 4, 1994), p. 2.

5. *The Press and Campaign '92: A Self-Assessment* (Washington, DC: Times Mirror Center for the People and the Press, 1993).

6. Ibid.

7. "Protecting Bill Clinton," *MediaWatch* (March 1992), pp. 6-7.

8. "Shilling for Bill and Hillary," *MediaWatch* (April 1992), p. 1.

9. Crowley's August 17, 1992 comments and Sesno's August 20, 1992 statements are included with the platform labeling and the 70 to 0 negativity count in "Network Convention Disparities," *MediaWatch* (September 1992), pp. 6-8.

10. Engberg's October 5, 1992 *Evening News* report featured in "Watching the Ad Watchers," *MediaWatch* (October 1992), pp. 6-7.

11. Smith's October 12, 1992 *CBS This Morning* comments quoted in "Harry Hurls," *MediaWatch* (November 1992), pp. 6-7.

12. Jennings' October 28, 1992 *World News Tonight* report featured in "Accentuating the Negative," *MediaWatch* (November 1992), pp. 4-5.

13. "A Very Comfortable Relationship," *MediaWatch* (January 1995), pp. 6-7.

14. Sherrill's May 4, 1993 *Washington Post* story and Carlson's May 10, 1993 *Time* story quoted in "Hard-News Hillary's Pliant Press," *MediaWatch* (May 1993), pp. 4-5.

15. "Selling the 'Job Creation Bill,'" *MediaWatch* (May 1993), pp. 6-7. Clift's comments on the May 15, 1993 *McLaughlin Group* quoted in "Clinton's 'Serious' Deficit Cuts," *MediaWatch* (June 1993), p. 1.

16. Friedman quoted from June 20, 1993 *Meet the Press* in "Clinton's Budget Cheerleaders," *Notable Quotables* (July 5, 1993), p. 2.

17. Media Research Center transcript of Angle's report on the September 2, 1993 *World News Tonight*.

18. "From *I Am Woman* to *Who's That Girl?*," *MediaWatch* (June 1994), pp. 6-7.

19. Lamer, Timothy W., "NBC Health Special Supports Clinton," *MediaNomics* (July 1994), pp. 1-4,

20. "Criminal Gaps in Crime Bill Coverage," *MediaWatch* (September 1994), pp. 6-7.

21. Quotes from CBS reporter Eric Engberg on November 2, 1994, *Time*'s Richard Lacayo in the November 7 issue, and a November 7 *Newsweek* photo caption quoted in

"Newt Gingrich, 'Radical Geek,'" *MediaWatch* (November 1994), p. 1.

22. Jennings' November 14, 1994 ABC Radio commentary quoted in "Peter Jennings: You Voters Need a Diaper," *Notable Quotables* (November 21, 1994), p. 1.

23. Alter's remarks on CNN's *Crossfire* October 21, 1992 quoted in "Liberal Bias: The Ongoing Denial," *Notable Quotables* (November 23, 1992), p. 2.

24. Nagourney, Adam, "Clinton: GOP Whining Paid Off, Bias Charge Resulted in 'Tough Press,'" *USA Today* (September 8, 1992), p. 4A. Clinton also claimed "J. Edgar Hoover didn't do much more to people than what's been done to me." Quoted in the *Newsweek* book *Quest for the Presidency 1992* (College Station, Texas: Texas A&M University Press, 1994), p. 46. The book was authored by Peter Goldman, Thomas N. DeFrank, Mark Miller, Andrew Murr, and Tom Mathews.

1. REGAINING CONTROL

1. Greenfield's interview published in Cunningham, Liz, *Talking Politics: Choosing the President in the Television Age* (Westport, CT: Praeger, 1995), pp. 83-94.

2. Otten, Alan L., "TV News Drops Kid-Glove Coverage of Election, Trading Staged Sound Bites for Hard Analysis," *Wall Street Journal* (October 12, 1992), p. A12.

3. "Clinton's Incredible Shrinking Ideology," *MediaWatch* (March 1995), pp. 6-7.

4. Cooper's July 22, 1991 *U.S. News* article appeared in "Clinton's Incredible Shrinking Ideology," op. cit.

5. Baer's October 14, 1991 *U.S. News* quote noted in "Clinton's Incredible Shrinking Ideology," op. cit.

6. Carroll's September 30, 1991 *Newsweek* quote and other 1991 *Newsweek* stories noted in "Clinton's Incredible Shrinking Ideology," op. cit.

7. Kramer's October 14, 1991 *Time* article and Carlson's December 30, 1991 *Time* piece noted in "Clinton's Incredible Shrinking Ideology," op. cit.

8. Myers' September 12, 1991 and October 3, 1991 *Nightly News* reports quoted in "Complimenting Clinton," *MediaWatch* (December 1991), p. 3.

9. Shields, Mark, "The Many Flavors of Snobbery," *Washington Post* (December 26, 1995), p. A23.

2. REGRETTING GENNIFER FLOWERS

1. "Convention Coverage Assessed," *Television Digest* (July 20, 1992), p. 6.

2. "Protecting Bill Clinton," *MediaWatch* (March 1992), pp. 6-7.

3. Clift, Eleanor, "Testing Ground," *Newsweek* (March 30, 1992), pp. 34-36.

4. Greenfield in *Talking Politics*, op. cit.

5. *Quest for the Presidency 1992*, op.cit., p. 45.

6. "Protecting Bill Clinton," op. cit.

7. Kramer, Michael, "Moment of Truth," *Time* (February 3, 1992), pp. 12-14.

8. Martz, Larry, "Headed for the Exit," *Newsweek* (July 1, 1991), pp. 22-24.

9. Laureen Hobbs' July/August 1992 *Spy* article quoted in Irvine, Reed, and Goulden, Joseph, "Blending News and Politics?," *Washington Times* (July 11, 1992),

p. B3.

10. Rosenstiel, Tom, *Strange Bedfellows: How Television and the Presidential Candidates Changed American Politics, 1992* (New York: Hyperion, 1993), pp. 65-67.

11. Flowers transcript quoted in "Media Let Clinton Lie," *AIM Report* (February-B 1992), pp. 7-8.

12. Media Research Center search of the Nexis news data retrieval system through the end of 1995.

13. Confirmed in the same Nexis search for Perry stories.

14. "Disparities in Infidelity Coverage," *MediaWatch Convention Watch* (August 19, 1992), p. 4.

15. Thomas's remarks on the August 15, 1992 *Inside Washington* quoted in "Dueling Jennifers," *MediaWatch* (September 1992), p. 2.

16. Both stories appeared in the "Periscope" feature at the front of the magazine. The first was "Taking Aim at the Bush Rumors," *Newsweek* (June 15, 1992), p. 6; the second was "Tale of the Tape," *Newsweek* (August 24, 1992), p. 4.

17. Mitchell's, Hunt's, and Miklaszewski's statements on the August 12, 1992 *Today* quoted in "Defending the Democrats," *MediaWatch* (September 1992), p. 3.

18. Thomas's August 15, 1992 *Inside Washington* remarks quoted in "Defending the Democrats," op. cit.

19. Media Research Center transcript of Gumbel's interview with James Carville on the August 13, 1992 *Today*.

20. Clift, Eleanor, and Miller, Mark, "Saint or Sinner?," *Newsweek* (April 11, 1994), pp. 25-26; Goldman, Peter, and Miller, Mark, "The Message Struggle," *Newsweek* (November 7, 1994), pp. 38-40.

3. MAINTAINING HIS POLITICAL VIABILITY

1. Rosenstiel, *Strange Bedfellows*, op. cit., pp. 71-72.

2. Morton's February 8 *CBS Evening News* declaration quoted in "Protecting Bill Clinton," op. cit.

3. News accounts included Colton, David, and McConnell, Darci, "Viet-era Letter Haunts Clinton," *USA Today* (February 13, 1992), p. 1.

4. Rosenstiel, op. cit.

5. Ibid.

6. Media Research Center transcript of February 12, 1992 *CBS Evening News*.

7. "Koppel Contradiction," *MediaWatch* (March 1992), p. 7.

8. Clift, "Testing Ground," op. cit.

9. Media Research Center transcript of February 12, 1992 *Nightline*.

10. Germond, Jack, and Witcover, Jules, *Mad As Hell: Revolt at the Ballot Box, 1992* (New York: Warner Books, 1993), p. 204.

11. Rosenstiel, op. cit., pp. 76-78.

12. Koppel's August 18, 1988 *Nightline* interview with Craig Fuller quoted in "Koppel Contradiction," op. cit.

13. Bury's February 13, 1992 *World News Tonight* report quoted in "Protecting Bill Clinton," op. cit.

14. Ibid.

15. Ibid.

16. Ibid.

17. Ibid.

4. THE INDUCTION NOTICE FIZZLE

1. Church, George J., "Questions, Questions, Questions," *Time* (April 20, 1992), p. 28.

2. Media Research Center Nexis check.

3. Maraniss, David, *First In His Class: A Biography of Bill Clinton* (New York: Simon and Schuster, 1995). The contribution is detailed on page 300; the *Oxonian* sentence on page 448. The Talbott boys' contributions, as reported by *Washingtonian* magazine, appeared in "No Probe From Strobe," *MediaWatch* (April 1992), p. 3..

4. Talbott's March 7, 1992 *Inside Washington* remarks quoted in "The Clinton Corps Reports," *Notable Quotables* (March 16, 1992), p. 1.

5. Talbott's April 6, 1992 *Time* essay quoted in "No Probe From Strobe," op. cit.

6. Ibid.

7. "Clinton Critic Seeks Space in Time," *Washington Times* (October 10, 1992), p. A8.

5. THE FIRST LEAKS OF WHITEWATER

1. Threlkeld's February 16, 1992 report quoted in "Shilling for Bill and Hillary," *MediaWatch* (April 1992), p. 1.

2. Carroll, Ginny, "Will Hillary Hurt or Help?," *Newsweek* (March 30, 1992), pp. 30-31.

3. Carlson, Margaret, "When Spouses Earn Paychecks," *Time* (March 30, 1992), pp. 30-31.

4. Carlson's January 27, 1992 *Time* story and Painton's January 20, 1992 piece quoted in "Marilyn vs. Hillary," *MediaWatch* (February 1992), p. 8.

5. Chancellor's March 17, 1992 primary-night commentary and Bury's March 23, 1992 *World News Tonight* story quoted in "Shilling for Bill and Hillary," op. cit.

6. News accounts included Schmidt, Susan, "Notes Indicate More S&L Work By Mrs. Clinton," *Washington Post* (December 19, 1995), pp. 1, 4.

7. Confirmed by Media Research Center Nexis news data search of Whitewater stories. The *Post*'s two late-summer stories were the only major-media mentions of Whitewater from April 1992 through Election Day. A Charles Babcock article on April 16, 1993 then marked the only major media mention from 1992 until the *Post* broke the story open with a front-page scoop on October 31, 1993. Later in the election year, Howard Kurtz returned to complaining about Clinton's rougher press treatment in "Media's Arrows Don't Seem to Wound Perot: Skeptical Reports About Undeclared Candidate Lack Intensity of Press Assaults on Clinton," *Washington Post* (June 11, 1992), p. A16.

8. "Double Standard for Sununu," *MediaWatch* (July 1991), pp. 6-7. The study noted that the *Post*'s attention to the Sununu story far outstripped coverage of congressional junkets by Dan Rostenkowski and the Ways and Means Committee, as well as then-House Armed Services Committee Chairman Les Aspin's use of military aircraft. After the study, the *Post* published one front-page story on Aspin.

9. Alter, Jonathan, "Press Affection, and Vivisection," *Newsweek* (April 6, 1992), p. 26. Alter failed to mention the cocaine dealer was Arkansas "bond daddy" Dan Lasater, who gave Clinton's brother Roger a job and was later pardoned by the Governor. Lasater's connections to Clinton through bond sales of the Arkansas Development Finance Authority (ADFA) remain under investigation. But a Media Research Center Nexis search showed *Newsweek* never even printed his name until its January 24, 1994 issue.

10. Boo, Katherine, "The Hillary Loophole," *The Washington Monthly* (May 1992), pp. 26-30.

11. Shepard, Alicia C., "The Second Time Around," *American Journalism Review* (June 1994), pp. 28-35.

12. *The People, Press and Politics, Campaign '92: Campaign and the Press at Halftime* (Washington: Times Mirror Center, June 4, 1992), pp. 39-41.

13. Greenfield, Meg, "The Folly of Reinvention," *The Washington Post* (January 23, 1995), p. A19.

14. *Dateline* producer Mark Hosenball (now with *Newsweek*) wrote about the Susan Deer case in "Arkansas Gothic," *The New Republic* (August 3, 1992), pp. 14-17.

15. Couric's July 16, 1992 *Today* interview with Mrs. Kelley quoted in "NBC: *Today* or Toady?," *MediaWatch* (August 1992), p. 5.

16. Aaron's January 1992 speech quoted in "Protecting Bill Clinton," op. cit.

6. THE GOLD DUST TWINS

1. Roberts' May 22, 1992 remarks on *Washington Week in Review* quoted in "Murphy Brown: Willie Horton in Maternity Clothes?," *Notable Quotables* (June 8, 1992), p. 1.

2. Clift's June 1, 1992 *Newsweek* piece quoted in "Murphy Brown: Willie Horton...," op. cit.

3. Morrow's June 1, 1992 *Time* essay quoted in "Murphy Brown: Willie Horton...," op. cit.

4. Morton's June 13, 1992 *CBS Evening News* commentary and Goldberg's June 13, 1992 *TV Guide* remarks quoted in "Two CBS Views on Quayle," *Notable Quotables* (June 22, 1992), p. 1.

5. Kaus's May 11, 1992 *New Republic* article quoted in "Another Media Vote for Bill Clinton," *Notable Quotables* (May 25, 1992), p. 2.

6. Gumbel's June 3, 1992 *Today* question and Zahn's June 22, 1992 *CBS This Morning* assessment quoted in "Wake Up to Wonderful Willie," *Notable Quotables* (July 6, 1992), p. 1.

7. All of the newspapers' front-page profiles of Gore appeared on July 10. Also Shapiro, Walter, "Gore: A Hard-Won Sense of Ease," *Time* (July 20, 1992), pp. 28-29.

8. Fritz, Sara, "Born to Politics, Gore Fits the Ticket's Needs," *Los Angeles Times* (July 10, 1992), p. 1.

9. Mitchell's July 13, 1992 *NBC Nightly News* quote was reported in "Family Values: Horton All Over Again," *Notable Quotables* (July 20, 1992), p. 2. Mitchell often returned to the Bush campaign's 1988 use of Willie Horton as a metaphor. On page 424 of their book *Mad As Hell*, Jack Germond and Jules Witcover recall that in the October 1992 issue of *Harper's* magazine, their "Harper's Index" reported that Willie Horton was mentioned 69 times in *New York Times* articles from January through August 1992, compared to only 33 times during the 1988 campaign.

10. Hickey's July 10, 1992 *World News Tonight* quote was reported in "Gore on the Planet: No Extremist?," *Notable Quotables* (July 20, 1992), p. 2.

11. Babcock, Charles P., "Gore Getting $20,000 a Year For Mineral Rights on Farm; Lease Arrangement Made by Father with Armand Hammer," *Washington Post* (August 15, 1992), p. A10.

12. Gore's legislative ratings from the American Conservative Union and the National Taxpayers Union.

13. Threlkeld's July 9 *Evening News* story and Spencer's comments during live convention coverage July 13 quoted in "Clinton and Gore: Conservatives?," *Notable Quotables* (July 20, 1992), p. 1.

7. THE BIG PICTURE

1. Quoted from interview by Media Research Center's David Tosatti in "Coffey's Grounds," *MediaWatch* (August 1992), pp. 2-3.

2. Jensen's July 14, 1992 New York *Daily News* report noted in "TV Ladies Lean Left," *MediaWatch* (August 1992), p. 2.

3. "Media Money Funds Democrats," *MediaWatch* (July 1992), pp. 6-7. A newer study of campaign contributions found major media figures donated five times as often and six times as much money to Democrats over Republicans in 1993-94. See "So Much for 'Corporate Conservatives,'" *MediaWatch* (September 1995), pp. 6-7.

4. Morrow's January 4, 1993 *Time* article quoted in "Two Very Different Conventions," *Notable Quotables* (January 4, 1993), p. 2.

5. Adams' 1984 research cited in "History of Uneven Coverage," *MediaWatch* (August 1992), p. 5.

8. LOOK FOR THE LIBERAL LABEL

1. Wooten's July 13, 1992 *World News Tonight* report quoted in "No Liberals in Sight," *Notable Quotables* (July 20, 1992), p. 1.

2. Greenlaw's August 12, 1992 CNN quote appeared in "Look Out for Labels," *MediaWatch Convention Watch* (August 17, 1992), p. 3.

3. "Networks Coddle the Democrats," *MediaWatch* (August 1992), pp. 6-8.

4. *Newsweek's* July 4, 1988 table of contents quoted in "Campaign '88: Dukakis," *Notable Quotables* (July 11, 1988), p. 2.

5. "Coverage of the Democratic Convention," *MediaWatch* (August 1988), pp. 6-8.

6. Rather, Bode, and Brokaw on July 13, 1992 noted in "Networks Coddle the Democrats," op. cit.

7. Schieffer's and Jennings' July 13, 1992 remarks noted in "Networks Coddle the Democrats," op. cit.

8. "Network TV Convention Disparities," *MediaWatch* (September 1992), pp. 6-8.

9. Ibid.

10. August 17, 1992 remarks by Jennings, Schieffer, and Roberts quoted in "Network TV Convention Disparities," op. cit.

11. Rather's August 17, 1992 remarks and Chung's August 20 interview noted in "Network TV Convention Disparities," op. cit.

12. Crowley's August 17, 1992 CNN preview, as well as Bierbauer's and Sesno's August 20 overviews noted in "Network TV Convention Disparities," op. cit.

13. Brokaw's August 17, 1992 remarks noted in "Network TV Convention Disparities," op. cit.

14. Miklaszewski's August 20, 1992 report noted in "Morning Match," *MediaWatch* (September 1992), p. 6.

15. Kolbert, Elizabeth, "Networks Focus on Shift to the Right," *New York Times* (August 19, 1992), p. A14.

9. THE AGENDA OF QUESTIONS

1. "Coddling Democrats & Discrediting Republicans," *MediaWatch* (September 1988), pp. 6-8.

2. "Network TV Convention Disparities," op. cit.

3. Mitchell's July 13 PBS/NBC interview noted in "Networks Coddle...," op. cit.

4. Media Research Center transcript of Randall's July 16 interview with Heflin.

5. Media Research Center transcript of Crier's CNN interview July 13, 1992 with Gore.

6. Media Research Center transcript of Cochran's July 14, 1992 NBC interview with Napolitano.

7. Shriver's July 14, 1992 convention comments to Waters, Cuomo, and Glaser collected in "Network TV Convention Disparities," op. cit.

8. Shriver's August 18, 1992 interview with Sullivan noted in "Network TV Convention Disparities," op. cit.

9. Media Research Center transcript of Shaw's August 17, 1992 interview with President Bush.

10. Media Research Center transcript of Sherr's August 17, 1992 ABC interview with Nyegaard.

11. Media Research Center transcript of Jennings' August 18, 1992 interview with Bennett.

12. Media Research Center transcript of Crier's August 18, 1992 interview with Mrs. Quayle.

13. "Morning Match," *MediaWatch* (September 1992), p. 6.

14. Paula Zahn's July 14, 1992 interview with Harkin quoted in "Networks Follow Democrat's Agenda," *MediaWatch Convention Watch* (July 15, 1992), p. 1.

15. Couric's August 17, 1992 question to Gov. Ashcroft quoted in "Morning Match," op. cit.

16 Smith's August 19, 1992 question to Falwell and Bauer quoted in "The Morning After," *MediaWatch Convention Watch* (August 20, 1992), p. 2.

10. COVERING CONTROVERSIES

1. "Coddling Democrats and Discrediting Republicans," op. cit.

2. "Networks Coddle the Democrats," *MediaWatch* (August 1992), op. cit.

3. Interview by Media Research Center's David Tosatti quoted in "Koppel Claims It's Not His Job," *MediaWatch Convention Watch* (July 17, 1992), p. 2.

4. Hedges, Michael, "Clintons Profited from S. African Investments," *The Washington Times* (July 9, 1992), p. A1. The *Los Angeles Times* mentioned the purchases in passing in a May 2, 1994 story.

5. Jennings' August 17, 1992 quote noted in "Creating GOP Controversies," *MediaWatch Convention Watch* (August 20, 1992), p. 2.

6. Roberts' August 12, 1992 *World News Tonight* report noted in "Networks Hail Hillary, Bash Bond," *MediaWatch Convention Watch* (August 17, 1992) p. 3. For an informative overview of Mrs. Clinton's writings on children's legal rights, see Evans, M. Stanton, "What Hillary Clinton Really Said About Children," *Human Events* (September 4, 1992), pp. 1, 15.

7. "Brokaw Admits Imbalance," *MediaWatch Convention Watch* (August 21, 1992), p. 3.

8. Brokaw's August 18, 1992 interview quoted in "Creating GOP Controversies," op. cit.

9. Chung's August 19, 1992 interview noted in "GOP, Still Out of Touch," *MediaWatch Convention Watch* (August 20, 1992), p. 1.

10. Chung's August 17, 1992 interview noted in "Win One for Connie," *MediaWatch* (September 1992), p. 3.

11. Rather's remarks on the July 13, 1992 *CBS Evening News* and Moyers' comments during CNN convention coverage the next night appeared in "Jesse Jackson's Fan Club," *Notable Quotables* (August 3, 1992), p. 2.

12. "Network TV Convention Disparities," op. cit.

13. Shaw's remarks during CNN's live convention coverage on August 20, 1992 quoted in "Republicans Only Want Real Americans," *Notable Quotables* (August 31, 1992), p. 2.

14. Media Research Center transcript of Mitchell on the August 21, 1992 *Today*.

15. Rabinowitz, Dorothy, "Watching the Reporters' Convention," *Wall Street Journal* (August 24, 1992), p. A7.

11. TWISTING THE TENETS OF FEMINISM

1. Koppel's opening of the August 18, 1992 *Nightline* quoted in "Intimidated by Hillary?," *Notable Quotables* (August 31, 1992), p. 1.

2. Duffy's August 24, 1992 *Time* quote noted in "Republicans on Women," *Notable Quotables* (August 31, 1992), p. 1.

3. Media Research Center transcript of Gumbel's July 20, 1992 *Today* interview with Mrs. Clinton and Mrs. Gore.

4. Media Research Center transcript of Woodruff's July 14, 1992 prime time convention interview with Mrs. Clinton.

5. Woodruff's August 18, 1992 interview quoted in "Woodruff Disses First Mrs.," *MediaWatch Convention Watch* (August 19, 1992), p. 3.

6. Media Research Center transcript of Woodruff's August 20, 1992 interview with Marilyn Quayle.

7. The July 13, 1992 *Capital Gang* Charen-Hunt exchange quoted in "Calling Hillary Liberal: Neo-Fascist Nonsense," *Notable Quotables* (July 20, 1992), p. 1.

8. Media Research Center transcript of Zahn's August 24, 1992 *CBS This Morning* interview with Mrs. Clinton and Mrs. Gore.

9. Media Research Center transcript of Couric's August 24, 1992 *Today* interview with Mrs. Clinton and Mrs. Gore.

10. Media Research Center transcript of Couric's August 20, 1992 *Today* interview with Mrs. Bush.

11. Carlson quoted in *The Homestretch: New Politics. New Media. New Voters?* (New York: Freedom Forum, 1992), p. 49.

12. DELIGHTING IN DOUBLE STANDARDS

1. September 14, 1992 *New York Times* headlines noted in "Another Day on the Campaign Trail," *Notable Quotables* (September 28, 1992), p. 1.

2. Achenbach, Joel, "Clinton and Gore: New Heart-throbs of the Heartland," *Washington Post* (July 22, 1992), Style section pp. 1-2.

3. Walsh's July 23, 1992 *Washington Post* story quoted in "Clinton's Magical Mystery Bus," *Notable Quotables* (August 3, 1992), p. 1.

4. Clift quoted from the July 25, 1992 *McLaughlin Group* in "Clinton's Magical Mystery Bus," *Notable Quotables* (August 3, 1992), p. 1.

5. Maraniss's story in the August 6, 1992 *Washington Post* quoted in "The Rush to Gush," *Notable Quotables* (August 17, 1992), p. 1.

6. Kurtz, Howard, "When the Media Are on a Roll, the Candidate Rides a Wave," *The Washington Post* (July 25, 1992), p. A12.

7. Klein's August 17, 1992 *Newsweek* report on the Democrats and his August 31, 1992 article on the Republican convention quoted in "Joe Klein on Bus Trips and Conventions," *Notable Quotables* (September 14, 1992), p. 2.

8. "Clinton's Conformity Cops," *MediaWatch* (October 1992), p. 8.

9. Rauch's September 28, 1992 *New Republic* article quoted in "Clinton's Conformity Cops," op. cit.

10. Media Research Center transcript. The ABC change received attention from a September 16, 1992 story by Associated Press reporter Scott Williams, "Peter Jennings: ABC's *World News Tonight* to Tighten Campaign Focus."

11. Kaus, Mickey, "Sound-Bitten," *The New Republic* (October 26, 1992), pp. 16-18.

13. THE DRAFT AND THE TRIP

1. Rempel, William C., "Induction of Clinton Seen Delayed by Lobbying Effort," *Los Angeles Times* (September 2, 1992), p. 1.

2. Bozell, L. Brent, "Clinton's Draft Story: No Feeding Frenzy," issued September 10, 1992 by Creators Syndicate. The press deflected Clinton's draft status with Bush's involvement in or knowledge of the Iran-Contra affair. Look at the divergence of the questions in a September 9-13, 1992 CBS/*New York Times* poll. First, they asked: "Do you think Bill Clinton has been telling the truth about how he avoided the draft during the Vietnam War, or hasn't he told the truth?" But the Bush question was worded: "When it comes to the Iran-Contra matter, do you think George Bush is hiding something the public ought to know, or don't you think so?" Featured in *The Polling Report* (September 21, 1992), p. 1.

3. Nagourney, Adam, "Clinton: GOP Whining Paid Off, Bias Charge Resulted in 'Tough Press,'" *USA Today* (September 8, 1992), p. 4A.

4. Keen, Judy, and Nichols, Bill, "Clinton and the Draft," *USA Today* (September 9, 1992), p. 1A.

5. Hedges, Michael, "Gore's Resume Raised Questions in '88 Campaign," *Washington Times* (July 16, 1992), p. A6. In an article for *The New Yorker*, Peter Boyer unearthed a Vietnam-era letter from Al Gore, Jr. to his father, then-Senator Al Gore, Sr., in which young Al said the "best example" of a "fascist totalitarian regime" was the U.S. Army. He wrote: "We do have inveterate antipathy for communism -- or paranoia, as I like to put it...my own belief is that this form of psychological ailment -- in this case a national madness -- leads the victim to create what he fears the most." The networks ignored that, too. See "Another Counterculture McGovernik," *MediaWatch* (January 1995), pp. 4-5; also Boyer, Peter, "Gore's Dilemma," *The New Yorker* (November 28, 1994), pp. 100-110.

6. Seper, Jerry, and Archibald, George, "Clinton Toured Moscow at War's Peak," *Washington Times* (October 5, 1992), pp. A1, A8.

7. Media Research Center transcript of Bush's interview on CNN's *Larry King Live*, October 7, 1992.

8. Ford, Gerald, "Clinton's Candor Is Issue," *USA Today* (October 9, 1992), p. 12A.

9. Clift's remarks on the October 10, 1992 *McLaughlin Group* quoted in "Attacks Off Limits?," *MediaWatch* (October 1992), p. 1.

10. Smith's remarks on October 12, 19, and 21, 1992 quoted in "Harry Hurls," *MediaWatch* (December 1992), p. 3.

11. Greenwald, John, "Anatomy of a Smear," *Time* (October 19, 1992), pp. 28-29; Alter, Jonathan, "The Smear Heard 'Round the World," *Newsweek* (October 19, 1992), p. 27.

12. Klein, Joe, "Bush's Desperate Game," *Newsweek* (October 19, 1992), p. 26.

13. Bozell, L. Brent, "Some In Media Try to Head Off Bush Surge," *Conservative Chronicle* (November 11, 1992), p. 27.

14. WHERE WAS WHITEWATER?

1. Media Research Center transcript of Brian Ross's September 15, 1992 *Dateline NBC* report.

2. Pauley's September 8, 1992 *Dateline NBC* interview quoted in "Hillary's Fan Club," *MediaWatch* (October 1992), p. 5.

3. Seigel's October 20, 1992 *Chicago Tribune* story and Radcliffe's October 30, 1992 *Washington Post* article quoted in "Hurray for Hillary," *Notable Quotables* (November 9, 1992), p. 2.

4. Quoted in the editorial "Arkansas Forbearance," *Wall Street Journal* (February 22, 1994), p. A20.

5. Official transcript from the Democratic National Convention.

6. Eastland, Terry, "Why the Press Quit on Whitewater in 1992," *Forbes Media Critic* (Summer 1994), pp. 26-38.

7. Ibid.

15. AD POLICE BRUTALITY

1. Cochran's July 21, 1992 *Nightly News* report quoted in "Clinton-Gore Truth Squad?," *MediaWatch* (September 1992), p. 1.

2. Cochran's August 27, 1992 *Nightly News* story quoted in "Clinton-Gore Truth Squad?," op. cit.

3. Greenfield's September 8, 1992 *World News Tonight* report quoted in "Watching the Ad Watchers," *MediaWatch* (October 1992), pp. 6-7. The Clinton campaign's finding of 127 tax and fee hikes contained in Maraniss, David, and Pianin, Eric, "Comparing Records: Clinton Rebuts List of 128, But Numbers Basically the Same," *Washington Post* (September 6, 1992), p. A1.

4. Jackson's September 24, 1992 *Inside Politics* ad watch quoted in "Watching the Ad Watchers," *MediaWatch* (October 1992), pp. 6-7.

5. Engberg's September 26, 1992 *CBS Evening News* story quoted in "Watching the Ad Watchers," op. cit.

6. Utley's September 26, 1992 and October 3, 1992 *Nightly News* reports quoted in "Watching the Ad Watchers," op. cit.

7. Moore, Stephen, "A Fiscal Policy Report Card on America's Governors," Cato Institute *Policy Analysis* (January 30, 1992), pp. 29, 39.

8. Myers' and Greenfield's October 2, 1992 evening news reports quoted in "Watching the Ad Watchers," op. cit.

9. Engberg's October 5, 1992 *Evening News* report quoted in "Watching the Ad Watchers," op. cit.

10. Jackson's October 2, 1992 CNN report quoted in "What If the 'Wrong' Ad Is Right?," *MediaWatch* (March 1993), pp. 4-5.

11. Duffy, Michael, and Thompson, Dick, "Behind Closed Doors," *Time* (September 20, 1993), pp. 60-63.

12. Kurtz's October 2, 1992 *Washington Post* story quoted in "What If the 'Wrong' Ad Is Right?," op. cit.

13. Kramer, Michael, "Moving In," *Time* (January 4, 1993), pp. 28-33.

14. Unbylined *USA Today* February 18, 1993 story quoted in "Wrong, Wrong, Wrong on Clinton's Tax Promises," *Notable Quotables* (March 1, 1993), p. 1.

15. Congressional Budget Office, *An Analysis of the Administration's Health Proposal* (Washington: Government Printing Office, February 1994), p. 38.

16. Rosenstiel, Tom, *Strange Bedfellows*, p. 272.

17. Woodward, Bob, *The Agenda: Inside the Clinton White House* (New York: Simon and Schuster, 1994), p. 47.

16. QUAYLE'S TURN IN THE PENALTY BOX

1. Reynolds' October 21, 1992 *Wall Street Journal* editorial quoted in "Clinton and Gore Ignored, Quayle Scored," *MediaWatch* (November 1992), pp. 4-5.

2. Samuelson's October 28 *Washington Post* column quoted in "Clinton and Gore Ignored, Quayle Scored," op. cit.

3. Wooten's October 14, 1992 *World News Tonight* report quoted in "Clinton and Gore Ignored...," op. cit.

4. Jackson's October 14, 1992 *Inside Politics* report quoted in "Clinton and Gore Ignored...," op. cit.

5. Media Research Center transcript of Gore's July 30, 1992 interview on *Prime Time Live*.

6. The *Human Events* article on *Putting People First* noted in "Clinton and Gore Ignored...," op. cit.

7. Charen's *Washington Times* column quoted in "Clinton and Gore Ignored...," op. cit.

8. Jackson quoted in "Clinton and Gore Ignored...," op. cit.

9. Wooten quoted in "Clinton and Gore Ignored...," op. cit.

17. NAILS IN THE COFFIN

1. Media Research Center transcript of Jennings' and Jamieson's ABC report on the October 27, 1992 *World News Tonight*.

2. *The Washington Post*'s October 28, 1992 story quoted in "The Clinton Boom Begins?," *MediaWatch* (December 1992), p. 1.

3. Media Research Center transcript of Jennings and Wooten on the October, 28, 1992 *World News Tonight*.

4. Jennings' November 25, 1992 report noted in "Media on Economic Growth: Whoops!" *Notable Quotables* (December 7, 1992), p. 1.

5. Nasar, Sylvia, "Is the Clinton Expansion Here? Rebound Seen, But a Slow One," *The New York Times* (November 30, 1992), pp. A1, D4.

6. "Tamposi Tempest," *MediaWatch* (December 1992), p. 7.

7. Ibid.

8. Wattenberg, Daniel, "The Lady Macbeth of Little Rock," *The American Spectator* (August 1992), pp. 25-32.

18. BIAS? WHAT BIAS?

1. Sesno's August 15, 1992 interview with Bond noted in "Reporters Indignant at Bias Charge," *MediaWatch Convention Watch* (August 20, 1992), p. 4.

2. The August 19, 1992 *Inside Politics* exchange between Clift and Broder noted in "Reporters Indignant...", op. cit.

3. Alter's August 24, 1992 *Newsweek* article noted in "Reporters Indignant...," op. cit.

4. Totenberg's August 15, 1992 *Inside Washington* quote noted in "Reporters Indignant...," op. cit.

5. Thomas's comments on the August 15, 1992 *Inside Washington* quoted in "Coming Clean," *MediaWatch* (September 1992) p. 1.

6. Andrews' August 14, 1992 *CBS Evening News* report noted in "Reporters Indignant...", op. cit.

7. Graham, Tim, "Convention Coverage: Microcosm of Media Bias," *The World & I* (November 1992), pp. 112-119.

8. Fineman's remarks on the September 5, 1992 *Reliable Sources* quoted in "Growing Opinion?," *MediaWatch* (September 1992), p. 3.

9. Rainie's September 25, 1992 remarks on C-SPAN quoted in "Taking Criticism Seriously," *Notable Quotables* (October 12, 1992), p. 1.

10. Berke's contention on the October 16, 1992 *Larry King Live* quoted in "Denial," *Notable Quotables* (October 26, 1992), p. 2.

11. Moyers's comments on the November 2, 1992 *Larry King Live* quoted in "Liberal Bias: The Ongoing Denial," *Notable Quotables* (November 23, 1992), p. 2.

12. "Viewers Decry Slant," *MediaWatch* (April 1993), p. 3.

13. Hewitt's statement in the May 20, 1992 *Boston Globe* quoted in "One CBS Vote for Ann Richards," *Notable Quotables* (June 8, 1992), p. 1.

14. "Viewers Decry Slant," op. cit.

15. Ibid.

19. THE POST-GAME SHOW

1. Utley's October 17, 1992 *NBC Nightly News* commentary quoted in "Blame Game," *MediaWatch* (December 1992), p. 3.

2. Crier's election-night analysis for CNN quoted in "The Houston Convention: A New Willie Horton?," *Notable Quotables* (November 9, 1992), p. 2.

3. Brokaw's and Chancellor's election-night remarks for NBC quoted in "The Houston Convention...," op. cit.

4. The CBS election night exchange quoted in "Our Poll Shows the Conventions Didn't Matter, But They Did," *Notable Quotables* (November 9, 1992), p. 1.

5. Schneider's report from shortly after midnight on election night quoted in "Mandate for What?," *MediaWatch* (November 1992), p. 1.

6. Wilkie's November 4, 1992 *Boston Globe* story quoted in "A Sweeping Mandate?," *MediaWatch* (November 1992), pp. 1-2.

7. Shapiro's November 16, 1992 *Time* article quoted in "Clinton, Sex God," *MediaWatch* (December 1992), p. 3.

8. Cooper's story from the November 23, 1992 issue of *U.S. News & World Report* quoted in "Coddling Clinton," *Notable Quotables* (December 7, 1992), p. 2.

9. Carlson's November 30, 1992 *Time* story quoted in "Sucking Up to Stephanopoulos," *Notable Quotables* (December 7, 1992), p. 2.

10. Cooper's story in the December 7, 1992 issue of *U.S. News* quoted in "Sucking Up to Stephanopoulos," op. cit.

11. Maraniss's November 23, 1992 *Washington Post* story quoted in "Sucking Up to Stephanopoulos," op. cit.

20. THE GREAT LIBERAL HOPE

1. Wills quoted from November 21, 1988 *Time* in "Campaign '88 Reviews," *Notable Quotables* (November 28, 1988), p. 1.

2. Morrow quoted from the January 4, 1993 *Time* in "Man of the Year," *Notable Quotables* (January 4, 1993), p. 1.

3. Klein quoted from January 25, 1993 *Newsweek* in "Clinton the Messiah," *Notable Quotables* (February 1, 1993), p. 1.

4. Abramson's January 8, 1993 appearance on C-SPAN quoted in "Most Popular Inauguration Ever," *Notable Quotables* (January 18, 1993), p. 1.

5. Kurtz's January 31 *Washington Post* article quoted in "Media Applaud Clinton Policies," *MediaWatch* (February 1993), p. 1.

6. Blumenfeld's January 24, 1993 *Washington Post* Sunday Style story quoted in "Clinton the Messiah," *Notable Quotables* (February 1, 1993), p. 1.

7. Friedman's statement from the May 21 *Washington Week in Review* and Oliphant's May 30, 1993 *Boston Globe* column quoted in "Clinton's Right On, But He's Screwing Up!," *Notable Quotables* (June 7, 1993), p. 1.

21. UNEXPECTED BEGINNINGS

1. Gibbs, Nancy, "Thumbs Down," *Time* (February 1, 1993), pp. 26-28. The *Los Angeles Times* editorial is also quoted in the article.

2. Cannon, Carl, "The Story in the Closet," *Forbes Media Critic* (1993 Premiere Issue), pp. 38-46. Cannon noted that *Chicago Tribune* reporter Mitchell Locin told him he used a question about gays in the military in "a story about off-the-wall things candidates get asked."

3. Weisskopf's February 1, 1993 blunder, along with the Kurtz and Byrd articles, quoted in "The Post Pre-Judges," *MediaWatch* (February 1993), p. 3.

4. Talking head counts, as well as Shriver's January 26 NBC special and Nissen's January 29 ABC story, quoted in "Media Applaud Clinton Policies," op. cit.

5. A CNN/*USA Today* Gallup poll found the percentage of Americans describing Clinton as "liberal" in polls conducted in July 1992 and late January 1993 showed an increase from 32 percent to 50 percent. Cited by CNN political analyst Bill Schneider on the February 2, 1993 *Inside Politics*.

6. Media Research Center transcript of Traver's January 29, 1993 appearance on C-SPAN.

7. Crockett's comment on the June 1, 1993 *Inside Politics* quoted in "Clinton, Decent and Faithful," *Notable Quotables* (June 21, 1993), p. 2.

8. "Scandals Skipped," *MediaWatch* (February 1993), pp. 1-2.

22. WORKING FOR THE WHITE HOUSE

1. Hunt's remarks on the December 12, 1992 *Capital Gang* were quoted in "Defending the Clintonites," *Notable Quotables* (January 18, 1993), p. 1.

2. Muller, Henry, "From the Managing Editor," *Time* (February 1, 1993), p. 12.

3. Fedarko's November 29, 1993 *Time* article noted in "Hurray for Halperin," MediaWatch (December 1993), p. 7.

4. Carlson's June 26, 1993 article and the June 9, 1993 *Washington Times* editorial quoted in "Knocking Sam Brown Down," *MediaWatch* (July 1994), p. 6.

5. Weisberg, Jacob, "Clincest," *The New Republic* (April 26, 1993), pp. 22-27.

6. Stern's 1990 reports noted in "Stern Justice," *MediaWatch* (May 1993), p. 2.

7. "A Very Comfortable Relationship," *MediaWatch* (January 1995), pp. 6-7. Primary research by Brent Baker.

23. THE VICTIMIZED STIMULUS

1. "Selling the 'Job Creation Bill,'" *MediaWatch* (May 1993), pp. 6-7.

2. Clift's April 19, 1993 *Newsweek* story noted in "Selling the 'Job Creation Bill,'" op. cit.

3. *CBS Evening News* quotes from the month of April 1993 quoted in "Selling the 'Job Creation Bill,'" op. cit.

4. Rather's September 28, 1989 *Evening News* report was originally quoted in "Crying Over Capital Gains," *MediaWatch* (October 1989), p. 1.

5. Hume's April 5, 1993 *World News Tonight* report quoted in "Selling the 'Job Creation Bill,'" op. cit.

6. Ibid.

7.Plante's April 7 *CBS Evening News* story and Myers' March 30 *NBC Nightly News* story noted in "Selling the 'Job Creation Bill,'" op. cit.

8 Harry Smith quoted in "Selling the 'Job Creation Bill,'" op. cit.

9. Garvin's May 14, 1993 *City Paper* cover story noted in "NPR: No Putrid Republicans," *MediaWatch* (June 1993), p. 2.

10. Dentzer's March 15, 1993 *U.S. News* column quoted in "Stimulus Support," *MediaWatch* (April 1993), pp. 3-4.

24. THE FABULOUS FIRST BUDGET

1. Mitchell, Dan, "Making a Bad Budget Even Worse," *Washington Times* (June 2, 1993), pp. G1, G4.

2. Smith's April 28, 1993 quote and Zahn's May 30, 1993 quote noted in "Clinton's 'Serious' Deficit Cuts?," *MediaWatch* (June 1993), p. 1.

3. Myers, Mitchell, and Schieffer quoted in "Clinton's 'Serious' Deficit Cuts?," op. cit.

4. Kramer's May 3, 1993 *Time* article quoted in "Clinton's 'Serious' Deficit Cuts?," op. cit.

5. Zuckerman's May 17, 1993 *U.S. News & World Report* column quoted in "Clinton's 'Serious' Deficit Cuts?," op. cit.

6. Clift's May 15, 1993 *McLaughlin Group* appearance quoted in "Clinton's 'Serious' Deficit Cuts?," op. cit.

7. *Newsweek* "Conventional Wisdom Watch" items from February 22, 1993 and March 1, 1993 noted in "Clinton: Mount Rushmore?", *Notable Quotables* (March 1, 1993), p. 4.

8. Klein's June 28, 1993 *Newsweek* article quoted in "Those Pesky Anti-Tax Republicans," *Notable Quotables* (July 5, 1993), p. 1.

9. Borger's June 18, 1993 appearance on *Washington Week in Review* and the July 5, 1993 *U.S. News* story on the Clinton budget quoted in "Siding with Clinton's Math," *MediaWatch* (July 1993), p. 1.

10. Borger, Gloria, "Running the Tough Gantlet," *U.S. News & World Report* (February 15, 1993), pp. 42, 44.

11. Mufson, Steven, "Remaking a Culture at the OMB: Panetta Seeks to Make Honesty a Budget Policy," *Washington Post* (February 14, 1993), p. H1.

12. Mitchell, Dan, "Making a Bad Budget Even Worse," op. cit.

25. HILLARY'S FAN CLUB

1. "The Honeymoon That Wasn't," *Media Monitor* (September/October 1993), pp. 4-5. Of course, Clinton had 1,695 evaluations to Hillary's 85 in the study period, but Barbara Bush four years earlier had only one. According to the CMPA's methodology, Bush had a better first six months (60 percent positive), but he was both less visible (35 percent less, by their measure), and he was trying to do less. Conservatives felt Bush benefited from not being Reagan at that time. While some "negative" evaluations are openly critical comments, the CMPA count also includes statements like skeptical "wait and see" remarks about the chances for legislation.

2. Drew, Elizabeth, *On the Edge* (New York: Simon and Schuster, 1994), p. 196.

3. Sherrill's January 11-13, 1993 *Washington Post* series noted in "Hillary Hair Update," *MediaWatch* (February 1993), p. 2.

4. Carlson's sidebar interview with Mrs. Clinton in the May 10, 1993 *Time* and her remarks on CNN's May 8, 1993 *Reliable Sources* were noted in "Hard-News Hillary's Pliant Press," *MediaWatch* (June 1993), pp. 4-5.

5. Carlson's May 10, 1993 cover story quoted in "Hard-News Hillary's Pliant Press," op. cit.

6. Carlson's June 1993 *Vanity Fair* article quoted in "Taking Hillary as Policy Wonk Seriously," *Notable Quotables* (May 24, 1993), p. 1.

7. Sherrill's May 4, 1993 *Washington Post* story quoted in "Hard-News Hillary's Pliant Press," op. cit.

8. Carlson's and Sherrill's quotes about the right appeared in "Hard-News Hillary's Pliant Press," op. cit.

9. Media Research Center transcript of May 8, 1993 *Reliable Sources* on CNN.

10. Carlson quoted from the March 7, 1994 *Washington Post* in "Hillary: The Working Woman's Mascot?," *Notable Quotables* (March 14, 1994), p. 1.

11. Carlson's May 7, 1993 appearance on C-SPAN's *Journalists Roundtable* quoted in "Margaret Carlson: President of the Hillary Clinton Fan Club," *Notable Quotables* (May 24, 1993), p. 1.

12. Cobb's April 12, 1993 *Boston Globe* story quoted in "Hillary Hilarity," *MediaWatch* (May 1993), pp. 1-2.

26. THE HEALTH CAMPAIGN

1. Rogers, Mark, and Graham, Tim, "Foreign Systems: Promoting Socialist Role Models," Media Research Center *Special Report* (September 21, 1993), pp. 1-4.

2. "Good Morning Liberals," *MediaWatch* (October 1993), pp. 6-7.

3. Devroy, Ann, "Post-Vacation Clinton Swims Toward Mainstream: Health Care, Trade Pact, Reinventing Government Give President Chance to Alter His Image," *Washington Post* (September 6, 1993), p. A1.

4. Rowen, Hobart, "Buffeted from Both Sides," *The Washington Post* (September 9, 1993), p. A21.

5. Stout and Levine's August 30, 1993 CNN interview quoted in Graham, Tim, and Lamer, Tim, "Do's and Don'ts for Reporting on the Passage of a Health Care Bill," Media Research Center *Special Report* (March 1, 1994), p. 4.

6. Goodgame, Dan, "Ready to Operate," *Time* (September 20, 1993), pp. 54-58.

7. Graham and Lamer, "Do's and Don'ts," op. cit. But a skewed ideological spectrum existed long before the health debate began. In MRC newspaper studies of various study periods from 1987-93, ten liberal groups allied with or to the left of Clinton on health issues (such as Families USA and Citizen Action) were labeled "liberal" in only 49 of 2,604 stories (1.9 percent), while the Heritage Foundation was labeled "conservative" in 217 of 370 stories (58.6 percent).

8. Schieffer on the September 28, 1993 *CBS Evening News*, Crowley on the September 29 *Inside Politics*, and Jennings on the September 24 *World News Tonight* quoted in "Hurrays for Hillary on the Hill," *MediaWatch* (October 1993), p. 1.

9. The October 11, 1993 *Time* article by James Carney, Michael Duffy, and Julie Johnson was quoted in "Hillary: Mesmerizing, Passionate Citizen," *Notable Quotables* (October 25, 1993), p. 2.

10. Goodgame's September 20, 1993 *Time* quote was noted in "Universally Behind Universal Health Care?," *Notable Quotables* (September 27, 1993), p. 1.

11. Congressional Budget Office, *An Analysis of the Administration's Health Proposal*, op. cit.

27. THE BIG RED "WRONG" RETURNS

1. Hattie Kauffman's September 22, 1993 *CBS This Morning* report quoted in "Watching the Ad Watch," *MediaWatch* (October 1993), p. 1.

2. Maceda's September 22, 1993 *Today* story quoted in "Correcting the Clintons' Critics," *MediaWatch* (October 1993), pp. 4-5.

3. Maceda's 1993 story and Bazell's 1995 story were compared in "HMOs Then and Now," *MediaWatch* (November 1995), p. 3.

4. Interview with Maceda quoted in "Correcting the Clintons' Critics," op. cit.

5. Ibid.

6. Jackson's October 22, 1993 *Inside Politics* story quoted in "Double Standards on the 'Fact Check,'" *MediaWatch* (November 1993), pp. 4-5.

7. Noted in "Fiction Roundup: The President's 'Tight' Budget," *Notable Quotables* (February 14, 1994), p. 1.

28. THE GREAT BEAST OF NEED

1. "S&L Story Spiked," *MediaWatch* (December 1993), p. 3.

2. Carney, James, "Friends in Low Places," *Time* (November 15, 1993), p. 54.

3. Graham, Tim, "NPR's Troopergate," *Comint* (Spring 1994), pp. 37-39.

4. Seper, Jerry, "Clinton Papers Lifted After Aide's Suicide," *Washington Times* (December 20, 1993), p. A1. Despite Seper's regular breakthroughs, his work went unheralded by the journalists who hand out annual prizes like the Pulitzers.

5. Berke, Richard, "Poll Says Conservatives Dominate Talk Radio," *New York Times* (July 16, 1993), p. A12, and Balz, Dan, "Misleading Medium of U.S. Politics: Talk Radio Callers Often 'Caricature Discontent,' Study Finds," *Washington Post* (July 19, 1993), p. A7.

6. Dowd's January 23, 1994 *New York Times Magazine* story quoted in "Maureen Dowd Admits the Obvious," *Notable Quotables* (January 31, 1994), p. 1.

29. THE TROOPER TRUTH SQUAD

1. "'Holier-Than-Thou' Hypocrisy," *MediaWatch* (January 1994), pp. 6-7.

2. Newsmagazine reporter quoted in Sabato, Larry J., and Lichter, S. Robert, *When Should the Watchdogs Bark? Media Coverage of the Clinton Scandals* (Washington: Center for Media and Public Affairs, 1994), p. 34.

3. Interviews with reporters from Sabato and Lichter, op. cit., pp. 16-38.

4. Gigot, Paul, "John & Bill, Anita & Gennifer, Sex & Double Standards," *Wall Street Journal* (December 31, 1993), p. 6.

5. Sorenson's remarks and Phillips' April 8, 1990 story quoted in "'Holier-Than-Thou' Hypocrisy," *MediaWatch* (January 1994), pp. 6-7.

6. *New York Times* stories quoted in "'Holier-Than-Thou' Hypocrisy," op. cit.

7. *Newsweek*'s 1994 and 1991 stories noted in "'Holier-Than-Thou' Hypocrisy," op. cit.

8. Ferguson's admission from Sabato and Lichter, op. cit; the *U.S. News* cover story on Hill appeared on October 12, 1992.

9. Graham, "NPR's Troopergate," op. cit.

10. Ibid. More on Totenberg's self-defense appeared in Graham, Tim, "Nina Totenberg, Partisan Journalist," *Comint* (August 1993), pp. 9-11.

30. PAULA JONES: NO ANITA HILL

1. Grove's February 14, 1994 *Washington Post* story quoted in "Paula Jones: She's No Anita Hill," *MediaWatch* (March 1994), p. 1.

2. Kaus's March 7, 1994 *New Republic* article quoted in "Paula Jones: She's No Anita Hill," op. cit.

3. Clift's February 18, 1994 remarks on C-SPAN noted in "The Two Faces of Eleanor," *MediaWatch* (April 1994), PP. 1-2.

4. Isikoff's fight was noted in "Paula Jones Story Fight?," *MediaWatch* (April 1994), p. 8.

5. "From *I Am Woman* to *Who's That Girl?*," *MediaWatch* (June 1994), pp. 6-7.

6. Gumbel's May 10, 1994 remarks quoted in "Bryant Blames the Victim," *Notable Quotables* (May 23, 1994), p. 1. When Katie Couric interviewed Anita Hill on October 7, 1992, she asked questions like these: "Twenty years from now, fifty years from now, when people look back at these hearings, how do you want them to think of you?" Quoted in "More Tough Questions for Anita Hill," *Notable Quotables* (October 12, 1992), p. 1.

7. Brokaw's May 9, 1994 appearance on the CNBC show *Tim Russert* quoted in "Is Clinton a Sexual Harasser? Irrelevant, or a Plus?," *Notable Quotables* (May 23, 1994), p. 2.

8. Carlson's remarks on the May 7, 1994 CNN *Capital Gang* quoted in "Margaret Carlson's Plain Old Washington-Variety Harassment," *Notable Quotables* (May 23, 1994), p. 1.

9. Graham, Tim, "NPR and Paula Jones," *Comint* (Fall 1994) pp. 37-39.

10. Ibid.

11. Gibson's June 16, 1994 interview quoted in "Paula Jones: No Anita Hill," *Notable Quotables* (July 4, 1994), p. 1.

12. *Time's* and *Newsweek's* dismissals noted in "Pooh-Poohing Paula," *MediaWatch* (July 4, 1994), p. 1.

13. Brock, David, *The Real Anita Hill* (New York: Free Press, 1993), pp. 309, 315.

14. *Time* Associate Editor Nancy Gibbs quoted in "Anita's Allies," *Notable Quotables* (October 28, 1991), p. 1. Gibbs also mentioned Sojourner Truth and Harriet Tubman.

15. The Jones charges appeared under Cooper, Matthew, "The New FOBs: Foes of Bill," *U.S. News & World Report* (May 16, 1994), pp. 26-27. The Hill stories appeared in Borger, Gloria, "Judging Thomas," *U.S. News & World Report* (October 21, 1991), pp. 32-37; and Borger, Gloria, "The Swearing Never Stops," *U.S. News & World Report* (October 28, 1991), pp. 34-38.

16. The networks also played this game, singling out the Republicans for cynical or hardball political tactics 28 times during their live coverage of the Hill-Thomas hearings. (Twice CBS referred to both parties, but the Democrats were never singled out.) On another twelve occasions, the networks claimed the Democrats were too soft on Thomas, detailed in "Hard & Soft on Clarence Thomas," *MediaWatch*

(November 1991), pp. 6-7. A more thorough examination of the advocates behind Hill is contained in Brock, David, *The Real Anita Hill* (New York: 1993, Free Press).

17. Thomas's statement on the May 7, 1994 *Inside Washington* quoted in "Newsweek's Harassment Hypocrisy," *Notable Quotables* (May 23, 1994), p. 1.

18. "St. Anita vs. 'The Dogpatch Madonna,'" *MediaWatch* (June 1994), pp. 4-5. Despite *Newsweek*'s character attack on Jones, near the end of their May 16 story came the revelation that Gov. Clinton sought out private investigators to hunt down rumors of sex-and-drug parties attended by Republican opponents. Needless to say, the networks didn't breathe a word of that story.

19. Klein, Joe, "The Politics of Promiscuity," *Newsweek* (May 9, 1994), pp. 16-20.

20. Klein's May 8 theorizing on *Face the Nation* was noted in "Is Clinton a Sexual Harasser? Irrelevant, or a Plus?," *Notable Quotables* (May 23, 1994), p. 2. The contrast between Hill and Jones also reinforced itself when ABC devoted a one-hour special and a *Nightline* on November 2, 1994 to additional accusers of Clarence Thomas. In one of the few witnesses that had not been heard from in 1991, a former co-worker, Kaye Savage, suggested that Thomas had one *Playboy* centerfold on his bathroom wall, and then later amended that to an entire wall covered with centerfolds. ABC's reason for broadcasting this claim was to suggest somehow that this made Thomas a more believable sexual harasser of Hill. But no one in the media thought enough about Paula Jones to notice this passage about Clinton in David Maraniss's biography *First In His Class* on pp. 351-52: "Clinton seemed delighted with himself in his first elected job. He had his own office with his own staff and his own private quarters. On the inside door of his private bathroom, he put up a life-size poster of fleshily abundant Dolly Parton in a skimpy outfit."

31. THE WHITEWATER WIMP FACTOR

1. Morton's March 28, 1994 CNN *Inside Politics* story quoted in "The Whitewater Wimp Factor," *MediaWatch* (April 1994), p. 1.

2. Kurtz's March 12, 1994 *Washington Post* story noted in "The Whitewater Wimp Factor," op. cit.

3. Kurtz, Howard, *Media Circus* (New York: Times Books, 1993), pp. 369-70.

4. Shribman's March 11, 1994 *Boston Globe* article, Gumbel's March 30 CNBC appearance, and April 4 *Time* chart quoted in "The Whitewater Wimp Factor," op. cit.

5. Zuckerman's April 11, 1994 column noted in "The Whitewater Wimp Factor," *MediaWatch* (April 1994), p. 1.

6. CMPA study publicized in Adalian, Josef, "Clintons Get Good Reviews on Affair," *Washington Times* (April 5, 1994), p. A3.

7. Blackman, Ann, and Burleigh, Nina, "Yes, We Made Lots of Mistakes: Clearing the Air with Hillary Clinton," *Time* (March 21, 1994). p. 38.

8. Clift, Eleanor, "Hillary: 'I Made Mistakes,'" *Newsweek* (March 21, 1994), p. 35.

9. "Why Clinton Can't Complain," *MediaWatch* (May 1994), pp. 6-7.

10. Ibid. Since the Media Research Center was founded in the fall of 1987 and the networks with a presence on the Nexis news data retrieval system do not reach

back that far, the tally of Iran-Contra specials could be even greater.

11. Ibid.

12. Ibid.

13. Keenan's January 12, 1994 CNN story quoted in "Keen on Whitewater," *MediaWatch* (February 1994), p. 8.

14. Rather's June 30 *CBS Evening News* report, Shaw's June 30 interview on *Inside Politics*, and Russert's July 31 *Meet the Press* question featured in "Whitewashing Whitewater," *MediaWatch* (August 1994), p. 1.

15. Rather, Braver, and Engberg quotes from the August 8 and August 12, 1994 *CBS Evening News* appeared in "The Ken Starr Conspiracy," *MediaWatch* (September 1994), pp. 4-5.

16. Ibid.

17. Ibid.

32. HILLARY'S CATTLE KILLING

1. "Why Clinton Can't Complain," op. cit.

2. Post-press conference quotes from Brokaw, Jennings, and Daugherty appeared in "Three Cheers for Slick Hillary," *MediaWatch* (May 1994), p. 1.

3. Duffy's May 2, 1994 *Time* report noted in "Three Cheers...," op. cit.

4. Dowd's April 23, 1994 *New York Times* story noted in "Three Cheers...," op. cit.

5. Tony Snow's column quoted in "Three Cheers...," op. cit.

6. Linda Greenhouse's question on the April 22, 1994 *Washington Week in Review* quoted in "Three Cheers...," op. cit.

7. Shannon's remarks on the March 31, 1994 *Fox Morning News* quoted in "Enid vs. Hillary," *Notable Quotables* (January 1, 1996), p. 2.

8. "Dumping on D'Amato," *MediaWatch* (July 1994), p. 1.

9. Bozell, L. Brent, "Whitewater Wimps: Watergate Reporters Woodward and Bernstein," Waterbury *Republican-American* (April 25, 1994), p. 11A.

10. May 1994 *Money* article quoted in "Why Clinton Can't Complain," op. cit.

33. THE POLICY WARS CONTINUE

1. "They're No Friends of Bill," *Media Monitor* (July/August 1994), pp. 4-6.

2. "Criminal Gaps in Crime Bill Coverage," *MediaWatch* (September 1994), pp. 6-7. Primary research by Andy Gabron.

3. Lamer, Timothy W., "Media Engulfed by Politics of Health," *MediaNomics* (August 1994), pp. 2-3.

4. Burleigh, Nina, "Ads They Refused to Run," *Time* (August 1, 1994), p. 19.

5. Lauter, David, "Town Hall Health Hearing Presents Few Cures," *Los Angeles Times* (March 13, 1993), p. A21. News stories on other foundation-funded studies include Sugg, Diana, "Job Woes Swell Ranks of Uninsured," *Sacramento Bee* (April 22, 1994), p. B1; Broder, David, "The Public Wants a Revolution, Unsure of Which Faction to Join," *Washington Post* (September 12, 1993), p. A28; Gentry, Carol,

"Reform? Battle Lines Are Drawn," *St. Petersburg Times* (May 28, 1993), p. 12A; and Sternberg, Steve, "Coverage Crisis Will Hurt 75 Million, Group Warns," *Atlanta Journal and Constitution* (April 9, 1993), p. A3.

6. Carter, Bill, "Foundation Giving $2.5 Million to NBC for Health Care Program," *New York Times* (May 4, 1994), pp. 1, 20.

7. "NBC Takes the Money and Runs...Left," op. cit.

8. ABC *Good Morning America* quotes from February 7-11, 1994 and the *Investor's Business Daily* editorial on the AARP and article by John Merline quoted in "Good Fawning America," *MediaWatch* (March 1994), pp. 4-5.

9. Foreman's July 25, 1994 *World News Tonight* story quoted in "Who's 'Strangling Fair Debate'?," *MediaWatch* (August 1994), pp. 4-5.

10. "Harry and Louise Get the Shaft," *MediaWatch* (August 1994), pp. 6-7.

11. Manegold's July 17, 1994, *New York Times* ad review noted in "Harry and Louise Get the Shaft," op. cit.

12. Wartzman's April 29, 1994 *Wall Street Journal* article and Pear's May 27, 1994 *New York Times* piece quoted in "Harry and Louise Get the Shaft," op. cit.

13. "Harry and Louise...," op. cit.

14. Ibid.

15. Ibid.

34. PROBING THE CONSERVATIVE MIND

1. Dionne, E. J., "Why They Can't Stand Clinton," *Washington Post* (December 28, 1993), p. A15.

2. Burleigh, Nina, "Clintonophobia!" *Time* (April 11, 1994), pp. 38-39. This article was the first news magazine mention of Paula Jones.

3. Devroy, Ann, "Clinton Foes Voice Their Disdain, Loud and Clear," *Washington Post* (May 22, 1994), pp. A1, A7.

4. Birnbaum and Perry quoted in "Clinton the Moderate Faces Raw Hate," *Notable Quotables* (October 24, 1994), p. 2.

35. RETOOLING THE CLINTON RECORD

1. August 3 and 18, 1994 *Larry King Live* discussions quoted in "Reporters Side with Bill," *MediaWatch* (September 1994), p. 8.

2. Couric's August 18, 1994 interview quoted in "Poor Bill Doesn't Get Enough Credit," *Notable Quotables* (August 29, 1994), p. 1.

3. Koppel's August 16, 1994 *Nightline* quoted in "Poor Bill Doesn't Get Enough Credit," op. cit.

4. York, Byron, "Big Al's Big Scam," *The American Spectator* (February 1996), pp. 39-43.

5. Media Research Center transcript of Jennings on the October 26, 1992 *World News Tonight*.

6. Smith, Ted J., *The Vanishing Economy* (Washington: The Media Institute, 1988), pp. 19-41.

7. Weisberg's September 6, 1994 *New York* article was noted in "Bill Clinton's Excellent Presidency," *Notable Quotables* (September 12, 1994), p. 1.

8. Media Research Center transcript of Jack Smith on the October 2, 1994 *This Week with David Brinkley*.

9. Schieffer's comments on the October 23, 1994 *Face the Nation* quoted in "Clinton Deserves More Credit," *Notable Quotables* (November 7, 1994), p. 1.

10. Media Research Center transcript of CNN's Bruce Morton on the October 23, 1994 *Late Edition*.

11. Media Research Center transcript of Fineman's September 9, 1994 appearance on the PBS show *Washington Week in Review*.

12. Birnbaum's October 7, 1994 *Wall Street Journal* story quoted in "Clinton the Moderate Faces Raw Hate," op. cit. Birnbaum repeated his theory later that day in an appearance on *Washington Week in Review*.

36. NEWT'S WELCOME WAGON
1. Final numbers appeared in "The November Surprise: TV News Coverage of the 1994 Elections," *Media Monitor* (November/December 1994), p. 3. The preliminary numbers on Gingrich were issued bypress release from CMPA.

2. Engberg's November 2 *Evening News* story quoted in "Newt Gingrich, 'Radical Geek,'" *MediaWatch* (November 1994), p. 1.

3. Lacayo's November 7, 1994 *Time* cover story quoted in "Newt Gingrich, 'Radical Geek,'" op. cit.

4. Hosenball's November 7, 1994 *Newsweek* story quoted in "Newt Gingrich, 'Radical Geek,'" op. cit.

5. Khalid's October 14, 1994 remarks on C-SPAN quoted in "Newt Gingrich, 'Radical Geek,'" op. cit.

6. Ibid.

7. Media Research Center transcript of Zahn on the November 17, 1994 *CBS This Morning*.

8. Donaldson's question on the November 13 *This Week with David Brinkley* quoted in "Newt's Honeymoon," *Notable Quotables* (December 5, 1994), p. 1.

9. Media Research Center transcript of Brokaw's November 15, 1994 *Dateline* report.

10. Ibid.

37. REAGANOMICS REDUX?
1. Brokaw's September 27, 1994 *Nightly News* report and Borger's October 3 *U.S. News* article quoted in "Architects of Gridlock Gone Bad?," *MediaWatch* (October 1994), p. 1.

2. Klein's October 31, 1994 *Newsweek* lament quoted in "The Lower-Tax Bribe," *Notable Quotables* (December 5, 1994), p. 1.

3. Chandler's October 2, 1994 *Washington Post* story quoted in "More Disastrous Reaganomics," *Notable Quotables* (October 10, 1994), p. 2.

4. Memmott's October 3 commentary quoted in "More Disastrous Reaganomics," *Notable Quotables* (October 10, 1994), p. 2; Memmott's October 10 commentary quoted in "Contract with America: Shoddy Reaganomics," *Notable Quotables* (October 24, 1994), p. 1.

5. Carlson's June 14, 1993 *Fox Morning News* prediction quoted in "Florio's Political Courage," *Notable Quotables* (June 21, 1993), p. 2. Clift's October 16, 1993 *McLaughlin Group* prediction noted in "*Newsweek* Pundits on the Election: Whoops!," *Notable Quotables* (November 8, 1993), p. 1.

6. Hickey's October 7, 1993 *World News Tonight* report quoted in "New Jersey: Florio Right on Taxes," *Notable Quotables* (October 25, 1993), p. 1.

7. Mitchell's October 20, 1992 *Today* remarks and Warner's November 29, 1992 *Capital Gang* statements quoted in "Before the Plan: Rooting for a Middle-Class Tax Hike," *Notable Quotables* (March 1, 1993), p. 3.

8. Smith's October 30 *CBS This Morning* interview with Gingrich quoted in "Contract with America: Shoddy Reaganomics," op. cit.

9. Russert's October 2, 1994 *Meet the Press* interview with Gingrich quoted in "Relentless Russert," *MediaWatch* (October 1994), p. 8.

10. Media Research Center transcript of Borger's appearance on the November 4, 1994 *Washington Week in Review*.

11. Alter's October 10, 1994 *Newsweek* story quoted in "More Disastrous Reaganomics," *Notable Quotables* (October 10, 1994), p. 2.

38. PSYCHOLOGISTS CALL IT DENIAL

1. The election night comments of Schneider, Roberts, and Ifill were quoted in "The Non-Ideological GOP Landslide?," *MediaWatch* (November 1994), pp. 6-7.

2. Media Research Center transcript of Ifill and Roberts on the November 11, 1994 *Washington Week in Review*.

3. Media Research Center transcript of Schneider on the December 1, 1994 *Inside Politics*. Schneider changed positions on the political utility of the Contract at least five times, as explained in "Call Him Mr. Flip-Flop," *MediaWatch* (February 1995), p. 8.

4. Klein's November 14, 1994 *Newsweek* article quoted in "The People Stink, And So Do We," *Notable Quotables* (November 21, 1994), p. 1.

5. Brokaw and Russert quoted from live November 9, 1994 NBC coverage in "Why Democrats Lost: Conservative Media Bias," *Notable Quotables* (November 21, 1994), p. 2.

6. The November 14, 1994 ABC Radio "Peter Jennings' Journal" commentary quoted in "Peter Jennings: You Voters Need a Diaper," *Notable Quotables* (November 21, 1994), p. 1. Jennings' December 5, 1994 apology quoted in "Correcting the People's Tantrum," *MediaWatch* (February 1995), p. 1.

7. Shafer, Ronald G., "Washington Wire," *The Wall Street Journal* (November 11, 1994), p. 1.

8. "Clinton's Incredible Shrinking Ideology," *MediaWatch* (March 1995), pp. 6-7. This methodology may seem incomplete. After all, using only stories with the words

"liberal" and "Clinton" excluded many more stories where Clinton was described as a "moderate" or "New Democrat." But it is very interesting that in instances where reporters could be expected to use the word "liberal" to describe Clinton, they often balked at the opportunity.

9. Nichols' October 18, 1994 *USA Today* story quoted in "Clinton's Incredible Shrinking Ideology," op. cit.

39. THE BENEFITS OF IRRELEVANCE

1. "Snoozing Watchdogs," *MediaWatch* (January 1995), p. 3.

2. "The Newt-Centric Media Universe," *MediaWatch* (February 1995), pp. 6-7.

3. "PBS: Clinton Fails the Liberal Litmus Test," *MediaWatch* (February 1995), pp. 4-5.

4. Ibid.

5. Gumbel's December 12, 1994 *Today* remarks quoted in "Bill Clinton, Overachiever," *Notable Quotables* (January 16, 1995), p. 2.

6. Jennings' January 5, 1995 *World News Tonight* interview quoted in "Taking Out Hankies for the President," *Notable Quotables* (January 30, 1995), p. 1.

40. A BOUNTY OF SCRUTINY

1. "Fighting the First One Hundred Days," *MediaWatch* (May 1995), pp. 6-7. Primary research by Andy Gabron and Clay Waters.

2. "Nap Time for Network News," *MediaWatch* (March 1995), p. 1.

3. Maraniss, David, *First in His Class*, op. cit., p. 441.

4. Media Research Center transcript of the November 15, 1994 *Dateline.*

5. Fineman, Howard, "The Warrior," *Newsweek* (January 9, 1995), p. 28.

6. Chung's interviews with Mrs. Gingrich and Mrs. Kelley quoted in "Connie Cons Newt's Mom," *MediaWatch* (January 1995), p. 1.

7. Moyers quoted in "'Balanced' Bill Moyers?," *MediaWatch* (April 1995), p. 2. The "McCarthy with a Southern accent" quote appeared in "NBC Goes Left with Moyers," *MediaWatch* (February 1995), p. 2.

8. NBC's November 23, 1994 *Today* story and the November 28 *Time* article quoted in "Jesse Helms, 'Prince of Darkness,'" *MediaWatch* (December 1994), p. 1.

9. Ibid.

10. Crier's January 27, 1995 *World News Tonight* report quoted in "Outrage of Not...," *MediaWatch* (April 1995), pp. 4-5.

11. Media Research Center transcript of Couric's April 6, 1995 *Today* interview with Mineta.

12. Media Research Center transcript of Bob Franken's April 6, 1995 CNN interview with Gingrich.

13. "All Over Ollie North," *MediaWatch* (November 1994), p. 3.

14. "No Jesse Jackson Gaffes," *MediaWatch* (January 1995), p. 4.

15. "Outrage or Not...", op. cit.

16. Downs' November 22, 1992 commentary on the ABC Radio program *Perspective* quoted in "Hugh Fumes," *MediaWatch* (January 1993), p. 3.

41. A CONTRACT HIT

1. "Fighting the First One Hundred Days," *MediaWatch* (May 1995), pp. 6-7. Primary research by Andy Gabron.

2. Rather's March 16, 1995 *CBS Evening News* remarks quoted in "In the Unbiased News Tonight...," *Notable Quotables* (April 10, 1995), p. 1.

3. Rather's February 28 *CBS Evening News* remarks quoted in "The Contract's Not Done Until Every Child's Dead," *Notable Quotables* (March 13, 1995), p. 2.

4. Jennings' January 12, 1995 *World News Tonight* comment quoted in "Correcting the People's Tantrum," *MediaWatch* (February 1995), p. 1.

5. Media Research Center transcript of Lauer's February 23 and 24, 1995 *Today* stories on school lunch.

6. Schieffer's March 21 *CBS Evening News* report, Johns' *NBC Nightly News* report, and Halsey's February 23 report for CNN's *World News* quoted in "Fighting the First One Hundred Days," op. cit.

7. Fernandez's May 20, 1995 *Today* interview with Reich quoted in "And Why Did *We* Support Clinton in '92?", *Notable Quotables* (June 5, 1995), p. 1. Thomas's remarks on the May 20, 1995 *Inside Washington* quoted in "Stupid Tax and Budget Cuts," *Notable Quotables* (June 5, 1995), p. 1.

8. Rather's June 13, 1995 special report quoted in "That About Sums It Up," *Notable Quotables* (June 19, 1995), p. 1.

9. Thompson's February 27, 1995 *Time* story quoted in "Republicans: Threat to the Human Race," Notable Quotables (February 27, 1995), p. 1.

10. Gleick's March 6, 1995 *Time* article quoted in "The Magazine That Cried Wolf," *MediaWatch* (March 1995), pp. 4-5.

11. Media Research Center transcripts of Simpson's February 26, 1995 *World News Tonight* and Rather's February 23, 1995 *CBS Evening News* reports.

42. TIMOTHY McVEIGH: NEWT'S PROTEGE?

1. Donaldson's April 23, 1995 question on *This Week with David Brinkley* and Schieffer's April 23, 1995 *Face the Nation* question quoted in "Oklahoma City: Republicans' Fault," *Notable Quotables* (May 8, 1995), p. 2.

2. Gumbel's April 25, 1995 *Today* remarks quoted in "Oklahoma City: Conservative Talk Radio's Fault?," op. cit.

3. Broder's April 25, 1995 *Washington Post* column quoted in "Oklahoma City: Conservative Talk Radio's Fault?," *Notable Quotables* (May 8, 1995), p. 1.

4. Lacayo's May 8, 1995 *Time* story quoted in "Oklahoma City: Conservative Talk Radio's Fault," op. cit.

5. Rather's January 18, 1995 *CBS Evening News* introduction quoted in "Chopping at the Competition," *MediaWatch* (November 1995), pp. 6-7.

6. Rather's April 27, 1995 *CBS Evening News* introduction quoted in "Chopping at the Competition," op. cit.

7. Juan Williams' April 23, 1995 *Capital Gang* statement, and Carl Rowan's remarks in the April 25, 1995 *Washington Post* quoted in "Oklahoma City: Republicans' Fault," op. cit.

8. Shribman's April 25, 1995 *Boston Globe* front-page story quoted in "Oklahoma City: Republicans' Fault," *Notable Quotables* (May 8, 1995), p. 2.

9. Couric's September 13 *Today* question quoted in "White House Plane Crash: Blame Reagan, Tom Clancy," *Notable Quotables* (September 26, 1994), p. 1.

10. Schieffer's October 30, 1994 *Face the Nation* question and Gumbel's October 31, 1994 *Today* question quoted in "White House Shooting: Talk Radio Inspired?," *Notable Quotables* (November 7, 1994), p. 1.

11. Gumbel's January 4, 1995 *Today* interview with Gephardt quoted in "Newt's Welcome Bouquet," *Notable Quotables* (January 30, 1995), p. 1.

12. Leonard's January 8, 1995 *Sunday Morning* declaration quoted in "Pol Pot, Gingrich: What's the Difference?," *Notable Quotables* (January 30, 1995), p. 1.

13. "Direct Mail Divergence," *MediaWatch* (June 1995), pp. 1-2.

43. A NEW OBSTACLE COURSE

1. "1991 Collaborators, 1995 Eviscerators," *MediaWatch* (June 1995), pp. 6-7. Primary research by Mark Honig.

2. Randall's 1988 report quoted in "1991 Collaborators...," op. cit.

3. Meserve's March 30, 1995 report quoted in "1991 Collaborators," op. cit..

4. Ibid.

5. Wooten's February, 24, 1995 *World News Tonight* story quoted in "1991 Collaborators...," op. cit.

6. Jackson's dates on *Inside Politics* quoted in "1991 Collaborators...," op. cit.

7. Randall in "1991 Collaborators...," op. cit.

8. Bozell, L. Brent, "Media Plan a Gramm Slam," *New York Post* (February 27, 1995), p. 21.

9. "Pouncing on 'Porn,'" *MediaWatch* (July 1995), p. 3.

10. Ibid.

11. Ibid.

12. Ibid.

13. Media Research Center transcript of Bode's remarks on the August 31, 1995 *Inside Politics*.

14. Gumbel's September 18, 1995 *Today* remarks quoted in "Powell: Last Chance to Stop Far Right Extremists," *Notable Quotables* (September 25, 195), p. 2; National Public Radio transcript of Liasson's September 20, 1995 report on *Morning Edition*.

15. Martin's November 8,1995 *World News Tonight* campaign eulogy quoted in "Pouting Over Powell," *Notable Quotables* (November 20, 1995), p. 1.

16. Fineman's remarks on the November 8, 1995 CNBC show *Equal Time* quoted in "Pouting Over Powell," op. cit.

44. MANGLING THE MEDICARE MATH

1. CBO cost estimates appeared in *An Analysis of the Administration's Health Proposal,* op. cit. Douglass's September 15, 1993 *CBS Evening News* report quoted in "The Media's More-Spending Bias," *MediaWatch* (October 1995), pp. 6-7.

2. "A Healing Media Avoid Fearmongering," *Notable Quotables* (May 22, 1995), p. 1; the Woodruff quote came from "In the Unbiased News Tonight...," *Notable Quotables* (April 10, 1995), p. 1.

3. Office of Management and Budget, *Budget of the United States Government, Fiscal Year 1994,* and earlier volumes, published in the Joint Economic Committee Minority *Economic Policy Update* (June 25, 1993), p. 4.

4. Lamer, Timothy, "Medicare Reporting Improving But...", *MediaNomics* (September 1995), pp. 2-3.

5. Rather's September 20, 1995 *CBS Evening News* story quoted in "Lying More Than Johnnie Cochran," *Notable Quotables* (October 9, 1995), p. 1.

6. Paula Zahn's September 25, 1995 *CBS This Morning* report and Robert MacNeil's October 2 report noted in "Lying More Than Johnnie Cochran," op. cit.

7. Media Research Center transcript of Linda Douglass's September 14, 1995 *CBS Evening News* report.

8. Brokaw and Myers quoted on the November 17, 1995 *NBC Nightly News* in "Basic News Without Budget Numbers," *MediaWatch* (December 1995), pp. 6-7.

9. "Untold Stories," *Wall Street Journal* (December 7, 1995), p. A14.

45. WHITEWATER BUBBLES AND BOILS

1. Media Research Center transcript of Schieffer on the July 30, 1995 *Sunday Morning.*

2. Merida, Kevin, "Republicans' Dive Into Whitewater Scores Some Points," *Washington Post* (August 14, 1995), pp. 1, 6.

3. "Media Bridge Over Silent Waters," *MediaWatch* (August 1995), pp. 6-7. *MediaWatch* analysts reviewed the same four evening shows from July 16 (two days before the Senate hearings began) to August 10. The time frame covered the four weeks of Senate hearings and one overlapping week of House hearings. For the three morning shows (ABC's *Good Morning America, CBS This Morning,* and NBC's *Today*) analysts reviewed through August 4.

4. Rather's July 1995 Whitewater language noted in "Media Bridge...," op. cit.

5. Ibid.

6. Ibid.

7. Ibid.

8. Ibid.

9. Media Research Center survey of August 14, 1995 news magazines.

10. "Nonpartisan Judge," *MediaWatch* (September 1995), p. 3.

11. "Wallace's Whitewash," *MediaWatch* (October 1995), p. 3.

12. Alter's August 23, 1993 *Newsweek* article quoted in "Defending the Deceased," *MediaWatch* (September 1993), p. 4.

13. Von Drehle's August 14, 1993 *Washington Post* story quoted in "Defending the Deceased," op. cit.

14. "Festering Foster," *MediaWatch* (November 1995), p. 1.

15. Ford's and Russert's Sunday *Today* exchange quoted in "Festering Foster," op. cit.

16. Schmidt, Susan, and Locy, Toni, "Papers Detail Clinton Friend's Contact Push; House Panel Reviews '93 Travel Office Firings," *Washington Post* (October 25, 1995), p. A4.

17. "Further Festering," *MediaWatch* (November 1995), pp. 1-2.

18. Ibid.

19. MRC Media Tracking System printout of the October 26, 1995 *World News Tonight*.

20. Alter's August 23, 1993 *Newsweek* article in "Defending the Deceased," op. cit.

21. Schmidt, Susan, "Whitewater Notes Sketchy on Meeting," *Washington Post* (December 23, 1995), p. A3.

22. Drew, Elizabeth, *On the Edge*, op. cit., pp. 23-24.

EPILOGUE: THE MEDIA MERRY-GO-ROUND

1. December 17, 1995 CNN special on Gingrich quoted in "Newt Gingrich, Political Liability?," *MediaWatch* (January 1996), pp. 4-5

2. December 26, 1992 CNN special on Clinton quoted in "Newt Gingrich, Political Liability?," op. cit.

3. Rankin's August 20, 1995 Knight-Ridder dispatch quoted in "Clinton's Brilliant Achievements," *MediaWatch* (October 1995), pp. 2-3.

4. Benedetto's September 5, 1995 *USA Today* "news analysis" quoted in "Removing Clinton's Negatives," *MediaWatch* (September 1995), p. 2.

About the Author

TIM GRAHAM has been Associate Editor of *Media Watch* and an Editor of *Notable Quotables* since February 1989. Graham is responsible for researching and writing *Media Watch*'s monthly Study and Janet Cooke Award articles.

Seven of Graham's studies were published in *And That's The Way It Isn't: A Reference Guide to Media Bias* (Media Research Center, 1990). He also assisted in writing the book *How To Identify, Expose, and Correct Media Bias* (MRC, 1994) and the broadcast news criticism section of Jude Wanniski's 1990 *Media Guide*. Eight of his essays on public broadcasting appeared in *Public Broadcasting & the Public Trust* (Second Thoughts Books, 1995). Graham's media analysis has also appeared in periodicals, including *Human Events, Diversity & Division, Comint, Chronicles, Reason, The World & I, The Washington Times, World, Heterodoxy,* and *The Detroit News.*

Graham is a regular talk-radio spokesman for the MRC and his television appearances have included appearances on CNN's *Reliable Sources,* the CNBC shows [Geraldo] *Rivera Live, Cal Thomas, Charles Grodin,* and *Business Insiders,* the Christian Broadcasting Network's *700 Club,* PBS's *This Is America with Dennis Wholey,* and the cable networks America's Talking, the NewsTalk Network, and National Empowerment Television.

Before joining the MRC, Graham served as campaign press secretary for Rep. Jack Buechner (R-Mo.) in 1988, and in 1987, he served as Editor of *Organization Trends,* a monthly newsletter on philanthropy and politics by the Washington-based Capital Research Center. Before coming to Washington in 1986, Graham served as a news reporter for the *La Crosse Tribune* and local radio stations in Wisconsin. Graham, a native of Viroqua, Wisconsin, is a 1986 Honors Program graduate of Bemidji State University in Bemidji, Minnesota.

MRC PUBLICATIONS

MediaWatch, a monthly newsletter that reviews news coverage of political and current events by the television networks, newspapers, and news weeklies. Also, "Newsbites" provide ongoing examples of bias, and the "Janet Cooke Award" examines the month's most distorted story. Plus: in-depth studies and analysis.

MediaNomics, a monthly newsletter mailed along with *MediaWatch*, that examines national news coverage of business and economic issues and Hollywood's economic message. The "Issue Analysis" section reveals long-term trends in financial reporting and a back page essay explains how reporters could better cover the economy.

Notable Quotables, a bi-weekly compilation of the most outrageous and sometimes humorous examples of bias from the media. A year-end awards issue presents the best quotes of the year as determined by a distinguished panel of judges.

The Family Guide to Prime Time Television, is published annually, and is the most comprehensive study of the year's prime time fare. *The Family Guide* provides information on what shows may contain subject matter that is either offensive or inappropriate for children, and what shows promote family-friendly themes.

MRC BOOKS

And That's The Way It Isn't:
A Reference Guide to Media Bias,
now in its seventh printing, provides
over 350 pages of summaries, excerpts
and reprints of 45 studies that demonstrate the media's liberal bias. A one-
stop resource containing all the facts
and figures, examples and quotes
proving the media's bias.

How To Identify, Expose, &
Correct Liberal Media Bias,
includes a detailed explanation
of how to identify eight types of
bias complete with real-life examples of each; step-by-step in-
structions on how to analyze
news stories and conduct studies
proving the media's bias; publish
a newsletter; and get reporters to
include conservative views.

Out of Focus: Network Television
and the American Economy
"does for TV viewers what *Consumer*
Reports does for car buyers,"
according to *National Review*. An
in-depth analysis of how both
news and entertainment shows
undermine the free enterprise
system.

MRC's Press Picks, includes over
700 recommended print, radio, and
broadcast media professionals that
are committed to fair and balanced
journalism.

MRC Publication Order Form

- ❏ *MediaWatch/MediaNomics* ($40 for 12 monthly issues)
- ❏ *Notable Quotables* ($24 for 26 bi-weekly issues)
- ❏ All three newsletters for one year ($50). Save $14!

- ❏ *And That's The Way it Isn't* ($14.95)
- ❏ *How To Identify, Expose, & Correct Liberal Media Bias* ($16.95)
- ❏ *Out of Focus* ($19.95)
- ❏ *MRC's Press Picks* ($7.95)
- ❏ *The Family Guide to Prime Time Television* ($9.95)

- ❏ Additional copies of *Pattern of Deception*

1-9 copies	$18.95
10-49 copies	$14.95
50+copies	$10.95

_____ number of copies at _____ each = _____

Name _____

Address _____

❏Check   ❏VISA   *Total Enclosed:*
         ❏MasterCard $ _____

Card Number _____

Expiration Date _____

MEDIA RESEARCH CENTER®

Make check payable to Media Research Center

Media Research Center, Publications Dept.
113 South West Street, 2nd Floor
Alexandria, VA 22314
or call us at 800-MRC-1423